W9-CFQ-623

"Wow, what a fascinating journey! I read this book front to back nonstop. Amazed at what it takes to pioneer; amazed about all the pieces of this puzzle; amazed at God. I owe so much to the early Christian music pioneers. This book has heart, humor, and seeps with wisdom."
—JOHN COOPER, Skillet

"Eddie DeGarmo has been a pioneer in translating the unchanging message of Christ in the ever-changing musical genres of contemporary music. Had it not been for guys like DeGarmo and Key being willing to risk the scorn of some pastors and churches to share the Gospel in a musical language that people like me understood, I'm not sure where my own Christian life would have gone. In addition to award-winning and life-changing music he wrote and performed, Eddie DeGarmo has successfully spent the second half of his adult life opening the doors for some of the top Christian artists in the world. His own music would have been enough for most people, but he has unselfishly invested himself in others and multiplied the reach of music as a medium for reaching the masses. You have loved his music. You will love the story behind the music and the many people he helped you to love in *Rebel for God*."
—MIKE HUCKABEE, former governor of Arkansas, host of *Huck-abee* on TBN

"Pioneer. Trailblazer. Legend. Visionary. Artist. Executive. Mentor. Friend. Follower of Christ. These are just some of the words I use to describe Eddie DeGarmo. I am so happy he has written down his incredible life story and journey. This book is a joyride to read. The Scripture says in Proverbs, 'We can make our plans, but the Lord determines our steps.' This is most certainly true of Eddie, and you will read it all in *Rebel for God*."
—CHRIS TOMLIN, artist, songwriter, author

"I knew he could rock out, write songs, look a little on the wild side, and love people. I didn't know he could craft his own story in such a compelling way. And he does it with honesty, humility, and humor. Spruced up faith can be boring because it misses the struggle that makes us who we are. None of that in *Rebel for God*. Eddie DeGarmo opens the front door of his remarkable journey and invites us into his tiny apartments, bad road vans, and music friendships. I like Eddie for a lot of reasons but the top one is that he kept his promise to his mother. When he left college as a young man for the music road, he promised he'd finish his degree. And decades later, after D&K, EMI, and semi-retirement, he came back to college. It was my privilege to hand him his college diploma. A man with more music business experience than any doctoral program could ever grant, walked the stage with college kids—because a promise is a promise. The success he knows has never ruined the simple man he has become. Read slowly, my friends. This feels a lot like holy ground to me."

—**DAN BOONE**, president, Trevecca Nazarene University

"In Eddie DeGarmo's book *Rebel for God,* you will read the story of one man's walk with Jesus in the highly competitive music industry. You will also come to know the roots and mission behind what we know today as Contemporary Christian Music. He was one of the pioneers of it. Though Eddie and I have never had the pleasure of working together directly, I consider it an honor to be a co-laborer with him and know him. I urge you to get this book and reserve time to read it, because once you start, it will be very difficult to lay it down."

—**BART MILLARD**, lead singer for MercyMe and writer of "I Can Only Imagine"

"Eddie DeGarmo and Dana Key didn't invent rock and roll—but they sure introduced it to Christian music and I became a fan. In the years following my first meeting D&K I was fortunate to become friends with Eddie. I don't know that I have ever known a person that was equally comfortable in the control room and in the boardroom. Eddie is an incredible artist in his own right and, at the same time, has keen business acumen. He is an amazingly well-rounded individual and a great friend."

—**MICHAEL W. SMITH**, multi-platinum artist, bestselling author, and acclaimed actor

"The compelling story in *Rebel for God* should inspire us all toward faithfulness. As Eddie DeGarmo was faithful in his calling as a musician, songwriter, and family man, God continued to bless his work and expand his influence by providing him even greater levels of opportunity. This successful pioneer and visionary of Christian music has impacted countless lives with his music, his message, and his earnest devotion to love God with his heart, soul, and mind and to love his neighbor as himself."

—**PETER YORK**, chairman/CEO Capitol Christian Music Group

"Eddie DeGarmo is considered a creative giant in our industry. His bold musical journey is a road map of where vision and innovation can lead if only we dare to walk out the Master's plan. The experience, wisdom, honesty, and heart Eddie reveals in *Rebel for God* is not only valuable but truly inspiring."

—**JACKIE PATILLO**, president and executive director, Gospel Music Association

"Eddie DeGarmo is one of those rare characters in the field of Christian music who has had a great career as an artist, writer, producer, businessman, and entrepreneur. Doing anything for fifty years is quite an accomplishment, but my friend Eddie did it with class and a whole lot of fun. For anyone who would like to know the history of 'Christian Rock,' *Rebel for God* is a must read."

> —**BILL GAITHER**, Bill Gaither Trio, Gaither Vocal Band, Homecoming Concert Series

"Typically, fans become enchanted by mystical perceptions of their idol's splendor. But, in this book, *Rebel for God*, Eddie DeGarmo catapults the readers past the glitz and glamor of the stage, and infuses them into the 'bloodline' of the real journey. Through the rhythm of his experience and the wit of his writing, you will feel the pain, the strain, and the elation of Eddie's passion for his calling in Christ. Definitely, a 'must-read!!!'"

> —**HOWARD RACHINSKI**, chairman/founder, Christian Copyright Licensing International (CCLI)

"If it weren't for Eddie DeGarmo, I'm not sure that my music ministry would have ever taken flight! In the pages of *Rebel for God* you will discover the fascinating story of a leader and musical innovator, someone who is wise, visionary, and passionate about God. For this man I am profoundly grateful!"

> —**REBECCA ST. JAMES**, singer and author

"Eddie DeGarmo is a unique combination: incomparably visionary with a clear grasp on the moment, insatiably creative, and able to work inside realistic business boundaries; a corporate force and yet compassionate and genuine. He is a lover of art and a lover of people, a sincere believer and a really good hang. Eddie and Susan have been good friends to me and Kristyn, and we always look forward to the next time we're able to get together. We're honored to commend *Rebel for God* to you."

> —**KEITH AND KRISTYN GETTY**, modern hymn writers

"I have had the great privilege of watching as Eddie DeGarmo navigated almost all of the remarkable changes, transitions, and developments described in *Rebel for God*. Across all the years and all the miles, he learned a host of invaluable life lessons. I am so grateful that in these pages he has gathered them, distilled them, and shared them. This is a treasure trove of wisdom disguised as the wild ride of a rebel soul. In other words, it is quintessentially Eddie!"

> —**GEORGE GRANT**, pastor of Parish Presbyterian Church, director of the King's Meadow Study Center

"Eddie DeGarmo is a Christian music entrepreneur. His humble character and practical work ethic is inspirational in both music and business. *Rebel for God* is an eye-opening story of God using one man to influence so many in a powerful and positive way. It's a must read."
—**JOHN SCHLITT**, Petra

"*Rebel for God* takes us on a journey of God's love, grace, mercy, and provision as He helped Eddie DeGarmo and the many people Eddie worked with see His plan and purpose unfold over a fifty-year journey. There are many stories that will make you laugh, think, and for those entering into music as a profession, sage wisdom. I recommend this book to anyone who wants to learn about modern Christian music, worship, or anyone who wants to be inspired by another person's profound journey following Christ."
—**MALCOLM J. HAWKER**, president/CEO, Christian Copyright Licensing International (CCLI)

"If you listen to Christian music or sing along in worship, much of what you hear has been influenced or made possible by the work of Eddie DeGarmo. From his beginnings blazing a trail for Christian Rock with D&K, to his work with bringing so many artists and their music to the world, he then was a big part of bringing modern worship music to masses around the world. *Rebel for God* gives us a behind-the-scenes view of a truly blessed life. Buying and reading this book will inform, entertain, and most importantly, encourage you."
—**SCOTT BRICKELL**, BrickHouse Entertainment

"As one who attempts a radical life of Christianity while also performing rock music on tours, records, training, and marketing, I applaud this deeply personal story of Eddie DeGarmo's groundbreaking life. What a pleasure to also read of my beloved Memphis music scene from the years of Eddie's career start, the Jesus movements large and small, and the future of ministry and commerce. Eddie's singular style, story, and directives are thought provoking, giving fans of Christians making music a personal revelation. Readers will resonate with the childhood dreams, rock and roll romp, stories of the hit or miss business of music and ministry, and depth of spiritual formation. I recommend to everyone who loves music, ministry, Memphis, and making it no matter what, to read *Rebel for God* and try to accomplish a fraction of what Eddie has in his story!"
—**KEN STEORTS**, president, Visible Music College

"I've known Eddie DeGarmo for many years, during which time he has been a positive influence for a number of leaders within the Christian music industry. In his new book, *Rebel for God*, you'll enjoy hearing his story and be surprised

by how relatable his journey has been. Eddie has been very impactful on my life and I hope that when you read this book he will leave a similar impact on yours."
—**DAVID PIERCE**, chief of ministry partnerships, K-LOVE and Air1 Radio

"*Rebel for God* is a fun ride through Eddie DeGarmo's forty-plus years of ministry and Christian music biz: morphing and transitioning from artist-writer to record producer to label head to publishing guru. Such great stories—some in which I played a part—that are insightful, inspiring, humorous, challenging, instructional; and they bear out what I've experienced in our decades of friendship and as co-workers in the fields of the Lord: Eddie gets ideas, seeks God's voice, then follows his gut and leaves results up to the heavenly Father. Sage wisdom for all of us."
—**BOB FARRELL**, artist, songwriter

"An enjoyable, surprising, and honest look into the life of a legend in Christian music, *Rebel for God* is filled with so many great stories. Whether it's as an artist, a producer, label owner, or a music publisher, Eddie DeGarmo's passion to impact culture and see people find salvation has stayed with him the whole time. If you love Christian music and have watched or experienced any of Eddie's incredible fifty years in music, then this book is an unmissable read."
—**STEVE McPHERSON**, director, Hillsong Music Publishing

"Eddie DeGarmo's brilliantly written book *Rebel For God: Faith, Business, and Rock 'n' Roll* is limitless in its honesty about life and love. It is one of the best life stories I have ever read that will put your faith back into why the only constant in life is change well lived."
—**EVAN LAMBERG**, president, North America Universal Music Publishing

"With style and wit, Eddie DeGarmo tells the story of his life in music—a life that just happens to run the entire spectrum from young musician struggling to keep his band on the road and food on the table, to certified rock star; from co-founding and running his own record label, to top exec in the largest commercial music company on the planet. *Rebel for God* is a memoir well worth reading."
—**STEPHEN R. LAWHEAD**, novelist and (first) manager of DeGarmo and Key

"Eddie DeGarmo is definitely my brother from a very different mother, so much so…I've often thought and even said, that Eddie DeGarmo is an African-American man trapped inside a Caucasian-American male's body…LOL…He is full of Memphis soul, full of vision, and obvious passion to top it off! It's been pretty mind-boggling watching my friend ascend over the years since our first acquaintance—when TobyMac, Kevin Max, and myself came to Nashville, Tennessee green as leaves in the spring of '89 chasing after a similar dream…Literally among the 'first' few Christian rock bands to exist … [from] DeGarmo & Key to Eddie's rocking solo career, to the grand-slam idea of our industry's first super successful rock opera called *!HERO*—in which he so graciously allowed me to star, and expand my own career territory—to his tenure in groundbreaking ideas and leadership at Capitol CMG Publishing, he has pretty much led a 'renaissance man' kind of life! Needless to say, as a mentor to myself and many of my contemporaries, Eddie remains the Southern gentleman, soft-spoken, uber kind…and always a man of his word, world-class example! All said, I am proud of my big brother and more proud for EVERYONE to hear HIS story, from HIS mouth, about HIS great adventure…This dude is truly *A Rebel* (with a cause) *for God*! BOOM!"

—**MICHAEL TAIT**, Grammy award-winning artist and songwriter/dcTalk and Newboys

"Eddie DeGarmo, a pioneer of Christian Rock, was instrumental in helping us find our true voice. *Rebel for God* provides great insight on where Eddie's wisdom, creativity, and passion to share the love story of Jesus through undeniable songs come from. I'm honored to be a small part of his legendary impact on the music industry."

—**MARK STUART**, Audio Adrenaline and the Hands and Feet Project

"*Rebel for God* by Eddie DeGarmo is just the right book at just the right time. The stories in this book will keep you turning the pages and the message of God's love for His creation will make you want to share it with everyone you know."

—**JOSH McDOWELL**, founder of Josh McDowell Ministry (a Cru ministry), and author of *More Than a Carpenter*

REBEL FOR GOD

REBEL
FOR GOD

Faith, Business, and Rock 'n' Roll

EDDIE DeGARMO

SALEM BOOKS
an imprint of Regnery Publishing

Regnery® is a registered trademark of Salem Communications Holding Corporation

Salem Books™ is a trademark of Salem Communications Holding Corporation

Cataloging-in-Publication data on file with the Library of Congress

ISBN 978-1-62157-808-6

Published in the United States by
Salem Books
An imprint of Regnery Publishing
A Division of Salem Media Group
300 New Jersey Ave NW
Washington, DC 20001
www.SalemBooks.com

Manufactured in the United States of America

10 9 8 7 6 5 4 3 2 1

Books are available in quantity for promotional or premium use. For information on discounts and terms, please visit our website: www.Regnery.com.

CONTENTS

To my lovely wife:
I dedicate this book to Susan. Without her standing beside me,
this phenomenal journey would not have happened.
I love you dearly.

To my daughters Breckon and Shannon and their
husbands, Marcelo and Michael:
You guys are marvelous people and have made our
family story grow so much stronger. You make me proud.
Thank you, my daughters, for your love to me, especially as
I traveled so much while you grew up.

To my mom and dad:
Your belief and support in me was undying.
You were always there with me while I chased my dreams.

To my brother Larry:
Thank you for following Jesus and showing him to me.

To my grandkids Paisley, Oscar, Edison, Stella, and Louie:
If God could do these things with a guy like me,
it's unimaginable the great and wonderful things he has
in store for you. Follow him.

Thank you, Jesus, for allowing me to travel with you through
this journey. It's been quite a ride.

FOREWORD
Louie Giglio, Pastor of Passion City Church and founder of Passion Conferences and sixsteprecords

Memphis in the 1960s. A Hammond B3. A Marshall amp. Elvis in a blue suit. A nation-wide controversy. Selling out venues, standing on stages, and traversing the world of the music business.

Sounds like the makings of great movie, right? Well, you're holding the screenplay in your hands!

Eddie DeGarmo's life would make an epic film, but it makes an even better book, and I'm so glad he's written so much of it down here.

Shelley and I have had the privilege of knowing and working with Eddie in a number of capacities over the years. When our budding relationship began in the summer of 1983, the songs of DeGarmo and Key were a part of our soundtrack. Together, they were giving a fresh and unique voice to a new generation of Jesus-followers and we were in the wake of their sound. Decades later, we had the privilege of partnering together in our shared passion to equip the Church around the world with songs that proclaim the Glory of God.

Eddie is brilliant, kind, a straight-shooter, and like this memoir aptly puts it, he's a Rebel For God.

But, he's not the kind of rebel who flashes his counter-culturisms for show or acclaim. He's the kind of Jesus-loving rebel that left behind the world's ways and never looked back from the Kingdom purposes God set before him. He rebelled against what the world called good and popular and right and successful, and chose instead to chase after righteous living, an eternal Kingdom and the fame of a Name greater than his.

Eddie is a true original, and like one of the hits he helped bring to the world, a real-life Jesus Freak.

Eddie is a masterful storyteller, and narrates the series of miracles that have made up his life with all the melody and delight you'd expect from a rock star turned record label exec and music publishing wiz. Turning these pages is like listening to Eddie's fingers dance over his Hammond B3, making the notes sing of the goodness and grandeur of Jesus.

Rebel for God is a retracing of God's purposes in the dissonant events of life that helps us see the Divine Hand at work in it all. It's full of the soul of Memphis, the gritty glamor of rock and roll, and the absurdity of 1980s hairstyles, all tied together by the cord of a faithful God leading his willing, faith-filled servant.

I love Eddie's story and I know it's nowhere close to being done yet. Yet, the chapters that have unfolded so far remind us that God is always at work, narrating and knitting the moments of our lives together into a perfect pattern that draws us deeper into the fullness of his plans. Our part is to say yes, and let him lead the way.

Rebel for God will remind you that nothing is wasted, and that no part of your story is unredeemable or purposeless in the economy and timeline of God. Beginning to end, this story is marked by his fingerprints, and you don't have to dust very far to find them.

Life is about stewardship of God-given capacity, and while it's undeniable that Eddie DeGarmo's capacity is almost larger than life, it's the humility and open-handedness with which he's chosen to steward his God-gifts that is most striking. He's generously and skillfully shaped the music of our generation by helping amplify the voices of artists like dcTalk, TobyMac, Audio Adrenaline, Chris Tomlin, Skillet, and a host of others whose names would make your jaw drop. He's given God everything, and left nothing on the table.

I, and believers around the world, have so much to thank Eddie DeGarmo for. You and I may never know the number of voices who will sing the anthems his hands have helped craft, but I know Heaven's chorus has grown under the careful craftsmanship with which he's brought us his melodies.

I'm grateful for Eddie's life and legacy, and for the songs he's touched that have given words to many seasons of my soul. It's impossible to imagine Passion without Eddie's partnership in helping the songs God's given us reach the world.

I'm so glad you've picked up this book, and cover-to-cover, you're in for a wild and thrilling ride. As you read, I challenge you to open your mind to greater possibilities than what you've dreamed, and to open your hands to God's plans for the talents he's entrusted to you. In doing so, you—like Eddie—will be in for more adventure, and more fun, than you ever thought possible.

For His Fame,
Louie Giglio

FOREWORD
TobyMac, Grammy award-winning artist, producer, and songwriter

was still in college about to graduate when I first met Eddie DeGarmo. I was in a group called dcTalk that recently signed a record deal with a small upstart indie label called ForeFront Records. It was a tiny label, but they were willing to take a chance on a pop/hip-hop band in those early days of our genre. We were down in Memphis putting the finishing touches on our first album, working in a hole-in-the-wall recording studio sitting squarely in a gritty part of town. I thought it was cool, though. One of ForeFront's owners, Ron Griffin, was working with us on our record. The label's other owner was Dan Brock. He let us know he arranged for us to go on tour to launch our album with DeGarmo and Key if we were willing. I really didn't know about D&K and didn't have much awareness of the CCM industry in general. Instead I was immersed in hip-hop, r&b, reggae, and pop music. I really didn't hear any hip-hop that was incorporating faith in its subject matter. So that was where the idea of dcTalk began to develop. A long story short, I met a couple of friends in college named Michael and Kevin who could sing the phone book, and that is when the dcTalk story began.

Unbeknownst to me, D&K had already been pioneering a new musical genre years earlier that was eventually called CCM—Contemporary Christian Music. So Dan Brock let us know D&K were going to drop by the studio since it turned out they were from Memphis. When Eddie came walking into the studio that day, it was clear that he had been swimming in the river of rock and roll. He had '80s hair bigger than seemed possible and a swagger to match his mojo.

We toured with D&K for a couple of years and while Dana was the front man on stage, I figured out early on that Eddie was the guy pushing most of the buttons. A few years later Eddie let us know he was also an owner in ForeFront Records. So, we connected the dots and saw that it was clearly a good business decision to put us out on tour with them. It was good for us as well, as touring with D&K was an important building block early in our career. We were just grateful to be playing our music in front of a room full of people every night. Along with taking us on the road, there were a couple of times Eddie stepped in when relationships became strained with the label. His laidback manner and friendly approach along with his veteran wisdom helped us find common ground and continue our journey with our label partner.

This book is Eddie's story and I am thankful that our paths crossed when they did or the dcTalk story might look a lot different. Eddie has been a forerunner in a lot of areas within the CCM industry. Obviously one of those is starting a label called ForeFront Records. It is where we learned the ropes and then broke out onto the national landscape with our platinum record *Free at Last* and then followed it with the double platinum *Jesus Freak*. We could not have done it without our partners at ForeFront Records.

We are forever thankful they took a chance on us, let us mature, and stretch artistically as they walked alongside of us.

I have observed Eddie as an artist, keyboard player, tour producer, record executive, music publisher, rock opera creator, husband, and father over the years. Watching any man balance family with success in the music business gets my attention. Over the years I have respected Eddie at close range and at a distance. If I had one word to describe Eddie it would be wise, and I don't throw that out loosely. Through all my encounters with him, Eddie seems to have the rare ability to stay focused on what matters. He is a patient listener who offers concise feedback, usually in the form of a few words that end up sticking with you for life. In other words, when you have a conversation with him he doesn't leave you with a hundred different things to think about. He usually boils it down to the one or two things that really matter. To me that is a great picture of his life. He has been involved with a lot of different ventures and he has had many victories, but he has never lost sight of the things that really matter. I am grateful to be one of those who have benefitted from his wisdom and am honored to call him my friend.

KEY CHANGES

—

"The only thing constant in life is change"
—**FRANÇOIS DE LA ROCHEFOUCAULD (CIRCA 1650)**
OR HERACLITUS (BC 500)
OR EDDIE DEGARMO (CIRCA 2016)

Change and constancy are like the two rails of train tracks. They run parallel and never touch but always go to the same place. Change is inevitable in this life, but God is constant. In fact, he is the only constant. He never changes. His principles never change. How we interact with those principles, or even how we understand them, might change. The effect we allow them to have on our lives might change. But God is called a solid rock for a reason. He is like a boulder in the middle of a rushing river. Or maybe he's like all of the stones on a riverbed. Time and circumstances rush over and around him. Waves might form. Ripples in the surface might make it hard to see the rock, but it's there—shaping the flow of the river. With each turn of the stream the view changes. We can fight it all we want. We can try to row against the current. We might even be tempted to just head to shore and watch it roll past us. But if we want to get anywhere it might be best to embrace the twists and turns as best we can; to navigate the transitions and enjoy the ride. And what a ride it is!

As I look back on my life thus far I can see several major transitions I've had to navigate. In fact, if it wasn't for transitions—and painful ones at that—I'd still be playing clubs and chasing girls in Memphis. I might even go so far as to say that how I've handled these transitions, or how they've handled me, may have more to do with the success I've experienced as an artist, a businessman, and a disciple than just about anything other than God's providence. There's a lot I don't know about how God works, but six decades into this journey I'm learning to see His hand all around me. These stories I'm about to tell you, from the wild and wooly to the deeply personal and painful, are shared not to build my brand or to cement my "legacy," but simply to demonstrate a few key principles I now realize have been central to my journey. From my earliest days behind the keys of a Hammond B3 to helming the largest Christian music publisher in the world, I'm ready to share it all. I hope if you find the thread running through my crazy ride it may help you stitch out your own incredible story.

With the benefit of hindsight I can now recognize at least five major transitions in my professional life. First I made the jump from being a lost kid with rock 'n' roll dreams and a major label record deal to being a transformed Jesus follower on a faith mission that would eventually absorb and redefine every rock 'n' roll fantasy I ever had. A bit later I consciously chose to shift my creative vision from full volume blues rock to more mainstream pop style. After realizing more success than I could have ever imagined as a rocker, I shifted my attention to the behind-the-scenes aspects of the business and launched an independent record company that became the largest independent Christian record company in the world. Years later I returned to my entrepreneurial roots after selling my record label to one of the biggest mainstream entertainment companies and launched a boutique music publishing firm. Then I became the president of the largest faith-based publishing company in the world. How did *that* happen? Then, based solely on what I hope was a call from God, I stepped away from it all and retired. Talk about a key change!

So these are the stories of my transitions. Some are funny. Some are painful. I believe all of them, however, reveal some important truths about life, faith, vision, mission, and what some people call "success." As Dana Key and I sang all those years ago, I do believe we are "Destined To Win," as one of our D&K song says, but how we get to that finish line, well, that's the thing, isn't it?

ONE

WHEN YOU'RE NOT LOOKING

I once heard a man speaking at a seminar deliver an interesting view of humanity. "There are three types of people in this world," he said. "There are people who make things happen, there are people who watch things happen, and there are people who wonder what happened!" I thought that was pretty funny.

Southern California is an interesting place. You're liable to run into anything—especially when you're not watching what's happening.

In the mid 1980s, Disneyland hosted a massive concert event appropriately named "Night of Joy." I was honored that my band, DeGarmo and Key, was chosen to perform on that big stage along with several other artists. That night the Magic Kingdom was packed to capacity. Frenzied, energetic kids, youth groups, college students, and families crammed happily into every action ride, show, castle, and pirate ship. The feeling was electric.

Growing up in Memphis, Disneyland was always revered as the crème de la crème of theme parks. It was the top dog, the ultimate.

However, I never knew anybody who actually set foot there. We all just watched and drooled from afar when Walt Disney appeared on our TV sets every Sunday night, glowing about what the newest attraction was and how it would change our lives forever. We watched it all happen for other kids and dreamed about being there ourselves.

I was twelve years old when I finally got to see it for myself. It was 1967 and my folks and I travelled to California on vacation to visit my Uncle Eddie and his family in the San Francisco Bay Area. My dad, always the consummate deal maker, somehow convinced a downtown Memphis Lincoln dealer to allow him to deliver a new Town Car—complete with suicide doors—to a customer in San Francisco. I'm not sure you can do that anymore, but Dad made things happen. That Lincoln was our over-the-top, luxurious, vacation transportation. It was the size of an aircraft carrier. My mom, dad, and I spent a week driving to California. We passed through Colorado, which was my first time admiring the Great Rocky Mountains. We were amazed by the Grand Canyon and excited by the lights of Las Vegas. Then we cruised across the Mojave Desert and up to San Francisco. Vacation wasn't a normal occurrence in my family. I was blown away.

Uncle Eddie was my father's youngest brother and one of seven kids raised by their mother during the Great Depression. Their father died of malaria when my dad was only five years old. My Grandpap Edward was a sawmill operator in the cypress swamps off the Mississippi river in the Arkansas lowlands. The mosquitoes got him. Dad and two of my uncles, Eddie and Jack, were always close growing up. They started a thriving business together in the late 1940s in San Francisco. Their company manufactured and sold different contraptions and inventions my father came up with.

One of the gadgets, called "The DeGarmo Ice Magic," was an ice scraper you could plug into your car's cigarette lighter. It was really a pretty good idea for 1949. It heated up to help melt the ice on your windshield. My dad, the inventor and salesman, was selling them out of the trunk of his car to hardware stores, grocery stores, and gas stations from the Sierra Nevada Mountains east of San Francisco all the way over to Lake Tahoe. His brothers ran the manufacturing operation back in the city. Things were going gangbusters until the scraper's blades started to fall out prematurely. Uh-oh! They began to fly back, returned as defective by customers and retailers. At first it was only one returned per day. Then ten. Then a hundred poured from the mailman's bag every day! The brothers didn't have the money to fix and replace them as fast as they were coming back. That's when Dad, Mom, and their three kids, (I wasn't born yet) skedaddled out of town in the middle of the night and hurried back east.

I didn't hear that story until years later when I was a grown man. Uncle Eddie came out to see DeGarmo and Key play in the Frisco Bay Area and told me the tale about the scandalous "DeGarmo Ice Magic." He was laughing so hard he almost couldn't make it through to the end. He said he and his other brother went to the office one morning to discover my dad had just vanished, never to show up again. No note. No anything. The ice scrapers came back by the thousands. The brothers did their best at first, then finally locked the doors of the business and went bust. Dad finally called them both and made up a few months later. After that, I think my dad and the brothers got right and drove the straight and narrow. Well, for the most part anyway.

Back to when I was a kid. When we arrived in the Bay Area on our vacation it was the "summer of love" in 1967. I was looking forward to spending a week with my cousin, David DeGarmo. David was a couple of years older than me. He was in high school and was quite the savvy young man. We were thick as thieves that week, trudging all over the city. We had a complete blast and it was a real eye opener for me. He showed me the Haight-Ashbury district, Golden Gate Park and Bridge, the Bay Bridge, and the city itself. San Francisco was remarkably beautiful and definitely freewheeling during that time; way different from Memphis.

At the end of our week together, and after Dad delivered the Lincoln to its owner, we planned to fly to Los Angeles and visit Disneyland as the pinnacle of our trip. It was decided David should accompany us. I was elated. Disneyland didn't let us down. It was indeed magical. I even remember seeing a young Jim Morrison and his band The Doors rise from the ground on a small stage in the Tomorrowland section of the park playing "Light my Fire." They were just getting started in those days and were not yet famous. I didn't realize who they were until much later when I looked back on it. I'll never forget it now.

———

Almost twenty years went by before I returned to Disneyland for our concert as part of the Night Of Joy in the mid-eighties. A lot of water surged under the bridge of my life between those visits. About three years after my childhood visit—totally caught up in San Francisco's hippie culture—my cousin David died of an accidental heroin overdose. He shot up the drug under his tongue so his parents wouldn't see the needle marks. That was heavy on my mind as I returned to the "Happiest place on earth." Things could have easily turned out that way for me I guess. Fortunately, God had another plan.

Our band bus rolled into Anaheim at about 8:00 a.m. and delivered us to a high-rise hotel directly across the street from the front gates of Disneyland. It was a normal blue-sky, pristine, southern

California morning. We rolled out of our bus bunks and wandered half dazed into the lobby as our road manager checked us in. If not for our tour bus parked immediately outside, we could have easily been mistaken for homeless people. Hair all fuzzed out, wearing sweats, cut-off shorts, ripped t-shirts, and blurry eyed, we looked a total mess. That was typical for us.

A few minutes later when I got to my room the phone immediately rang. It was my bandmate, Dana Key. He invited me to come down to the restaurant and have breakfast with him. "Sure," I said. "Give me a few minutes to clean up and I'll be down." Cleaning up, for me, meant getting my hair under control. I had some kind of hair in those days. My wife and daughters said I could easily be confused with "The Beast" from *Beauty and the Beast*. Others said I looked like a wrestler. I liked that description better.

The hostess desk and cash register in the lobby restaurant was directly across from a double set of glass exit doors. I could see people sitting at booths and tables in the large dining area beyond the chest-high hostess desk. There were a couple of hipster street looking guys standing there paying their bill to the waitress from behind the cash register as I strolled up. The hallway was too narrow for me to pass behind them so I walked up between them and the hostess desk, smiled, and said, "Excuse me." The two guys graciously backed up to the glass exit doors, allowing me to pass by in front of them. When I walked into the restaurant, oddly, every eye in the place was trained on me. Suddenly I heard a woman's bloodcurdling scream from behind me and I turned around just in time to see those two men running through the glass exit doors as the waitress continued to scream.

They robbed the place!

I briskly stumbled over to the row of booths where Dana was sitting. He looked up astonished and gasping for air saying, "Do you have any idea what just happened? Those guys had guns trained on that waitress! We were all watching! You just walked up and said, 'Excuse me' and they raised their gun arms just like a tollgate at a parking lot and let you pass by. Then, they lowered their guns and finished the hold-up! Unbelievable! Eddie, you are Mr. Magoo!"

I have thought a lot about that morning since then; whether those guys knew whether I saw their guns or not. Maybe they thought I was some kind of bad-*** longhaired dude not to be messed with. I like the thought of that but I'll never know for sure.

Like they said at that seminar, there are people who make things happen, people who watch things happen, and people who wonder what happened. When the speaker laid it out like that we all laughed. What he said was funny, but I have found myself falling into the third category more than I like to admit.

"What happened?" The story of my life. It's definitely been exciting.

TWO

IN THE DAYS OF THY YOUTH

Memphis, Tennessee sits proudly upon a bluff overlooking the Mississippi River. They call it the Bluff City, actually. That's where I grew up. I never understood the nickname until I got older. They say the river bluff makes the tornadoes jump over Memphis. Maybe that's true, but it seems I do remember a couple of them wreaking havoc a little east of downtown when I was a kid. I guess they just didn't jump far enough to get past the hood or the suburbs for that matter. Downtown was the only area that seemed to be spared. Across the Big Muddy river, the land is as flat as the back of your hand, with cotton fields stretching for miles in every direction. That's where West Memphis is. It's actually in Arkansas and things are just a little bit different there. More about West Memphis later; it's important.

Downtown Memphis was extremely vibrant and alive in those days. Front Street, next to the river, was lined by cotton companies in both directions. They traded it, shipped it, picked it, sold it, or did whatever else could be done with cotton. They mostly made money. Every fall, during the harvest, you could see thousands of cotton bales stacked upon the cobblestones next to the river, waiting to be loaded onto barges. The businessmen and workers inspected and moved them around, circling them almost like vultures on the hunt.

Memphis could still be hot in October. It seemed everyone—whether dressed in suits or work clothes—was drenched with sweat. The city hosted the annual King Cotton Parade and it was quite a big deal back then. I represented my fourth grade class at the festivities one year. It was a proud moment and an honor when I was chosen to be the ambassador of my class at the King Cotton Parade! This was back in the late fifties and early sixties. When I met the girlfriend of my life years later she worked at a cotton company on Front Street, as did her father before her. Two things seemed to be the lifeblood of Memphis back then—cotton and music. The latter still runs through my veins to this very day.

Beale Street intersects with Front Street and South Main right on top of the river bluff above the muddy Mississippi. It's like you can smell the catfish when the breeze blows just right off the river. It's been called the Home of the Blues. I lived just a few miles south in a neighborhood called Whitehaven. When I was a kid my older brother and I, and sometimes a friend or two, would hop on the city bus and ride down to go hang out on Beale Street. I was only eight or nine years old. It was safe to do that back then. Incredible! In those days, Beale Street was lined with the coolest and most outlandish rock 'n' roll and soul clothing stores, a lot of pawnshops, and some infamous soul food restaurants. The century-old buildings were weathered and tattered and in serious need of fresh paint.

The streets had open air produce markets on the corners with vendors who called out when you passed by, "Hey boy, you wanna buy a slice of watermelon for a dime?"

Old black men sat on apple crates, played bottleneck guitar, and sang the blues all down the street. I remember a band called "The Three Tuffs" except there were four of them. One of the guys played bottleneck slide on an acoustic guitar with open tuning. One played a guitar with only five strings instead of the normal six. One played an upright bass made from a washtub and a string. The drummer beat a cardboard Stag Beer box with drumsticks. I asked the guitar player why he only had five strings. "Well, I only got five fingers," he said. "It only seemed right I didn't need that extra string." Made sense to me. I later found out the Rolling Stones' Keith Richards did the same thing. Guess it made sense to him too.

The drummer did fantastic things with that Stag box. He hit it in different places for different sounds and raised and lowered it with his foot for more bass resonance. The kids today do the same thing with the five-gallon plastic buckets. But this guy played a Stag Beer box! "Why that brand?" I asked.

"No other beer box sounded right 'cept Stag," he said. I was smitten. That was cool.

My family moved from Detroit to Memphis in 1959. My folks were both from backwoods, northeast Arkansas towns called Marked Tree and Piggott. They were country kids who grew up in the cypress swamps and farm country of the rural backwoods. They didn't know each other growing up, but both went north to Detroit during the beginnings of World War II when they were "all grown up" teenagers hoping to find work in the factories and help the war effort. I think a lot of folks did that then.

Strangely enough, my father was in the Army's horse cavalry back in Kansas during 1939 before we entered the war when he fell ill with a very bad case of dysentery. Uncle Sam thought he was sure to die and discharged him, giving him only six months to live in 1941. He received a pension of seventeen dollars a month all of his life after he was sent home. That doesn't sound like a very good deal. My dad wasn't allowed to re-enlist during World War II. I'm pretty sure he always felt guilty about that, seeing how all his friends went off to fight the good fight overseas. He just never died like the Army said he would. He met and fell in love with my mother in Detroit and started our family there. Though they lived up north for twenty years, they always had a longing to move back to the South. In June of 1959 Dad bought an old truck, packed us up, and headed back to Dixie. I was four years old. My folks were known as Cliff and Marge.

I'm the youngest of four boys. My oldest brother, Shelton, is eleven years my senior. Then came Mike and Larry. I came into the world almost six years after Larry. That worked out pretty well for me, actually. I was the only one at home from seventh grade through high school. I got all the attention.

When we moved from Detroit to Memphis our parents dropped us four boys off at my grandparents' farm outside McDougal, Arkansas. It was the month of June in between school years. We stayed with them for about a month while Mom and Dad went to Memphis to find us a place to live. That was when I first learned what chopping cotton was all about. My grandparents were good people, but thought it was right that we worked while we stayed with them on the farm. As I mentioned I was only four, so I'm sure I didn't work very much, but my brothers did. My grandma took us out to the fields every day with a hoe and had my brothers chop the weeds away from the cotton plants. I just remember it being hot and dirty and watching out for snakes. My grandma seemed to always have killed a copperhead or two with her hoe and stretched them out for us kids to see. I also remember my brothers hating chopping cotton with a passion. We learned to pick it later that year. We hated that too. Those are my earliest Southern memories; cotton, heat, dirt, snakes, and sweat. It all fit together pretty well.

On Thanksgiving Day, 1959, my family bought and moved into our house at 4080 Whitehaven Park Circle. Graceland, Elvis's home, was just a quick walk through the woods up and across Highway 51 from us. That's when music came alive for me. Elvis Presley personified rock 'n' roll, and his mansion captured my imagination. That kind of success and fame became the goal and purpose of my life. In many ways, music became my god by the time I hit adolescence. I dedicated myself at the altar of rock 'n' roll completely.

Growing up in Whitehaven was fantastic. It was just a few miles south of downtown, but far enough away to feel pretty rural. We only had a few stores, but Elvis lived there! When I was in first grade our school bus passed Graceland every morning. Sometimes we kids would see The King outside riding a horse in his pasture. Sometimes he would wave at us as we went by. I actually trick-or-treated from him on Halloween once. I remember the kids lining up the driveway of Graceland waiting to catch a glimpse of him. I was a little vampire and Elvis gave me a one-dollar bill he signed. I did what every other little punk would have done. I spent it the next day. I can't believe I did that!

My interest in music actually started back in Detroit. My mother played piano in our small Missionary Baptist church. She was really good at it. We had a piano in our basement, and I began to play around on it at the age of three. She taught me little melodies, very simple songs and such. Those were dear times with her I will never forget. She gave me lessons until I was five or six. Then she was done. I was unruly so she farmed me out to an evil piano witch. That didn't go so well until the witch bought me a Beatles songbook in 1964. Then she turned into a piano goddess! Smart, she was.

I can also remember the first record I was old enough to put on the record player and play all by myself. It was "I Got a Woman" by Ray Charles. I played it over and over again all day long. It must have been my big brother's record. My folks probably wouldn't have bought me "I Got a Woman" when I was only four. I know it was my brother's record player because it wouldn't work right one day so I painted it with blue-gray house paint I found in the basement. I painted the whole darn thing, turntable and all. It ruined the record player and it about ruined my behind after my father found out. That was a bad day.

A couple years later, down in Memphis, on the first day of the first grade, I met a kid who became one of the most important people in my life musically and spiritually. Dana Key was kind of a big kid who surrounded himself with his own greasy kid-gang of minions. I can still see his dirty, smudgy face when we squared off on the playground. He asked me if I wanted to be part of his gang.

"No way," I said. "I'm going to get my own gang and be the leader."

That's how we met. We competed with each other for the rest of our lives. We were friends, and truly loved each other, but we really acted more like blood brothers. I still recall, in the fourth grade, when we looked through the Sears and Roebuck catalog at the musical instruments. In the early years he was going to play trumpet and I was going to play trombone. I'm glad that didn't stick.

THREE

CHASE THE WIND

M y older brother Larry took up guitar around the time I met
Dana. He was in high school by then and got pretty good at
playing and singing. My father was an okay guitarist too, but
was even better on the harmonica. He picked up harmonica as a
kid while hopping trains around the country during the Great
Depression. He said they were really popular because you could put
them in your pocket if you had to jump off the train. He could play
rhythms and melodies at the same time. I marveled at it. Dad and
Larry sometimes played together in the living room.

Larry formed a neighborhood band with three or four other
kids from around the block. They practiced in my brother's upstairs
bedroom after school. I often sat in the corner and listened to them
play. It was magical. I was totally into the drums. I just couldn't
believe how cool it was to hit on things and keep a beat. When the
kids left to go home, I would sneak in, sit at the drums, and try to
make beats. By this time, my mother and father were home from
work and the noise drove them crazy. They yelled up the stairs for

me to leave those drums alone and come down and practice piano. Let's face it; playing piano is not the coolest thing for a fourth grade boy to do. The other kids spent afternoons playing football and baseball while I had to practice my stupid piano. Drums seemed cool, though. You got to hit things.

My mom and dad joined us all up to the Graceland Baptist Church when we moved to Whitehaven. I can still see the pastor, my dad, and the other deacons all taking a smoke on the church steps under a blue sky after the Sunday service. It was the early sixties and in the South after all. It seemed everyone smoked—even the dogs and cats. I tell folks I had a "smoking permit" in high school allowing me to smoke cigarettes at school. I don't think my grandkids believe me when I tell them. That was before we knew smoking killed you. Now, we've come up with better and quicker ways to kill ourselves: drugs, gangs, junk food, and all kinds of other bad stuff.

Remember, I said earlier West Memphis figured importantly in my story. It's known these days as the Truck Stop Capital of America. That's something when you think about how many truck stops there are. It's where the highly traveled I-40 and I-55 interstate highways intersect.

West Memphis was also known for the Southland Greyhound Park—the one and only place where legalized gambling was allowed around Memphis when I was a kid. Every night on the evening news the announcer gave the odds on the Trifecta or Quinella, or all sorts of crazy schemes a person could bet on and maybe win a little money. The Baptists didn't think kindly of gambling, of course. Well, one night my dad, being the good Baptist that he was, decided to go over and bet on the dogs. He ended up winning $1,200, which was a small fortune in 1964. He took me out the next day, probably either out of guilt or his hatred of my drum playing, to Berl Olswanger Music on Union Avenue and bought me a Farfisa Combo Compact Organ and a Gretsch amplifier. It was the same keyboard many of the famous British invasion and American rock bands used. I was beside myself.

That is how I got started in Christian music—at the dog track.

God may have taken a few years to work out his plan properly with me, but that was the start of my apprenticeship. During my years as president of Capitol CMG Publishing, I purchased the exact model of that little organ and set it up outside my office with a picture of me playing the original one with our band when I was ten years old. It was a great reminder of where I came from and also a good story to tell to aspiring artists and writers.

I was nine years old when my dad bought me that organ. It caused quite a hoopla at home. All of a sudden it was cool to be a piano player in the neighborhood. It also drew some pretty snide remarks from my brothers. They couldn't believe my folks spent that much money on me. Frankly, I can't believe it either. We were a totally middle class American family and that sum was downright outrageous. I think it was the "sin money" from the gambling escapade that did the trick.

I was quickly invited to be in my brother Larry's band. All the band members were in high school and I was just going into the fifth grade, but I had the organ and amplifier. It's probably what got me in the band. We named our band The Chants. I practiced every day like clockwork. I learned songs from vinyl records by picking the needle up over and over again and copping the licks. I probably drove my poor family crazy. I couldn't pass by a piano without sitting down and banging out a tune. That was my daily passion from then on.

One of my big moments came on the last day of the fifth grade. My teacher came to me and said there was going to be a celebration for the whole elementary school in a couple of weeks and our principal wondered whether or not our little rock band would play a few songs for the student body. I went home elated and asked my brother and the band if they would be willing. Of course he agreed, but they needed permission to get everyone out of high school that day. The parents of the band members wrote notes and, thankfully, it all worked out. We played three songs that day at Graves Road Elementary School; "Gloria" by The What (Van Morrison's first band), "Louie, Louie" by The Kingsmen, and "You Really Got Me" by The Kinks.

The place went wild while we played. It was glorious. All the girls wanted to talk to me after I got offstage. I couldn't believe it. It was kind of sicko when I look back at it. I was somebody! Our dear ol' dad even showed up unannounced with a bunch of big amplifiers he rented. He wanted us to sound good. He was always into it that way.

That was the day I dedicated my life to becoming a rock star. Hell or high water, I was going to make it big someday. Unfortunately, for the next several years I visited hell first.

My first real conflict happened at our church. Our band was a dance band. All the kids wanted to do when we played was dance. There were dance TV shows like "American Bandstand," "Hullaballoo," "Dance Party," "Where the Action Is," and others. The Methodists, Catholics, and several other churches sponsored weekend dances in their gyms or youth meeting rooms.

The message I heard from our church, loudly, was simple. "The Baptists don't dance, son."

That's pretty much all I remember hearing from my church for several years, actually all the way through my high school years. But it was the sixties and I was bent to be all about it in every way—good or bad. I was sold. I found my destiny.

Later on that year our band hit a road bump and proceeded to drive off a cliff. We started playing out fairly frequently. It seemed it was always for a dance at a skating rink, a church, or swimming pool party. One day the whole band met with me and told me they were going to kick out our drummer and get a kid who played better and owned better drums. But the drummer and I were tight as ticks so I quit the band out of loyalty. It turned out to be divine intervention.

Not long after, Larry's band played at a senior graduation house party where the parents were gone and the kids got up into some heavy drinking. Later that evening my folks found my brother passed out in our old, funky, nasty fishing boat in the carport. The band left him out there, totally fractured by the alcohol. I guess they were too afraid to knock on the door. He was crazy drunk and a complete mess. He probably could have died out there. My parents and I found him by his moaning and dragged him into the house and into his bed.

In the morning, all hell broke loose as my parents handed out Larry's sentence. He was banned from his rock band forever and grounded from any activities completely for the three very long summer months. That's pretty hard medicine for a kid just about to graduate high school. My folks further humiliated him by cutting his hair close to the scalp while he was still drunk and passed out. I know they were just handing out what they thought was tough love. We never questioned their motive. But it was really tough.

After that Larry gave up on music and went to work at a local grocery store. Many years later he still felt he was judged too harshly by our parents and that one mistake took him away from the music he was so good at playing.

"Maybe that messed my career calling up," he once told me.

For me it was just the beginning. Music wasn't just a hobby for me. I was completely "ate up with it." Larry's tragedy sidelined him, but I kept on keeping on. That kind of passion can be a good thing, like a cool drink of water, or it can be bad—like a disease you can't control. For some of us music gets deep into our souls and roots itself in there. There was no stopping me.

Dana Key and I formed our first band in the sixth grade. We named ourselves "The Sound Corporation." We were a four piece: Dana on guitar, me on keys, Andy Owens on bass, and Donnie O'Neal playing drums. Around the time Christmas came Larry showed up at one of our band practices.

"You guys need a manager," he said. "Someone just like me."

He then began to tell us if we were going to be a band we had to look like a band. It was time to dress accordingly and get some real threads. He was right about that. Years later as a record executive, I said to my artists, "If you can walk through the mall without people suspecting you are an artist, singer, or in a band by the way you dress and carry yourselves, you've missed the mark." Image is important.

Then my brother, our new manager, also said there was a battle of the bands at the Mid-South Fair and he thought we should enter. We had a few months to get ready. Over that span we practiced as much as possible and played every possible gig. My dad was a real estate agent at that point and sometimes we set our amplifiers up and played on the driveway at his open houses. It was then I first really experienced how music could draw a crowd. People stopped their cars in the street, got out, stood, and listened. My dad was a pretty good marketer.

I've discovered through the years that performing live is where the rubber meets the road for an artist. It changes everything about how you sing, play, look, and smile. You've heard "Strike a pose." Well, that actually happens when you perform in front of a crowd. Everything gets much more intense, focused, and refined.

Later in life when I was a music executive, my first question to young artists was, "Where have you been performing?" Too many times I heard excuses. "Well, I have to work here or there to make money and I haven't had as much time to sing and play as I would prefer. But, if you could help me with a deal and support I could do it more."

To that I replied, "But, you said you are a singer," or "You said you are a guitar player. Singers sing and guitar players play. I didn't ask you if you were getting paid for it. That's not the important matter for now."

Many times artists gave me a puzzled and discouraged look after that exchange. I would then say, "You know, you have to want it more than me. It never works out in the end if you don't."

It was the beginning of the seventh grade when the band competition rolled around for Dana, the guys and me the next September at the Mid-South Fair. We were rock solid tight. We also had our knee-high black suede Beatle boots, white pants, light blue turtleneck sweaters, and love beads around our necks. We probably looked like a commercial for the TV show *Laugh In*. But hey, it was 1967. We were scared to death when we performed that Saturday afternoon at the fairgrounds. It was probably 95 degrees in the place and we were wearing sweaters. I have to say though, we killed it.

There were several dozen bands competing from all over the mid-south. When it was our turn to perform, we played "Mustang Sally" by Wilson Pickett, "You Keep Me Hanging On" by Vanilla Fudge, and "For What It's Worth" by Buffalo Springfield. Every group got to play three songs. Ours weren't necessarily the happiest pop songs of the day. We were way too hippie-psychodrama for that fluff and we wanted everyone to know it. We were cool.

The band that came on behind us was much better at playing the socially accommodating game than we were. When they started playing, all but the drummer had their backs to the crowd and one by one they were introduced over the music. "Danny on bass"—then he would turn around to face the crowd very quickly with a huge smile. "Jimmy on guitar," and so on. They were all wearing blazer jackets and ties. I have to admit, even back then Dana and I laughed and thought it was extremely cheesy. That band went on to win the competition based on their showmanship. We came in second place. We won in every other category—musicianship, performance, etc. But those guys had a show and we didn't. I learned a hard lesson that day.

I think it was Les Paul who said, "People hear with their eyes." Les Paul invented the electric guitar way back when. When he first presented it to the public it was just a board, kind of like a two by four with strings on it, and it didn't go over well. In fact, it bombed. He went back to the drawing board and came back out with a version that looked similar to the acoustic guitar form. It was a hit and it caught on big.

"People hear with their eyes." If you think about it, Les Paul is completely right. It is certainly true when it comes to live performances of all kinds of popular music. Most of our concert memories are visual. Try it out. What do you remember most about your favorite concert? More times than not, we remember what we see more than what we hear.

After that surprising defeat Dana and I spent a lot more time thinking about how we looked and moved on stage.

FOUR

TOO FAR TOO LONG

T hings started to get serious in the music business for me during the latter half of ninth grade. I met a fellow in high school by the name of Dunk Carter. He was a rhythm guitar player who just moved to town. Dunk wore a jacket with a threadbare American flag sewn on the back with red, white, and blue peace symbols on each arm. This meant to me he couldn't be half-bad. He knew a man who had a recording studio in the poor and funky part of downtown Memphis. This man's name was Lewis Willis. Dunk was old enough to drive and invited me to go to the studio with him one Saturday to meet the owner. I'm not sure how long it took me to say yes, but it couldn't have been more than half a second.

Dunk and his brother picked me up that Saturday morning and we drove a little north of downtown Memphis to a seedy part of town where 2nd and Looney cross. All I saw was an old furniture store with a neon sign blinking the name "Willis Furniture." There was also a big pelican painted on the plate glass window along with the words, "Pay a little down on a big bill."

I laughed and asked Dunk, "What is this strange place?"

He assured me the studio was in the back and we proceeded inside. I noticed a small hewn stone African American church across the street, and an old dilapidated little grocery store at the corner I later discovered made the best bologna sandwiches in town. As we entered the building we passed by several pieces of new and used furniture for sale in the showroom on our way to the back.

There sat Lewis Willis, smoking a cigarette. He rose and walked to me, extending his hand and introducing himself. Lewis had a debonair look to him in his turtleneck and blue cardigan sweater adorned with the customary suede elbow patches. He respected me as an equal, even though he was an adult white man in his late thirties and I was a fourteen-year-old punk kid. That meant something to me. He began by showing me around the tiny control room of the studio. He had a two-track recorder and a modest mixing board. He asked me all sorts of questions about the music I liked. Then we walked back out through the furniture to the room where the musicians played while recording. It was pretty dark in there. Dim red and blue lights highlighted the walls and ceiling. In the middle of the room, in front of a microphone, was a lanky, tall, black man who was also smoking a cigarette.

He walked over to me and stuck out his hand. "Hey there," he said. "I'm L. H. I sing lead in this here band."

Despite the darkness L. H. was wearing sunglasses. I also noticed he had a goatee. He was older than Dunk and me; old enough to have chin whiskers. As my eyes began to focus in the dim light, I saw a couple more musicians sitting in isolation recording booths positioned around the corners of the room.

That afternoon I joined L. H. and The Memphis Sound. We were a seven-piece soul band with a rhythm section, a trumpet, and a sax. Over the course of a rehearsal or two, we realized we needed a lead guitar player and I suggested to Dunk he call my friend Dana Key. Dana joined us shortly after that, playing lead guitar as our eighth member.

That was my first experience playing in an inter-racial band. For that matter, it was the first time I had a meaningful relationship of any kind with black kids. It was a blast and opened my eyes in a thousand different ways. We got to know each other quite well over the next few months as I was baptized into the world of soul music, Lewis Willis, and Allied Recording Studio. It was wonderful. It seemed back then music transcended all the racial barriers in Memphis.

My dad was a real estate man. Before that he was a Buick man. When he was discharged from the Army and went to Detroit in search of work he ended up going to work for one of the Buick dealerships in town. He started as a mechanic and worked himself up to service manager over a few years. One day, a mechanic showed up on the job drunk and Dad got into his face about it. I guess the ole boy was of a pretty good size. Anyway, he ended up taking a swing at my father, caught him on the jaw, and sent him tumbling across the floor. Dad got up and chased him out of the place with a big monkey wrench. He's lucky the guy took off running because Dad would have taken his head off with that monkey wrench had he caught him. He'd probably still be in jail.

Dad got pretty rough and ready growing up in Arkansas and Texas during the Depression. He'd fight a buzz saw if he thought it had it coming. He ended up going to the hospital after the mechanic ran off. He lost a few teeth in the process and had his jaw wired shut for a while until it healed up. He carried a bit of a scar there for the rest of his life. After that incident, my father decided he wanted a more peaceful job so he went into selling real estate and building houses.

My mother owned beauty schools and beauty shops. She and Dad started the first one when I was in the fourth grade. My mom started attending beauty school when I was in the first grade, when she had time during the days with me in school. After she graduated, she ran a beauty school for another fellow for a couple of years while learning the business. She and my dad opened the first DeGarmo Beauty School in Whitehaven. It did pretty well, so they opened a second one a few years later and then a string of beauty salons. I feel pretty lucky to have had both my mom and dad be so entrepreneurial as I was growing up. It taught me a thing or two about business just by watching them and living through it. I learned first and foremost that if you are the owner there is not a single job beneath your dignity. If the floor needs sweeping, you sweep it. If the windows need washing, you wash them. Also, you work before and after all the employees leave. That is just the way it is. It's your business. I swept a lot of hair and mopped a lot of floors in those days when we cleaned all those places on Sunday afternoons.

My mother worked a job when I was one and two years old in Detroit. Then she stayed home with me after the move to Memphis until I started school. When she started back to school and work, my folks hired a maid, and a nanny of sorts, to be with us boys while they worked all the time. They were always black women and they were always great to be around. We sassed them and they chased us and my mother gave them permission to whack us if we needed it. We usually did.

Every morning and evening their men folk would drop them off and pick them up in some sort of jalopy car. I never thought anything about it as a small boy. As I said, my dad contracted houses. He built them and sold them. Many Saturday mornings, he and I would get into his pickup and ride into shantytown. He drove up and down the street talking to the black men, asking whether they wanted to work for a day or two or sometimes more. We picked up four or five men in the back of his pickup and he took them to work on his houses and then took them back home at the end of the day. I never thought twice about it, being a kid and all. That was just the way it was.

I remember being with my dad one morning and us seeing a young black man sitting in my father's favorite coffee shop for the first time. My dad looked my way and said, "Look there, son. Things are a changing!" That was the South in the late fifties and early sixties.

Since our schools and churches were still segregated, the time I spent playing music with black kids was the first time I had ever been around them for any length of time. I found out very soon those kids were exactly like me, other than often being much better musicians than I was. They worked at it harder. Maybe they wanted it more. Music was a way out of poverty for them. Being in an integrated band did raise an eyebrow or two around our schools and the town in general. We thought that was awfully cool.

Sadly, L. H. and The Memphis Sound didn't last very long. We were a hot band while we were around, though. One important thing that happened was the other underage kids in the band and I had to get our parents to sign work permission papers with the state and city giving us permission to work underage in places and clubs that served alcohol. Our parents signed them after Lewis went and met with them each personally and promised he would look after us. He and my dad were Masons and it turned out they had a common bond of trust on that level. Lewis did try to keep watch over us. He was good that way. The problem, though, was we learned how to sneak around him pretty well.

Slowly, as L. H. and The Memphis Sound dissolved, we reformed by replacing members with kids we knew from our end of town. We changed the name of the band to "Globe." We became an all-white soul band—which was even more peculiar in Memphis at the time. L. H. introduced me to musical masterpieces I'll never forget; artists like Otis Redding, Booker T. and the MG's, The Barkays, Eddie Floyd, and Al Green. I learned how to feel the back side of the beat, which is a different place altogether. It's greasy back there. You can ask any drummer worth his salt what the difference is.

My favorite keyboard player was Booker T. Jones. I saw him play once with The MG's, at the YMCA in Whitehaven. He played "Green Onions" for what seemed to be at least fifteen minutes, on his Hammond B3 organ. Later I met the songwriting team of David Porter and Isaac Hayes, the writers behind big hits like "Hold On I'm Coming" and "Soul Man." It was a new world for me, and a good additional influence from the British Invasion bands so popular at our suburban schools.

Lewis formed an alliance with the legendary producer Willie Mitchell and Hi Records. Hi was just beginning to top the charts then with artists like Al Green, Ann Peebles, and Anita Ward. Hi Records operated a studio called Royal Recording just around the corner from Stax Records in Memphis. Hi had some success with The Bill Black Combo and the saxophonist Ace Cannon in the late fifties and early sixties. By the late sixties they had turned to Memphis soul music. Royal Recording Studio is still in operation today with notable artists like Bruno Mars and Paul Rogers recording there recently.

Lewis communicated with Willie that he was managing and recording an all-white soul band named Globe. We were a ten-piece band by then, including two horn players and three singers. The year was 1969. We were playing all over town and around the mid-south three nights a week and were appearing regularly on well-known local TV shows out of Memphis like *George Klein's Talent Party*, *Swingshift*, and others. Those local shows hosted many notable artists in those days. I remember seeing James Brown, Wilson Pickett,

Herman's Hermits, Sam the Sham, The Pharaohs (the band behind "Wooly Bully"), and many others.

Memphis music was on fire with Stax Records and Hi. Stax was arguably one of the largest independently owned record companies in the world and Hi Records had begun a string of dominating global hits with Al Green. Several other major labels had offices in Memphis as well. There was a band on every corner and it was like music was in the water.

April 4, 1968, was the day Martin Luther King Jr., was assassinated in Memphis. So much changed after that day. There were riots in the streets. The National Guard drove tanks through our city. Troops were everywhere. There was a lockdown curfew after dark. Many buildings were burned and looted in the parts of town where the recording studios were. Interestingly, Lewis Willis told us, the old family furniture store was not harmed in any way even though buildings on both sides of the street were ransacked and several set on fire. Lewis was a friend to many in the neighborhood as was his father before him. They sold furniture and allowed people to pay (or not) on credit for fifty years. He was passed over by the riot. Like the pelican on his front window promised, "A little down on a big bill."

Later on, when I started dating Susan, my wife, I learned she marched with Dr. King and the Memphis Sanitation workers a few weeks before he was killed. She was only fourteen at the time. Most folks will tell you about the heightened tension felt everywhere in Memphis between the races after that horrible event. Even the music wasn't above it.

Through our manager Lewis Willis, Globe signed a record and publishing deal with Hi Records and Willie Mitchell in 1970. I was fifteen at the time. We recorded a few singles at Allied Recording Studio, which grew to occupy the entire furniture store by then. The guys in the band helped Lewis build the new studio by working nights and weekends. We would do anything to record.

Lewis arranged for us to do a session at Royal on a Saturday soon after we signed. I was elated. They had a Hammond B3 there and a Leslie speaker just like Booker T. played and I couldn't wait to play it. When we unloaded our guitars and amps that day I felt like I had died and gone to heaven.

We walked into the cavernous old building on South Lauderdale Street goggle-eyed. It was an old movie theater converted into a recording studio. Stax, just around the corner, was also an old movie house. It seemed the high ceilings really suited the recording process. It made everything sound big.

We didn't really get to dive deep into any serious music that day. We did a few takes though. Mostly we just listened to Willie Mitchell tell stories of who recorded there and how much promise he saw in us. It couldn't have been a better day. Over the next year or so, we recorded many times at Hi's Royal Studios. We even recorded at Stax Studios some, as well as Allied, which was our home turf.

Allied bought a Scully eight-track recorder so they could compete with the bigger studios. I heard it was the same type of machine The Beatles recorded *Sgt. Pepper's Lonely Hearts Club Band* on. Many years later my wife and I met George Martin, The Beatles' record producer, at the Grammy awards at Radio City Music Hall in New York and had a wonderful conversation. He was sitting alone in the foyer that day for some reason, and my wife simply struck up a conversation with him. She got his autograph. She reminds me I didn't.

In August 1969, everything in the music stratosphere tilted. That was when the Woodstock Music and Art Fair happened in upstate New York. Woodstock was the largest music festival that had ever happened. It was three days long with back-to-back performances of every artist imaginable. There were four hundred thousand people there. I didn't get to go. I was only fifteen, but the next summer in 1970 was when I became "experienced" as Jimi Hendrix would say. *Woodstock* the movie was released.

At that time, it was only being played at the outdoor drive-in movie theaters in Memphis because it was restricted by age to attend. You had to be eighteen to get in. Dana and I were dying to see the movie. Dana became a total Jimi Hendrix freak and just had to see him play the "Star Spangled Banner" on his guitar complete with simulated dive bombs on the guitar's whammy bar. Not only did I want to see that, but I was just as much into Joe Cocker, Santana, and Sly and the Family Stone.

We had to come up with a way to get in. Dunk Carter's big brother was eighteen, so we devised a plan for him to drive his parents' Oldsmobile Delta 88 to the drive-in. That was a really big car. Dunk planned to lie down in the rear seat floorboard under a blanket and Dana and I could hide in the trunk. Off we went!

Woodstock changed everything. Our soul band transformed into a rock band with horns. We were doing some pretty original stuff for the day. We were definitely influenced by Santana, Hendrix, and Jethro Tull, as well as horn bands like Sly and the Family Stone, Chicago, and Tower of Power. We were getting somewhere musically and Hi and London Records, their distributor, loved the new hybrid sound. We started to record some originals, looking for that special first single. We were playing out all over the place in the mid-South and were fairly popular. My dream was coming true, the dream I first had when my school bus passed by Graceland every day. It seemed being a rock star was where it was at.

FIVE

LIVIN' ON THE EDGE OF DYIN'

The only time I saw my father cry while I was growing up was when my older brother Mike shipped out for Vietnam in 1968. We were all together at the Memphis airport when Mike was flown away. He recently graduated Officer Candidate School in the Army and was a second lieutenant. We fortunately didn't hear the statistics until later just how long second lieutenants survived in combat in Vietnam. It wasn't very long. Some only lived minutes. They were targets. A few months after Mike was in the country, he was severely burned on his legs and ended up in a hospital in the Mekong Delta. He spent several months recuperating there and eventually made it home safely, thank God. He was a proud veteran, but to his dying day the after-effects of that war tortured him. It was devastating.

Our oldest brother Shelton didn't have to serve because he didn't pass his physical, but my brother Larry volunteered for the draft when he was nineteen, shortly after Mike shipped out. He knew he was on the short list to be drafted. He learned that by volunteering, a recruit was offered some limited level of choices of where to go, what his job would be, and so on. Larry ended up being assigned to Germany. While he was stationed there, he sent me a poster bearing a large photo of a marijuana cigarette with a sign stuck in it that said, "Keep off the Grass." Ironically, I immediately hung it on my bedroom wall. Much later when Larry came home, he told me the drug culture invaded the Army as well, and he had his own struggles with it in Germany. He sent me the poster hoping somehow his little brother wouldn't go down the same path.

Mike and Larry were different people when they came home. Obviously they had grown into men, but they both seemed so unsettled. Wartime definitely took a toll on them and our family. A few years had passed since they were in the house and I guess they were trying to find their place in civilian life. I was in the twelfth grade playing in the band and doing pretty well. Globe was popular around the mid-south and we felt like we were about to make it. But both of my brothers were acting completely crazy and out of control. They went out together carousing all night on an endless party. I knew my parents were concerned. Heck, even I was concerned, though I was living in my own dark world of the same sort of thing.

Larry went out and bought a big motorcycle and began to ride around with a biker gang. That certainly didn't sit too well with our family. We were just a normal, suburban, middle class family and not at all immersed in the motorcycle culture with its peculiar tribes and behaviors. Several nights I came home from a gig long past midnight on a Friday or Saturday and found Larry passed out from drinking or taking drugs. Sometimes he'd be lying next to his motorcycle in our carport on the bare, cold, concrete. I helped him into the house and upstairs to bed. Occasionally, the next morning I attempted to talk to him about it, but he didn't want any part of that. He told me to stay out of his business and leave him alone.

One night I got home in the wee hours of the morning from a gig we played about fifty miles north of town. I remember it was winter because frost was a problem on the windshield of my old Ford Econoline van. The defrosters didn't work and I had to roll down the window and freeze to death to see where I was going. I remember being very high once driving around and my friend ripping his underwear off of himself in the passenger seat next to me without even undoing his pants. He proceeded to use his shredded underwear to clean the frost off my windshield. He just reached down grabbed and ripped! I couldn't believe he did that. Gross!

This particular night when I pulled into our driveway at home I saw Larry's motorcycle parked, but no Larry lying close by. I got out of my van quietly, closed the door, and walked into our house through the door entering the breakfast area. I saw a lone figure silhouetted in the dark at our table. It startled me. I reached over and grabbed for the light switch. As the light came on and my eyes adjusted I saw Larry sitting at the table. On one side of the table was our oversized family Bible and on the opposite side of the table stood a fifth of whiskey. Larry stared at one for a second, then turned his head and stared at the other. He was completely silent. It was like the Bible and whiskey were dueling it out over the control of his mind. He didn't utter a sound. The sight was beyond bizarre.

"What is wrong with you?" I asked. "Are you going crazy?"

He motioned for me to come over and said, "Take a seat. I need to tell you a story."

Larry emotionally told me that while he was in Germany he fell in with the wrong crowd and found himself deeply involved with drugs and all that goes along with that lifestyle. He said over time he became quite despondent and disillusioned with just about everything he once held dear. "Things grew quite bleak for me," he explained. Yes, he was homesick, but it was more than that.

One night he was invited by a fellow soldier to attend a small meeting made up of soldiers. They met to discuss and study the Bible together in the city of Heidelberg. He told me for the very first time, he heard he could have a relationship with God way deeper than just going to church or anything he ever experienced. It could be a personal relationship. He heard Jesus would forgive him of his sins if he simply asked, and then Jesus would help him navigate this crazy life, not only on a daily basis, but on a moment-by-moment basis.

Larry then said, "Eddie, I dedicated my life to Jesus that night. That was just a few weeks before I was due to be shipped home. Things became very clear for me for the first time. I knew God loved me and had a plan for my existence far beyond random fate. Things made sense. Then I came home. I became intimidated and afraid to share with anyone about my encounter with Jesus in Germany for fear of being labeled a religious fanatic or 'Jesus freak.' I was especially afraid to tell you. I didn't know what you would think of your big brother. So, I bought the motorcycle and tried everything possible to drink my life away and forget the promise I made to Christ that night in Heidelberg."

Then Larry said the most remarkable thing to me. "Eddie," he whispered, "God won't let me go. No matter how hard and fast I try to run, God won't let me go."

That story is what I call experiencing my first epiphany. An epiphany is defined as a moment of sudden intuitive understanding; a flash of light, or a sudden and profound understanding of something; or an appearance or manifestation of God. Larry's story was all three of those things to me. I understood and knew at once that something supernatural had dramatically taken hold of him. I just wasn't completely sure what it was. It bothered me.

The next day Larry put his motorcycle up for sale and immediately stopped his carousing and partying. He began to attend church and told me daily he was praying for me and my soul. Over the next few months he actually drove me away from him with his continual preaching. He was driving me nuts. Our band was doing well. I certainly didn't need the religious distraction. After all, I was born an American and grew up Southern Baptist. I even got baptized when I was eight years old. I would fist fight you if you said anything bad about Jesus. I didn't need anything deeper.

Larry bugged me constantly about it, saying, "There is more to it, Eddie. Jesus can be real and walk alongside you every day." I hated hearing that! Especially over and over, all day long.

Larry and I grew up sharing a bedroom. Our two older brothers roomed together down the hall. Larry and I were still rooming together after he came home from the Army. We had grown but the house was still the same size. I recall us getting ready to go to sleep one night and Larry started in on me with his Jesus preaching.

I screamed at him, "Shut up! Leave me alone. You are driving me insane."

He did shut up that night. I also remember looking up from my bed in the darkness totally exasperated and praying, "God, he is either right or I am right. I want to know the answer."

I found out later you need to be careful when you ask God things like that. He will surely tell you. "Seek and you shall find," the Bible says.

Later that spring, in March 1972, the band was playing a dance in Ripley, Tennessee, at the town's recreation center. It was on a Saturday night and before I left for the gig, I finally succumbed and promised Larry I would attend church with him the next morning. I hadn't attended any church in several years and was rather skeptical about churches in general. There was a special guest speaker in town named David Wilkerson. Larry thought I would enjoy hearing him because he had a rough and tumble story of working with gang members in New York City. I didn't get home from the dance until around 4:00 a.m. When Larry came to wake me in the morning, I told him I got in too late and that he should go away. I still recall hearing his footsteps as he turned to leave. Then a miraculous thing happened. I just sat straight up in bed and called out for him to wait. I knew I was going.

We drove across town to a church I wasn't familiar with. That morning I heard David Wilkerson speak and a young guitar player/ singer named Dallas Holm perform. I had never seen anyone play guitar at a church service before and was taken aback by it a little. Nothing remarkable happened that morning other than the guitar playing, really.

Larry asked if I would be willing to go see a movie made about the morning speaker's life. It was called *The Cross and the Switchblade*. I agreed to go on one condition; that Larry would then accompany me to Overton Park later that afternoon to see some local bands play. The Overton Park Shell during that era hosted some of the best rock bands and performers in the world. I saw The Allman Brothers, Deep Purple, ZZ Top, Seals and Crofts, Grateful Dead, Poco, and many others in concert there through my high school years. Elvis even performed there in the fifties. Globe played there a few times on the stage with other local bands. The shell seemed to have a concert every weekend during the warmer months. Overton Park also became the place in Memphis the hippies would hang out during the sixties and early seventies. You could get into all kinds of mischief there, from strange religions to Frisbees to drugs. It was where we all gathered on weekends.

After seeing the movie, it was my turn for Larry to hang with me. We drove to Overton Park to hear the bands play. I had been with Larry all day, and now it was his turn to be with me and my people. It was a warm, beautiful, and sunny March afternoon in Memphis.

The skies were blue, the trees were just beginning to bloom. The gray winter was passing by. Spring, flowers, music, and the smell of pot were everywhere in the air. There were several thousand people on the great lawn of the park. A stage was set up at one end and one of my friend's bands was playing. The sound system suddenly squealed loudly with feedback and everyone held their ears.

My friend, the band's singer, then screamed over the mike "F-—k! Sorry about that!" I looked at my brother, embarrassed by what my friend said. Then my brother and I began to walk through the crowd. Right then, Dana Key walked right up and faced me. His eyes were very swollen and red. He was obviously really stoned, drunk, or both.

He asked "Where you been all day? We've been having a blast."

About that time Dana turned to see my brother standing next to me and immediately turned and ran off. He probably didn't want to get preached to. It was in that moment I had my second epiphany. The difference between my life and my brother's life became immediately and vividly apparent to me. For the first time my eyes were completely opened to who I was and what I had become, juxtaposed with who my brother was, and what he had become. Also, for the first time in my life, I felt ashamed. I asked Larry if we could leave.

That evening we went back to hear David Wilkerson again. He spoke about something I never heard before. That one day Jesus would come back to this earth and take his children home. I realized I was deathly afraid of facing Jesus and that particular thought bothered me greatly. Why was I afraid if my life was so together with God? When the invitation came at the end of the service, I went forward and was ushered backstage to a room. I remember the guitar player, Dallas Holm, coming into that room. I immediately made a beeline over to him and asked if we could speak.

I explained to him about my band, success, and the dilemma I faced. "If I give my life to Jesus, will I have to quit my band?" I asked.

He gave me a very simple, honest and to the point response. "I don't know that answer," he softly said, "but you have to be willing to."

As I have thought about what he said through the years, I've come to the conclusion it was divine truth. It hit me hard in my gut and gave me just enough strength to take the next step. I prayed with Dallas Holm that night and asked Jesus to forgive me. I dedicated my entire life to him.

Later, when Larry dropped me off at home, I went immediately up to my room to be alone. I had my room to myself again as Larry recently married and moved out. I then knelt by my bed and wept. I wasn't necessarily a person who ever cried and that felt strange enough to me. But the reason I was crying was not out of joy. I didn't feel joy at all that night. I thought to myself, "What have I done? I've given my life to Jesus and what if he demands I quit my band? I can't go back now." That was foremost on my mind.

What an ungrateful twit I was. The God of the Universe saved my soul just hours before, gave me the gift of eternal life, and I was so completely self-centered I couldn't even be thankful for just a moment of time. I felt awful immediately as the truth of who I was covered me like pond scum and my selfishness became apparent to me. Exhausted, I then asked God to forgive me, and I tried to sleep.

SIX

GO TELL THEM

The next day was a Monday. I awoke early, half excited and half frightened about my mysterious encounter with God the night before. I had to go to school. I jumped in my van, started it, and hit the road without talking to anyone at home.

There was a ritual of sorts that happened every day before school in the parking lot. The students who had cars parked, visited, smoked cigarettes, ate junk food for breakfast, and traded stories from the weekend. It was like tailgating at 7:00 a.m.

Graduation was just six weeks away and it was a main topic. That particular morning, I was quiet. I was so quiet, in fact, my friends asked me what was up. I didn't know what to say about what happened the night before. I stayed awkwardly silent, waiting for the bell to ring.

I was a fairly popular kid in school, mainly because of our band's local notoriety. I didn't play sports and was working most weekend nights somewhere with the band. My circle of friends was tight. Outside the band, my main social scene in high school was camaraderie with a wild fraternity that I was a member of. We even had a frat house—in high school! We didn't practice Christian behavior, or even intelligent behavior in that lion's den. It was just a hang out where we would get into all kinds of mischief.

During my initiation and hazing the year before, the other pledges and I were made to streak naked on Highway 51 in front of Graceland at 8:00 p.m. on a Saturday night. There we were, in our full glory, prancing by the front of the most famous house in Memphis, in nothing but our birthday suits. Traffic was heavy so we had quite an audience. Some cars followed us with their high beams on while others honked their horns and hollered. I still can't believe I did it. It didn't seem like too big of a deal back then. People should be arrested for streaking right past Elvis and Graceland.

But that Monday morning I didn't even want to see my fraternity brothers. I just didn't know what to say to anyone. I walked into the school, on my way to my first class, and immediately ran into Dana. I believe it was Providence. He strutted up to me and asked why I left so early from the concert at Overton Park the day before.

"I found Jesus," I blurted uncontrollably.

Dana smirked. "I didn't know he was missing."

"I'm serious, Dana," I said. "We need to talk." I suggested we skip class and Dana agreed.

Let the record show, it did not occur to me that Christians weren't supposed to skip class. I was in the flock for less than twenty-four hours at that point. We ended up ducking into a janitor's closet off one of the classrooms. Fortunately, there was a light bulb in there hanging from the ceiling by a wire. I picked a Bible up from our chorus teacher's desk on the way to the janitor's closet. I remembered that Mrs. Tyler always kept it lying there on her desk. It's funny how God shows you things as you go along.

Once we got situated in the closet, on mop buckets and boxes, I explained to Dana what happened to me the day and night before in great detail. I told him about how my eyes were opened when I saw him stoned at the park. I explained how I asked Jesus to forgive me of my sins, how I committed my life to him forever, and how I didn't really understand what it all meant or how it would play out. I simply told him I felt like it was right, and I was changed. I opened the Bible to a random place and began to read. I didn't have a clue what I was reading.

Dana stopped me mid-sentence and exclaimed, "Stop! I want what you have. I have been going through the same weird confusion and nothing makes any sense in my life. I want to give my life to Jesus too."

In that janitor's closet at Hillcrest High School, in March 1972, Dana Key committed his life to Christ. Nothing would ever be the same for either of us ever again.

Coincidentally, we had band practice on Monday nights. We practiced downtown at Lewis's studio. Being a recording studio, it was the perfect practice room. Dana and I got there early that night to set up. As the rest of the band began to arrive, the air in the room got pretty thick. You could cut it with a knife. Maybe I was nervous because I planned to share what had happened to me the same way I did with Dana.

After everyone was set up I asked if I could say a couple of things. That probably really freaked them out, as I had never asked to do that before. I went on to explain the journey I was on and where it ended the night before. I explained I made a decision to follow Jesus. I also shared about Dana's decision to follow Jesus in the closet at school.

They looked at me with complete dumbfounded confusion. It was as if I had just said I joined the French Foreign Legion and was going to Africa to find Tarzan and Jane.

"Wow. That's great, Eddie. Awesome for you. And you too, Dana—now, can you play that new song by Yes?—or somebody? Just play anything by anybody—quickly!" Those were the kind of comments I got back. Some couldn't even find words. They offered no response but blank stares.

That was an important moment for me. To stand in front of my peers and share Christ with them was a big, big deal. You see, our band was known for its somewhat loose and risqué attitudes, songs, and performances on stage. So, for me to drop this bomb on them might as well have been like saying I was an alien from space beamed in from Mars or Pluto.

I've thought about that moment many times. I wonder whether it was wise for me to say that stuff in a group setting, or if it would have been better to explain it to them individually. Sharing with the group like that did have a galvanizing effect on me, though it also had a dividing effect amongst us as well.

I call that entire day my third epiphany because God suddenly invaded my life like a majestic force. It was also clear to me things had changed forever in the band. The train was off the track. The cat was out of the bag, and no one knew how to get it back in. There was definitely no turning back.

Over the next few weeks, the differences between the other members' point of view and ours became painfully clear. We had conversations about what songs were appropriate to play, what was appropriate to wear, and what we should, or should not, say from stage. It was weird, to say the least. I never imagined I would suddenly feel so dramatically different about so many things and would feel the need to vocalize those feelings. I'm sure it blew their minds. One day I was this, and the next day I was that. It blew my mind as well. I also shared the Gospel with many of my friends at school during that time. I was a man on a mission.

A couple of months after that fateful band practice, we had a gig at the Enlisted Men's Club on the large naval base in Millington, just north of Memphis. We played there many times so I didn't think much about it. Larry called that afternoon and said he had a free evening and wondered if we needed any help.

"Sure!" I said, enthusiastically.

Anyone who has moved a Hammond B3 organ and all the amplifiers, speakers, and rest of the machinery of rock 'n' roll knows help is always needed. We got set up that night at the club and, as usual, noticed and remarked about the male to female ratio in the place. There were probably three hundred men and ten women in the club.

For the most part the guys would clown around, drink a little too much, and occasionally dance with somebody. It was mostly harmless, but I forgot about an important ritual that happened every time we played there. About mid-way through our second set, the sailors cleared the area in front of the stage to create a roughly sixty foot wide semi-circle of chairs right in front of the band. The soldiers sat in the chairs and a series of scantily clad girls appeared from backstage, shimmy around each guy, and do what was basically a soft-porn exotic dance and tease in front of them. If a guy "got lucky," she might sit in his lap, or slip off a little piece of clothing.

We always played a long sultry instrumental for about ten or fifteen minutes while the girls did their version of private table dances for each guy. This night was no different. We decided to play "Green Onions" by Booker T. and the MG's because it was easy to stretch out. As the song started and the girls came out, I glanced over at Larry, sitting to my right about six or eight feet away. Oh my gosh, was I uncomfortable. I couldn't believe how embarrassed I was to have to do this in front of the guy who led me to the Lord.

That night I had my fourth epiphany. God revealed to me, in that moment, I was meant to leave the band. I had an immediate and profound understanding. That was the first head-on collision between my faith and the world of entertainment. It was definitely a moment of destiny. It was also far from the last such revelation.

This was hard stuff for me. I dedicated everything in my life to making it in the music biz and now I was ready to give it up. I knew as I grew in my understanding of the things of God, my relationship with the band was increasingly like the relationship between oil and water. I shared how I felt with Dana, somewhat worried about how he might react. "Man," he said, "I never thought you'd say it. I'm so ready to quit too."

Dana wasn't as ready for my next step. I told him I was putting all of my keyboards and equipment up for sale. "If God sells them," I said, "it will be a sign for me to quit music." I was confused and needed some direction and guidance. I advertised my keyboards at good prices in several newspapers for a few weeks. Good news was, I couldn't give the stuff away.

It actually took a few months to leave the band. We had several gigs on the books, and we didn't want to leave the guys hanging. In the meantime, prom and graduation came. Dana and I drew really close during that time because of the bond of our new faith. We went to prom together with our dates in my dad's full-size Lincoln Continental with suicide doors. We were a sight to see, all dressed up in tails and top hats. I even carried a cane and wore white gloves. I'm pretty sure I looked like a vampire.

After our graduation ceremony, our friends all went out to party the night away. Neither of us had any desire to do that anymore. We knew what it meant and where it could lead. So I picked Dana up at about midnight, and we drove about sixty miles south to Sardis Lake. We slept on the beach and watched the sun rise the next morning. It was kind of a bummer to spend our graduation night that way, but it was also a defining experience for both of us. We knew we were changed through Christ. We just didn't quite know what to do with ourselves at that point. Old things passed away, and as we were being made new it was a weird feeling. It was like suddenly seeing in color for the first time after a lifetime of black and white.

Within weeks we were both starting to write songs about our new faith and what God did in our lives. This was no pre-meditated thing, mind you. We just wrote about what was important to us. That was how our generation worked. One day we're writing songs about cars, or girls, or Vietnam, and the next we're writing about Jesus.

We never had a discussion about what style of music we wanted to do. Rock 'n' roll was second nature to us. Had we grown up on country music, I'm sure that's how our songs would have sounded. But we'd cut our teeth on Memphis rock and soul. It was our language. At that time neither of us were aware of anyone else playing rock music about Jesus. Later we discovered several other artists around the world were doing the same thing, but at that point the only Christian music either Dana or I were exposed to was hymns at church and Southern Gospel. Both our dads were fans of Southern Gospel music.

Once Dana and I were officially out of Globe I went and met with Lewis Willis and told him about the new songs we were writing together. We were still under contract with Hi Records and Hi Publishing even though we were out of the band. Lewis let us use the studio for rehearsal so we could work up a few of the songs. We rounded out the band with a drummer named Max Richardson who was a previous member of Globe. I asked him if he was interested in helping us develop this new kind of music we were calling Jesus Rock. We didn't have any money, and no gigs to play, but we had a vision. He agreed and we got to work.

We didn't have a bass player, so I played the bass notes with the pedals of the Hammond B3 organ the way Felix Cavaliere did in The Rascals on their hits "Good Lovin'" and "People Got To Be Free." Neither Dana nor I had ever sung in Globe, but we didn't have any other singers available so we did it ourselves. All three of us played and sang. It was pretty cool. The plan was to get the songs together and then see if Lewis, Hi Records, or their distributor London Records were at all interested in working with us.

Dana, Max, and I recently moved out of our parents' houses and got a cheap, one-bedroom apartment in a ramshackle mid-town building. We lined up our three twin beds like an army barracks along the wall in the bedroom. The neighborhood was funky. The apartment was tiny. We were loving life.

There was a fellow that lived primarily on the street who went by the name of Dancing Jimmy. The thing was, Jimmy only had one leg. He had another spare leg he would wear occasionally. You could always tell when Jimmy was down and out. He would take off his prosthetic leg and sit on the street corner and beg with one pant leg rolled up. When he would raise enough money to buy cigarettes, wine, or maybe a sandwich, he would fetch his other leg he had hidden close by in the bushes and put it on quickly to make a beeline for the liquor store around the corner. We guys would go visit him in the afternoons and hear his stories of war, lost romance, and just how screwed up politics was in the world.

Across the hallway from our apartment lived an old gal who wore what looked like a Beatle mop-top black wig she bought from a dime store. Sometimes she would wear it backwards. She was always sweet to us boys. It was an interesting neighborhood. We would leave our front door unlocked at night so if anyone needed a place to sleep they could come in and find a couch or the floor. Sometimes, we would wake up to find two or three young folks we didn't know from Adam sleeping in the living room. People just dropped in to crash late in the night after carousing at the music clubs down the street in Overton Square. It was the Jesus Movement, and there was ample good ministry going on.

Dana and I had started to hear that there was a tiny support system for "Jesus Music" coming together around the country, but we still knew nothing about it. Dana came in to the apartment one summer afternoon clutching an LP called *Only Visiting This Planet* by Larry Norman. He was visibly excited and said, "You are not going to believe this!" He proceeded to play the entire album on the turntable. I was truly amazed. It was the first time I realized that there were other artists besides us making this kind of music. I also noticed that the record was released on Capitol Records, a major label. Maybe that meant they saw potential in Jesus Rock. I thought maybe there was a way we could someday commercially release an album as well.

Truth be known, I was a rebel without a clue. I didn't have any idea if I could actually make a living in this new genre of music or not. I just knew that I felt compelled to do it. It was my calling, and I was just naïve enough to think God would make a way.

SEVEN

EMMANUEL

After that summer I started as a music major at Memphis State University. That didn't work out so well, but we'll get to that later. There were no classes for what I needed to learn. I was going to have to figure it out as I went. I met a guitar player named Tony Pilcher, who was in one of my music classes. Tony and I had a lot in common and hit it off from the start. He grew up playing in rock bands like ours and gave his life to Christ about the same time as Dana and I. In fact, as the phenomenon known as the Jesus Movement took root in the U.S. and the UK, millions of longhaired kids like us were coming to faith. Turned out there were lots of other rock 'n' roll Jesus freaks out there, we just hadn't met them yet.

I invited Tony to come jam with us at the studio. He was a great addition to the band and came and went several times over the next few years. We became a four piece; two guitars, keys, and drums. I still played bass with my feet. We practiced with a vengeance, two or three times a week for the next month or so. It was finally decided we needed to find a place to play publically.

Every band needs to gig. You really learn what works and what doesn't when you play in front of an audience. The only venues we knew of, however, were clubs, frat houses, corporate parties, dances, and bars. Churches, in the South anyway, didn't host Jesus rock bands. So, we tried a few gigs at bars. We found out quickly folks didn't usually come to bars to listen to Jesus rock bands. They were especially turned off by what we had to say between the songs. We were evangelists. That didn't go over so well. I've carried that lesson with me my entire career.

The first time I experienced any kind of censorship of my music was when Hi Records said they didn't want us to write songs that openly shared our faith. They just had no idea what to do with those songs. That was a massive hurdle for us to jump. Artists don't want to be censored. Could we find a way to perform our Jesus music in bars and clubs? Every band needs an audience and a place to play. The bars didn't want to hear about Jesus. The label had no idea what to do with us. The churches weren't the slightest bit interested in our loud rock 'n' roll. Where would we fit?

We began to invite friends and people we met around town to come to Allied Record Studio for our rehearsals. As that group grew we started to become known as the "Christian Band" around Memphis. We thought it was too prideful at that point to honor the band with a real name. "Christian Band" suited us just fine. We painted big red crosses on all of our equipment with blood dripping off the crossbar. It all fit nicely.

One cold night in January of 1973, Tony Pilcher brought a girl from his neighborhood to our band practice. Her name was Susan. I still recall meeting her and being a bit shy about it. She was very pretty. We started every rehearsal with a prayer. That night we prayed earnestly for Susan, even though the rest of us didn't know her. Later on she shared with me that was the first time anyone ever prayed for her. She was struck and moved by it.

I didn't see Susan again until February nineteenth. I remember the date because it was her birthday, and she was throwing a party at her home. I decided I would go see how she was getting along. At her party we talked for hours on end. She made me laugh by saying the most interesting trait about me at band practice that night was I played bass pedals with my sock-clad feet, and I had really cool looking boots that laced up the sides. Other than that she thought I was stuck up. On a more serious note, she shared with me, the day after she came to our rehearsal she gave her life to Christ. She said she didn't know how to pray, she certainly didn't know how to recite the Sinner's Prayer, but she said, "I told the Lord I want what those guys have."

That night at her birthday party I could sense the overwhelming joy she had living in her soul. That was magnetic to me. Joy is a powerful thing in a person. It's rare. A few months later Susan and I started dating. A few months after that, we got married. We've been married since October 1973. She is still my girlfriend to this day. I affectionately call her my first "groupie." I usually get smacked when I say that.

After Susan's birthday party, things began to clear up and focus a little more for the band. Lewis met with us and heard our new songs. We did some simple two-track demos of a few of them he took over to play for Willie Mitchell.

Lewis came back with a resounding message. "No. Hi and London are not interested. They didn't sign you guys to do music about God, and they don't understand or have any desire to market religious rock music." After that episode they released us from our contracts. That was when I first realized there were underlying rules to be followed in order to market and sell music. Making music is different than marketing music. Oh well, it was just another hurdle I had to learn to jump.

For some reason, though, Lewis still saw something in us and continued to allow us to practice at his recording studio. We began to invite other friends who in turn invited other friends, and before you knew it on a given night we could have a hundred or more people at our rehearsals. One night we had over two hundred people show up in the big old converted furniture store.

One thing led to another and we started to get invitations to play in public and away from the confines of the studio in other venues. That's when things got really interesting.

Our band was invited to accompany a regionally known evangelist at a rally at Union University in Jackson, Tennessee. We were going to play music to attract a crowd and then he would come up to the platform and speak. That was the plan, anyway. Union, being a respected Southern Baptist school, was known for its great biblical teaching and its conservative leanings. I respected it then, and I still do now. That particular day, as we were setting up our Marshall amplifiers, Leslie speakers, and our sound system, I noticed that the auditorium looked as though it was probably built at the turn of the twentieth century. It was completely constructed of hard wood with zero sound baffling. The floor, walls, and ceiling were a beautiful, polished wood and had certainly been built long before electric sound amplification had been invented. I wondered if that wood had ever experienced anything like our crazy brand of rock 'n' roll. That evening the auditorium quickly filled up with students and folks from all different backgrounds. After a brief introduction we started attacking the first song and immediately the young folks were completely into the music. However, the adults looked to be in a state of shock. They had never had seen or heard anything like us before.

They all looked like they were sick to their stomachs and wanted to throw up. I think that racket is probably still vibrating in those walls to this very day! It was a beautiful thing. But about midway through the first song a leader from the university and the featured evangelist of the evening ran up on stage and waved his hands for us to stop.

The evangelist looked directly at Dana and screamed, "You have ruined this program!"

"Amen!" Dana immediately responded. "What did you expect?" He could always be the consummate smart aleck. His timing was impeccable.

Actually, he was dead right. What did they expect? We were a rock band! After that intrusion, we were powered down and not allowed to play anymore—much to the chagrin of those attending. We were asked to pack up and leave. That's not the only time we were shut down for being too loud and offensive, mostly by those dang adults in charge. The young people loved us, but the establishment was wary. And we were just getting started.

Folks in the South weren't accustomed to long-haired boys playing rock 'n' roll and preaching about Jesus at the same time. I recall on more than one occasion playing in some backwoods town, setting up on a flatbed trailer in a parking lot somewhere, or on a street corner, and people were stunned. They looked at us like the guys in Globe did when we shared our faith with them, like we were goons from outer space.

Sometimes folks got offended and threw stuff at us. Yes, we have actually been pelted with half-rotten tomatoes. It was mostly the religious folks who got that upset. Sometimes people jeered and cussed at us. Many times though, people came to the Lord. It was an amazing time. We were blazing a trail, as it were. Dana and I used to joke in those days, we should always leave the truck running for a quick getaway "just in case some church person wanted to 'lay hands' on us."

One early Sunday morning during the "Christian Band" era in the spring of 1973, I woke up after sleeping over at my parents' house and went downstairs to find my father watching one of the local church services on TV. My folks hadn't been regulars at any church in years. They stopped going about the time I started playing in dance bands, and the Vietnam War was raging and sought my brothers. But they would watch church on TV sometimes. As the TV pastor got into his sermon he got pretty wound up. He was shouting about folks being deceived by the world and the devil, and how Satan would trick you into thinking you were doing the right thing but it would ultimately lead you to the pit of Hell.

"Take this rock 'n' roll music about Jesus for example," he shouted with a grimace. That stuff is straight from Satan himself! This fellow, Eddie DeGarmo, (that's right, he said my name) is the ringleader who's going to destroy our young people's hearts and minds with this smut. He'll lead them to a fiery hell as surely as I stand here!"

As the preacher's frenzy went on my father's head turned slowly toward me. His eyes locked directly on me with a snide look. Then he said, "Boy, what in the world have you gotten yourself into now?"

Later that month, we were invited to play at another local Christian college by some students we played for several times before when we were in Globe. The next week I received a call from the college saying they had to cancel. They didn't realize we played "Christian rock" music now and their church denomination didn't permit rock music with Christian lyrics. Talk about weird.

So, we were asked by club owners not to come back, shut down by an evangelist, preached against by TV preachers, and now canceled by a Christian college that used to let us play there when we were a mainstream band. It was a cross-cultural train wreck. It felt like trying to push magnets together when the poles repel each other. I was a little hurt, and a little confused by the reactions. What did God lead me into? The kids liked it, but the establishment on either side of the aisle, mainstream and religious, didn't.

Now, there's a rock 'n' roll story if there ever was one. It turned out the controversy was what drove the press machine wild. The newspapers and magazines couldn't keep themselves from writing about us—kind of like people not being able to turn their eyes away from a car crash.

EIGHT

LOVE IS ALL YOU NEED

Susan and I were married on October 21, 1973. She likes to say our first baby girl was born nine months and fifteen minutes later. I say it was really nine months and five minutes! Wow! As I have looked back and laughed about our wedding day and how we sent our families into shock about it, I'm pretty sure everyone must have thought Susan was pregnant, but that wasn't the case. That's because we decided on Friday to get married on the following Sunday. Also, we were both at the mature age of nineteen. Yikes! We were just head over heels in love. That was it. During our first year of marriage, we saw many things that brought enormous change to our lives. The central, earth-shaking event, of course, was having a baby. I was still nineteen when our daughter was born. Susan had just turned twenty. I recall when I got home that day and heard the news for the first time. Susan said she had something very important to share with me.

"Eddie," she whispered, "I went to my doctor today. I'm pregnant." She studied my face, looking for a reaction. She had no idea how I would respond to the news.

My first reaction was shock; like the kind of shock that hits you when someone throws a plugged-in hair dryer into the tub while you're taking a bath. But very quickly shock turned into beaming pride. Susan and I decided immediately we should thank God and pray about what to do next.

Again, rebels without a clue. I was only working part time while going to college. She was working part time as well. We didn't have any money. Susan came over to my easy chair and sat in my lap while we prayed. Just as we said "amen" the phone rang. I answered and my friend Greg was on the line. Greg was a fellow I met while living with Dana in our one room apartment in midtown Memphis. We went down to Overton Square one night to share our faith with those coming in and out of the rock clubs there. I shared my faith with Greg and we prayed together sitting on a bench. He dedicated his life to Christ that night.

"Eddie, this is Greg," he said. "I've been working as a maintenance manager at a large apartment complex and we need to hire a couple of guys. I know you know some stuff about fixing things. Are you interested? Job pays $3.25 a hour."

In 1973, $3.25 per hour was a dang good job. My calculator brain quickly added that up—$130 a week. My gosh! We hit the jackpot.

I immediately said, "Yes!"

God took care of us again. It was a miracle. We both had to do a lot of growing up during that time. I finally had to drop out of college to take the full time maintenance job at the apartment complex to pay the bills. Susan worked as long as she could, right up until the baby was born. We were just kids trying to figure life out. But when our baby girl was born I was so proud of her—and her momma. She was the first girl born into the DeGarmo family in a long, long while and was very special to all of us. I was beside myself, acting like the completely smitten papa.

The band went into a holding pattern after we got married. As I mentioned, both my parents were entrepreneurs, so that way of thinking came easily to me. I rose through the ranks at the apartment job pretty quickly, becoming a supervisor in no time at all. I think that may have been because so many others on the crew kept quitting. Even though it was challenging to take care of hundreds of apartments, my upbringing gave me an edge. In addition to that entrepreneurial spirit, I learned to fix most anything on a house or commercial building. It drove me crazy as a teen when my dad made me work for him on the weekends building houses before I'd head out for gigs with the band on a Friday or Saturday night. That's the busiest times for bands. I hated construction work in high school and didn't like it much better as a young adult, but I sure am glad I knew something about it.

After a couple of years at that work, I started a contracting business of my own. I focused on painting at first and then expanded into other areas of remodeling and construction. I had one other fellow working with me and we built the company up pretty quickly.

Early on I learned a huge part of any successful business is simply being dependable and doing what you said you would do. It's amazing the results those simple disciplines can produce. The phone was ringing. We landed a contract with the county to re-furbish several HUD homes vacated for one reason or another. It was good work, to be sure, but it was also really nasty work. Several of the homes were repossessed or abandoned. One had the very sad story of being the site of a grisly murder-suicide in the family room. We were hired to re-do the house and I found myself cleaning up blood spatters and removing pieces of human skull from the ceiling where some poor soul fired a shotgun into his mouth.

The job definitely paid the bills, but I was completely miserable doing it. I have needed to apologize to Susan more than once for being a miserable sourpuss and for being so down in the dumps during those days. I was definitely one of those people who "wondered what happened" to me.

In my mind, I was going about my merry way when God up and saved me. So, I quit my band, got married, dropped out of college, had a baby, and was working a job I hated with a passion. Where had my dreams gone? Up in smoke! I prayed for answers, but God seemed totally silent on the subject. I felt trapped by my responsibilities. I was supposed to be a rock star—right? Instead, I found myself working a grungy day job I despised just to get by.

I couldn't see a way out and blamed God for it. I was angry, bitter and really, very short-sighted. Truth be known; I was just plain old stupid. I was in turmoil and made sure everyone around me knew it. My poor unfortunate wife suffered the brunt of my self-absorbed attitude. I couldn't deal with my defeat and took it out emotionally on anyone in earshot. I knew God called me to play music for him, but I couldn't see a way past my dilemma; a dilemma I created for myself. I still had an immense amount of growing up to do. God was just getting started with me.

Construction workers tend to rise quite early in the morning. That's pretty much the antithesis of playing in a rock band. I set my clock for 5:30 and was on the job by seven in the morning. There was one particular morning late in 1975 I will never forget. I woke up to get myself ready, swung my legs out of bed to the floor, and rose from the bed to step down the hallway to the bathroom, only to fall flat on my face. My right leg went out from under me and wouldn't support my weight. Susan immediately awoke and asked me what happened. I didn't know. I just fell down. As I tried to regain my footing and stand, excruciating pain radiated all through my lower extremities. I couldn't stand up straight to save my life. Susan immediately got up to help me, but all I could do was roll back into the bed.

Needless to say, we called and set up an appointment with my family doctor. This was the same guy I saw growing up. He gave me my first shot as a kid and fixed the arm I broke playing football. I knew him pretty well. Fortunately, his office was just down the street and he agreed to see me that afternoon. Susan arranged for my mother to come babysit our little girl so she could drive me to see the doctor. After Dr. Parrott's examination he came to a judgment fairly quickly about what had likely happened to me.

"How did you hurt your back?" he asked.

I had no idea what he was talking about. I have pondered that question for more than forty years and I still don't really know the answer. Maybe the injury was the result of lifting a Hammond B3 and all that band gear around. I did that enough times, and it all weighs a ton. Maybe it was putting a 220-volt, heavy air conditioner in a window all by myself. Those things were beasts. Seems I remember doing that a time or two. Maybe I hurt myself working construction. Maybe it was simply the hand of God. I'll never know for sure, I guess, until I get to the other side.

Anyway, the good doctor explained my back was in bad shape. I was suffering from compression of my spine and discs around the various nerves going into my legs. I was twenty-one years old. He ordered me to bed rest and began to set appointments for me to visit various specialists. This was in the dark ages of back surgery in the mid-seventies, and none of the doctors wanted to perform that on me, especially because I was so young. They ordered me to complete bed rest for three months before they would make any decision.

What a weird time that was. Susan was awesome and took care of me every day. I got pretty out there, though, on pain meds and living inside my depressive state of mind. There was a popular show on TV called *Ironsides* starring Raymond Burr. He played a detective bound to a wheelchair because of paralysis. I watched that show's reruns religiously every night because I was sure that was to be my fate as well. To that fact, the doctors told us my chances of paralysis were 60 percent if they had to resort to surgery because it was so intricate and so easy for them to make a mistake. I had more tests, and they said the discs in my spine looked like someone squirted a tube of toothpaste inside my back.

Over those three months our money ran clean out. We were dead broke. My mother and dad were great to be there for us when they could. My mother also encouraged me to seek out public assistance. She said, "Eddie, that's what we pay taxes for."

She was dead right, but that was very difficult for me to face. I was raised and always taught to pull myself up by my own boot-straps. That was the American way. I timidly called the Memphis public assistance office and explained our situation in great detail. They sent a nice lady by to visit us soon after and to personally assess our situation.

I still remember it like it was yesterday. She told us to qualify for any assistance, we couldn't own anything, including a car or other valuable personal property regardless of the circumstances. It was a pre-requisite. To qualify for Aid for Dependent Children, (or "welfare" as it's known today) you had to be totally destitute. We had to sell our car and anything else standing in the way. Even then, the public assistance lady only brought us a few bags of canned food and a little money. We were grateful, but I was completely humbled. That was good for me. My pride was beginning to subside. It hurt not being able to provide for our family. It was good for me, though, to learn some things that everyday people have to face. I've been a supporter of a safety net for folks ever since. We needed one so desperately. Without it, I'm not sure what we would have done.

After the ninety days of bed rest I went back to visit the neuro-surgeon and other specialists. There was no improvement so they ordered the prescribed surgery—the only alternative to correct the problem. I had every test possible to determine the location of the ruptured discs. Turned out there were two in the lower lumbar section of my back. It was late January of 1976 when they decided to take the last resort and operate on me. The doctors met with us and told us the risk of paralysis was great, and the recovery period would be a year or more. It would be a long time until I could work. When I could re-enter the work force, construction or heavy labor were out. I would have to figure out something else to do. We knew we couldn't survive that long on our own, so the decision was made, after the urging of my parents, to move into their home with them.

Oh my gosh! What happened? Not only could I be paralyzed in my legs, but we were going to be living with my parents in the house I grew up in. I felt completely out of control in all aspects of my life.

Fortunately for us, we had maintained a modest health insurance policy for our small family. It was a blessing, but it was the bare bones economy model. Because of the length of stay required in the hospital for my surgery and recovery, the policy only paid for a bed for me in a ward. That turned out to be okay because I made friends with the other guys in the room, and it helped me not to be alone so much. That was quite a life experience.

I was admitted to the hospital a couple of days before my surgery for additional tests. When they rolled me into the ward there were two other men in the room. One was a very old, feeble looking black man. He didn't say much but he waved at me. He was probably too weak to do much else.

The second day I was there Susan noticed he hadn't moved all morning, so she called out to him. He didn't respond.

Susan whispered to me, "Eddie, I think he may have died."

Okay, that freaked us both out! Susan went and fetched a nurse and sure enough the old gentleman left this world that morning, right there, one bed over from mine. That was the first time I was ever close to another human being while he died. Oh, the thoughts crashing through my mind!

The night before my ten-hour surgery was to begin, long after Susan and my family left to go home, our pastor and the college minister from our church dropped by to pray with me. It was like being trapped in a bizarre dream. A movie called *Jeremiah Johnson* was playing in the background on the TV in the room. Impassioned and highly upset Indians were chasing Robert Redford for his character's violation of their tribe's spiritual resting place, and it was all happening while these two men prayed with me. Somehow I felt connected that night with Jeremiah Johnson and his quest for normalcy. It's funny how you remember strange things that shape you. It was all pretty weird; "surreal" definitely summed it up.

The next morning, as they rolled me to surgery, I told the guys in my room I'd be back before they knew it. The old man who died and met eternity was removed, and another fellow moved in to his bed by the end of the same day. He was also an old black man who talked about as slow as any man could and still be breathing. They put a pacemaker in him about a week later, and Susan and I remarked at how much it sped him up. He was really funny and very genuine in his concern for me.

The other fellow in the room was a Jehovah's Witness pastor. We talked theology for a couple of days, each trying to convince the other of his particular corner of the truth. He knew how to quote the Bible much better than I, and that bothered me a great deal. I liked him even though I knew in my heart what he was saying about several basic and important elements of the faith just weren't true. It sent me on a quest to learn why I really believed certain things, a quest that has lasted my entire life.

Hours later, when they returned me to the room after surgery, it was dark outside. I was gone all day—sun-up to sundown. Susan and my mom were there to greet me, thankfully, but I was in a great deal of pain and could hardly talk above a whisper. They rolled me into the room and some nurses came by to set up an apparatus above my bed, kind of like a trapeze I could reach up to, grab ahold of, and adjust my body in bed ever so slightly.

As the pain medicine began to wear off, I couldn't breathe. It felt exactly like someone drove a truck over my back and stopped with its tires setting squarely on me. I had an incision up the center of my back about six inches long. My mom called for the doctor to quickly come and step up my pain medicine. Before long I was completely in la la land from the narcotics. I remember it so vividly because all the while the other two men in the room were telling me to hang in there and it would be all right.

After Susan and my folks left to go home, I felt lower than I ever felt in my life. It was that night I experienced my fifth, and thus far final, epiphany to this very day. I was lying there, completely doped up on morphine, staring at a trapeze above my bed, not knowing whether I would ever actually walk again. A man died in my room one bed over from me the day before. The Jehovah's Witness pastor in the bed next to me wouldn't stop proselytizing me. It was like some bizarre three-ring circus set up all around me and I was performing in the center ring with a top hat and cane.

It was in the wee hours of that night, shrouded in the darkness of that hospital room, when God spoke to my soul in perhaps the clearest way I have ever heard him in my life.

He said directly to my heart, "Eddie, all of those things that stood in your way, and you thought blocked you from doing my will with your music are not there anymore. You have nothing left. Now you can do what I asked you to do."

That was the most freeing experience I have ever had. I had nothing more to lose. There was no fear anymore. I was on rock bottom. Finally, I was free to do what God asked of me.

When Susan came to the hospital later that day I told her all about my experience with God. She was as excited as she could be looking at me bandaged head to toe. It would be a long road ahead for us.

Shortly after that we did what any warm-blooded, unemployed, American couple would do after moving in with their parents and experiencing a life-altering injury. Susan got pregnant.

NINE

ONE STEP CLOSER

The DeGarmo and Key Years

Jim Dickinson was a legend in Memphis. He was a genuine, homegrown icon. Jim grew up loving the blues, playing the blues, and eating the blues for breakfast. He did a lot to preserve the legacy of the blues and rock 'n' roll in our city. His credits include playing with The Rolling Stones, Bob Dylan, Ry Cooter, Arlo Guthrie, and many others. Jim actually played the piano on Guthrie's massive hit "City of New Orleans." He was also an excellent record producer. He was behind some truly groundbreaking albums, including a couple by the pioneering alternative power-pop/alternative band Big Star. They took their name from a local grocery store chain and went on to help create an entire genre of music.

Jim's sons started a band called North Mississippi All Stars. They tour the globe continually with notables such as Robert Plant and others. They are definitely carrying on their father's work and legacy.

Jim Dickinson was also Susan's uncle.

I vividly remember the first time I met him. It was back when we were first married and went to Susan's grandmother's annual Christmas party. Katherine Hicks Andrews was from old Memphis family stock and was firmly rooted in social prestige. She lived in East Memphis where the magnolias grew strong and mighty. She drove a red Cadillac with fins on the rear end as high as the heels on her shoes. She meant business and carried that air about her. I confess I was a bit intimidated by the sight of her at first, but I liked her. My family was just pure old middle class. Everyone had a pickup truck, or a muscle car up on blocks in their yard—two if you were showing off. Susan's grandmother was high spirited, spunky, and classy.

When Susan and I drove up to her house for the Christmas party I remember thinking the front yard was about the size of a football field. It would have held a lot of cars on blocks if my family lived there.

Grandma Andrews greeted us at the front door, framed by a blue billowing cloud of cigarette smoke. It was as if she aimed a chimney directly at us, as we stood on the front step in the crisp December air. Again, it seemed like everybody smoked in those days—even Santa Claus and the kids.

When we entered the room I was taken aback by the elegance of the furnishings—all fine antiques upholstered in rich crimson and dark green velvet. At the far end of the room sat an ivory white baby grand piano. I never saw a baby grand piano in anyone's home before. Susan informed me her grandmother was a fine piano player who specialized in the big-band songs of the thirties and forties. She also let me know not to be too surprised if I was asked to play and sing a Christmas carol or two. It seemed like the family was chock-full of piano players. Susan's Uncle Al, who was also there, went to high school with Elvis. He played music out with him a few times back in the day. They had the same sideburns.

Al survived the disease of music and went on to become a successful businessman. He sold Coppertone and other concoctions made by Schering-Plough in Memphis. He was smart.

Over in the corner stood Jim Dickinson. He reminded me of The Muppets' drummer, Animal, in the best way. He was all rock 'n' roll style. He even sported a gold tooth. He was completely out of place in the social surroundings of the Christmas party. Jim caused quite a stir in the family when he married Susan's aunt, Mary Lindsey, a few years earlier. She was a lovely East Memphis prep school socialite, and Jim was known as the down and dirty rock 'n' roll and blues musician. When the family all got together many would whisper about Jim and Mary Lindsey and their escapades as a couple.

As soon as we walked through the door Susan marched me right over to introduce me to Jim. We hit it off. We both looked like animals. We talked some pretty good Memphis music lingo that night. I told him about my recording days with Lewis Willis and Willie Mitchell. He told me about his band "The Dixie Flyers."

"So what are you doing now?" he asked.

"Well, all that has changed for me," I replied. "I got saved, so now I'm writing and playing Jesus rock music."

Jim's eyes widened, and he became totally animated.

"That is so out!" he exclaimed. "I want to record you guys."

That was Christmas of 1973.

A few months later Jim took Dana and me into Ardent Studios on Madison Avenue and recorded four demos on our band in early 1974. Ardent was known as "The rock 'n' roll studio in Memphis." ZZ Top recorded all of their albums there. Even Led Zeppelin made a record there. It seemed everyone in rock 'n' roll knew about Ardent.

Dana and I were in hog heaven, but totally scared to death. When we entered the enormous recording room of Studio A, I felt like Bugs Bunny seeing the giant carrot patch for the first time. We were completely in awe. The ceilings were over twenty feet high and the studio walls were hardwood with alternating sound baffles. Little could I know DeGarmo and Key would record several albums in that very studio over the next years.

We recorded four demos over the course of four days. We began around 6:00 p.m., after Dana and I got off work or school, and recorded into the wee hours of the morning.

I learned much from Jim over those four late night sessions. His philosophy about rock 'n' roll was the best I've ever come by. "Eddie," he said to me late one night, "Always remember rock 'n' roll is built on the tension between good and evil. When it leans too far in either direction, it loses its right to exist."

I was so glad to have the chance to work with Jim, though we were still a couple of years away from finding our musical path, and I had a lot more growing to do. The four demos he recorded for us became an important musical introduction for us years later. His philosophy was important, too, especially to a young man thinking about using rock 'n' roll to talk about Jesus.

It was fun recording with Jim, but that was before my back injury happened and life came to a halt. The "Christian Band" Dana and I were building went fairly dormant as I struggled to make ends meet, but with the surgery and recovery it was as good as over. After the surgery, while living at my parents' house with Susan and our one-and-a-half-year-old little girl, it was time to figure out what I was going to do next.

In the meantime, I was able to re-enroll and was going to Memphis State University full-time to try to get a plan for our future. However, I felt deeply I needed to contribute something financially to our family. Whatever job I got would have to be in the evenings because of school, so I did what came natural to me and formed a dance "cover band." We named ourselves "Slingshot" and started

booking gigs at dances, bars, and clubs around town and the surrounding area. That was easy for me in some ways, and very difficult
in others. I hadn't been around that lifestyle in a long while and it
made me uncomfortable. However, those days were part of the journey. I still had some growing up to do.

Those were difficult times. Susan was holding down a day job, I
was going to college during the day and off playing in clubs at night
and various venues on the weekends. All of this was combined with
the drama of living with my parents. Yuck!

For me, playing music back in the club scene was a vivid wakeup
call. I'm not at all making a judgment about people who feel compelled to make their livings there, for that's certainly respectable. For
me, however, I felt this divine tug on my heart to use my music as a
calling card to share the Gospel and my story of faith. I tried playing
"Jesus Music" in clubs before and found it was challenging at best to
share one's faith publically from the platform in that setting. People
can throw stuff. As I have said, I actually think one could be far more
effective sitting at the bar speaking and sharing with folks in one on
one conversations.

A few months after I started gigging with Slingshot, Dana Key
called and asked if he could come by and see me. I know it was spring
because the flowers were blooming, and as we sat outside in my parents' backyard, I could hear a lawnmower off in the distance. It was
strange for Dana to visit me at my parents' house. It was like being
back in high school. I felt awkward, like I was trapped in some sort
of time warp. I was married and had a little girl, but I was still in my
old room.

As we sat in a couple of worn out lawn chairs, Dana told me why
he came. "I've been thinking, Eddie," he said. "I just can't believe
God would lead you on this journey for no reason. When you came
to high school that day and told me you found Jesus, I knew

something radical happened to you. I sensed a real difference in your eyes, and I wanted to have it too. Now, four years later, and after the 'Christian Band' days, you are back playing in the same old clubs. I'm here to ask you to get our band back together. God has bigger plans for us. I know it."

I was stunned and elated at the same time. I looked in Dana's eyes and said, "What you have shared with me today is like a breath of fresh air." I knew deep down in my soul I needed to take a step of faith and trust God to show me the way. I give Dana the credit for getting us back together to heed God's calling on our lives.

I then said, "Dana, I'm on welfare, food stamps, and am going to college on the state's dime. I'm still living with my parents with a wife and baby. Let's do what God called us to do. Why not? I'm all in!"

When Susan got home from the mortgage company, she wasn't necessarily in the best of moods. She was six months pregnant with our second child and had been standing on her feet all day collecting sweaty money from people who would sometimes take it out of their shoes, shorts, or brassiere. No joke. That is the truth. I said, "Honey, (I always start out with that when I want to get my way) Dana came by today and asked me if I would be willing to get our Christian band back together. He went on to say God wasn't through with us yet."

Susan looked at me with tired eyes and said, "Well, we live with your parents, are on welfare, and I'm pregnant. We've got nothing to lose. Do it. I agree with Dana. We are not through this journey yet. Do it and do it quick."

I just smiled.

Later that evening I shared with Slingshot that I would be leaving, and Dana and I were getting back together to write music about God and our faith. I think they were actually relieved to get rid of me. I just didn't fit anymore. They knew it too.

Dana and I started to do shows as a duo. It was just the two of us. We performed that way publically for a few months. We simply called ourselves "DeGarmo and Key."

TEN

WAYFARING STRANGER

At that point Dana was working part-time for Youth for Christ while attending Bible College. I worked for Youth for Christ before I had my accident and Dana was able to help me get back with them leading a high school Campus Life club. I earned fifty dollars a week. Susan and I were grateful.

We lived with my parents for ten months with our two-year-old daughter during 1976. During that seemingly endless period of time, Mom and Dad decided to retire and move back to Arkansas to my mother's family farm where she grew up. My grandmother was in her eighties and needed someone with her. I think my dad had a vision of the *Green Acres* sitcom in his mind. I spent many of my summers at their farm growing up. Even though my grand-father passed away when I was five, my Uncle Gene took over. We kids called him Uncle Beaner-stalker. My brothers and I loved going there and spending time in the country. It was idyllic to me.

Many years later, in the mid eighties, Susan and I—with our two little girls in tow—went to visit my folks at the farm for Easter.

We enjoyed going to their little country church that still had my brother's initials carved in the back of one of the pews. I guess he wasn't listening to the sermon much that day.

We arrived mid Saturday afternoon before Easter. I came home from the road in the morning and had just enough time to pack a bag of clean clothes before we needed to get in the car and drive up to the farm.

It was Easter, 1984, when a remarkable thing happened to me at the farm. We loaded up the old Volkswagen to drive the 120 miles north from Memphis to get there. We went through Rector and had a blast on the rollercoaster highway leading to Crowley's Ridge and on to the farm. The girls squealed with delight going down the hills, airborne in the back. If you have ever been to Rector, you know there is not much to it. There is an old car dealership that went out of business in the 1940s and rumor has it they kept their inventory of cars when they shut down. They were all still supposedly stored in pristine A-1 condition hidden in the old closed and sealed up brick building. That was the local folklore anyway.

Rector also had a one-chair barbershop with the old-fashioned red and white barber pole outside the door. Now, my dad was the sharp dresser in his day. He was a real estate man, always wore a suit and tie, and always wore shined shoes. Once, when my brothers and I were kids, we visited the farm to see our grandparents. I can remember us four boys sitting all across the back seat in my dad's Chevrolet Impala, driving home to Memphis one Saturday afternoon. Dad had an appointment to show a house later that day and wanted to look his best.

He decided to drop in that little barbershop in Rector on the drive back to Memphis to get a fresh haircut and shave before his appointment. We all sat out in the car sweltering while he was inside. He came out about fifteen minutes later and all seemed well for a little while.

Dad cranked up that old Chevrolet, and we took off in a cloud of dust down the road.

I noticed my Dad kept looking at himself in the rearview mirror. I could tell he was studying his hair cut. Something just didn't sit right with him. Then I heard him cut loose with a little profanity.

"Damn if that barber didn't cut off one of my sideburns. He only left me with one!"

You've got to understand what this meant. This was 1966, when everybody in Memphis, including women and pets, sported sideburns to match Elvis and to show solidarity with the King. This was not an ordinary size sideburn. It was an XL size Elvis sideburn. The old man was steaming. We didn't dare laugh then, but I do now.

Susan, our girls, and I loved our visits to the old farm. It seemed the whole world slowed to a halt there. The farm sat three miles outside McDougal, Arkansas. The biggest and closest town was called Piggott. They had the Hoggard Funeral Home in Piggott. No lie. Truth can be stranger than fiction. It just all fit together. Piggott's claim to fame was being the filming location for the Andy Griffith movie *A Face in the Crowd*. That was a popular movie when it came out in 1957.

On this particular visit to the farm with Susan and our little girls, we were planning on joining my folks at New Hope Baptist Church in the little hamlet of Pollard for Easter morning services. Seems like my whole family, except my brother Mike, are planted in the church cemetery out back. My oldest brother Shelton had a Harley Davidson carved on his tombstone. It looks good, but he should have had it set up on concrete blocks like he used to do with his hot rods back in Whitehaven when we were growing up. It would have fit his persona better.

But I digress. Let's get back to the story from 1984. Somewhere around eight in the evening that Easter eve I began to notice a little toothache in the back of my mouth. Around ten o'clock it was hurting very badly. By the time the girls, Susan, my parents, and I finished our tradition of playing a game of Scrabble and decided to roll it up and go to bed, I was in a heap of pain. My only remedy was to take an aspirin. There were no dentists, doctors, or emergency rooms open for a toothache victim in McDougal or Piggott.

We all went upstairs to bed. We always rolled the sheets back to check for spiders at the farm. It was tradition. There was an old closet halfway up the staircase in the landing. I would usually hide in it and reach out and grab the girls as they passed by. We were sure a farm ghost haunted that old closet. I huddled in that closet as the deranged farm ghost and scratched the walls as the girls ran past. They screamed and giggled a little.

Every hour my toothache got worse and worse. Somewhere around 2:00 a.m., I decided I had to get out of bed and go downstairs to moan and sit it out. Nothing worked. I was in a great deal of pain. As the sun began to rise that Easter morning I wrote the lyrics to the song "Destined to Win," which was fated to be one of D&K's most popular songs ever.

It seems like more often than not, there is some suffering to endure before the blessings come into our lives. It was that way with me. It took a toothache, and staying up all night in wrenching pain, for "Destined to Win" to be birthed. It's just like God to do it that way.

So, my parents decided to retire and move to that beautiful family farm in Clay County, Arkansas, while Susan and I lived with them after my surgery in 1976. Their move from Whitehaven, Tennessee to the farm happened slowly over a few months. I hope we didn't run them off when we moved in.

As I mentioned, Dana and I were working for Youth for Christ then, occasionally performing our musical duo gigs at small gatherings or coffee houses around town. Dana called me one day and told me *Campus Life Magazine*, which was a big deal in its heyday, called to let him know it was sending a writer to Memphis to cover a story about a high school kid in Dana's Campus Life club. The young man had been operating as a drug dealer when he had a lightning bolt conversion to Jesus. He created quite a stir in his local school by shouting his miraculous salvation story to everyone he met.

Dana called me to let me know about the magazine writer, and then asked if it would be all right for the man to stay with us for a couple of days. With my parents moving out he knew we had some extra room. He and his wife Suzy had a tiny place. I immediately agreed.

ELEVEN

MATTER OF TIME

A couple weeks later *Campus Life Magazine* sent a young writer, a fellow named Stephen Lawhead, to Memphis to stay overnight with Susan and me. His task was to cover the story about the young ex-drug dealer in Dana's high school club. Stephen and I hit it off quickly. It turned out he was also the music critic for the magazine's "What's New" feature. Every month *Campus Life*, which had the largest magazine subscriber base of Christian high school students of its day, reviewed new music and films. Stephen was the critic.

That first evening, after he interviewed the kid he came to see, Dana dropped Stephen off at my folks' house. We spent the next several hours together, sharing our stories. I told him how Susan and I met during the "Christian Band" days, and how Dana and I came to Christ and left our mainstream rock band and recording contract behind to follow Jesus. I also told him about my back injury and how, as a result, Susan and I lost everything we owned and had to move in with my parents or be out on the street. As I told him the tale his eyes widened with every twist and turn. At the end of my story, Stephen said, "Man, I need to write a story about you guys. You can't make this stuff up."

Then he asked, "Did you record any of your Jesus rock music?"

"Only four songs Susan's Uncle Jim helped us with," I responded.

"Can I hear 'em?"

"Sure, let's go upstairs to our room." Mind you, this was mine and Susan's bedroom that doubled as our tiny living room.

"I got a stereo in there with a reel to reel tape recorder."

That night I played Stephen Lawhead the four demos Jim Dickinson produced for Dana and me a couple of years before. That evening at my parents' house changed all of our lives forever.

Stephen shared with me his dream of becoming a novelist. In time he would prove to be just that. Today, Stephen Lawhead is a world renowned, best-selling author of many books, including the *Song of Albion* series, *The King Raven Trilogy*, *The Pendragon Cycle*, *Byzantium*, and many more. Back then, though, he was a young man from Nebraska with an oversized mustache making a living as a magazine writer. We had a lot of dreams in common.

After I played the demos for Stephen on our reel to reel tape recorder, he asked if he could take a copy back to Chicago with him and listen a few more times. He went on to say, "This is really good, but something tells me you guys can do better."

Stephen left to return to Chicago the next morning. I didn't hear from him for a couple of weeks. I shared with Dana I played our old demos for Stephen and he seemed to like them. Dana didn't realize Stephen was the music critic for the magazine either. Both of us were excited but also unsure what any of it meant.

Over the next few weeks my folks continued to move to the family farm in Arkansas. They also owned a couple of small rental homes in Memphis, which proved to be crucial to the beginning of DeGarmo and Key over the next few years. One house became a lifesaver for Susan and me and our little family.

My folks came to me one day and sat me down for a discussion. Dad said, "Son, you've been through a lot. The good news is you are now back in college. Your mama and I have been talking. You know we own that little rental house on the north side of town. We are happy to let you guys live there, rent free, for as long as you stay in school. We've sold this house, and we are going to the farm."

Susan and I took a drive out by the little rental house. We were appreciative, but it really needed a lot of work to make it livable. I was good at fixing things, and Susan was good at decorating things, so we went to work. I had to lift the floors with a jack to make them level and replace the floor furnace, which was all the heat the little six hundred square foot house had. We painted it inside and out, and I was able to trade our hot rod van to a carpet company to install new carpet on all the floors and new linoleum in the kitchen and bath. We made it our own and that little house became a blessing to our family.

The neighborhood was a bit of a revelation, however. It had definitely seen better days and was in serious decline, but we made some great friends. Next door lived Mr. Bill and Mrs. Katy. Mr. Bill retired from being a heat and air repairman. Mrs. Katy still worked at a factory around the corner. They had a parrot named Mike that would whistle at our girls when they passed by and shout "Hello" to them. It was funny and creepy at the same time. Across the street lived a little boy about five years old named Gator. He kind of looked like an alligator, actually. So did his mom. But she was the sweetest lady.

Down the street lived a little boy named Randy who played with our girls. Sometimes Randy showed up with bruises. Too many bruises, if you know what I mean. We tried to figure out what was

going on, but never could get to the bottom of it. So, we just loved on
Randy. Sometimes you might see someone walking down the street
who'd had a little too much to drink. We had a couple of fights break
out in front of the house, and one time a woman tried to run down
her husband in a pickup truck for cheating and running around on
her. Other than that, the neighborhood was fine. It was home.

When Susan left the mortgage company to deliver our second
baby girl, Shannon, her company decided not to offer her the job back.
She went on unemployment. It was needed. In those days, employers
could get away with that sort of thing.

Life was full of miracles during that time. Stephen Lawhead called
me and said he had been listening to the demos over and over. He then
said, "I think you guys should write some more songs and figure out
a way to record them."

Dana and I spent the next month getting together every chance
we could to write songs. I took a part-time job at an apartment complex doing maintenance work. I could fix most anything back then,
before computers. Now, it seems harder. You need a technical degree
and little fingers to replace all the transistors, chips, and stuff.

I was in college in the mornings, working at the apartment complex in the afternoons, and running a high school Campus Life club
three nights a week. Susan did her part too. She was home with our
girls. She did some sewing from time to time and sold the pieces. She
also signed us up to be "tasters" in the test-marketing efforts of a local
food processor and distributor. We got all kinds of stuff delivered to
us weekly to taste test and report back to them. We never died. Life
was good. Some of it tasted good. Some—oh well, it was free.

In the meantime, Dana and I wrote a new batch of tunes and were
trying to figure out how to record them. I mentioned to Dana we
ought to go visit Lewis Willis, our old rock band manager, and ask
for his advice. I knew that would hopefully perk old Lewis up.

We played a couple of our new songs for Lewis at Allied Recording Studios down on Looney Street in the hood north of downtown Memphis. "I'll tell you what," Lewis said. "I'll give you boys a week of studio time and help you record your songs for three hundred bucks."

That was basically the cost of the tape.

"I only have one condition," he went on to say. "I want to take them over and play them for Willie Mitchell and London Records when we are done. I want to see what they think of this new "Jesus Rock 'n' Roll."

We agreed immediately, but told Lewis we would need a few weeks to raise the three hundred greenbacks and find a couple of musicians willing to help us out.

I went to work on finding us a band. I met a bass player at our church who came out of the local rock scene about the same as Dana and I. His name was Mel Senter. Mel played on those demos for free. We later offered him a spot in the band. He declined and went on to become a pediatrician. Mel always was smart.

For drums I went to Max Richardson. Max played with Globe in the beginning. He had been on a spiritual journey that began when Dana and I became Christians. I'm still not sure he has found what he is looking for all these years later. Max did a great job playing on those early demos, though.

Dana and I went into Allied Recording Studios in June of 1977 and spent a week, almost around the clock, with Lewis Willis. We came out with seven new demos of our songs. We were really pleased. It was comfortable for us in that old funky studio down by the muddy river. We helped Lewis build that place during our high school years. I met Susan there. She and I went there sometimes in the Christian Band days when no one was around to make out. It wasn't fancy, but it was home. Lewis helped us tremendously by producing those seven demos.

True to our word, when we finished we gave Lewis first shot to pitch the demos to Hi and London Records. He came back discouraged and said, "Boys, they really like your sound and music. They just can't figure out how to market and sell rock music about God."

I think Lewis deeply regretted their decision. He really wanted to work with us.

I immediately sent a copy to Stephen Lawhead. He called me as soon as he listened and in his soft-spoken way he said, "This should do the trick. Do you mind if I send it around to a few folks?"

TWELVE

READY OR NOT

During the first year of D&K we were flat broke. At one point our cupboards were actually bare. I called Dana and told him I needed to raise a few bucks to buy some groceries for our little girls. I asked him if he had any ideas or knew of someone who needed an odd job done. He said he was dead broke too. He invited us over later that afternoon and decided to get some folks together to pray about it. Susan and I packed up the girls and drove over. We went inside, gathered with the band and began to ask God for food. After a minute or two I decided it was my time to pray out loud. As soon as I started my first sentence, though, there was a startling knock on the front door. Since I was closest I got up and answered it. There, standing on the porch, was our friend Buddy Abbott, with a sack full of groceries under each arm.

"I was driving home from work and the strangest feeling came over me," he said. "I felt like I was supposed to stop and buy you some groceries. So here I am!" Buddy then handed me the bags of groceries.

Needless to say, I was freaking out. Buddy and I walked back into the room and we all freaked out together, shouting and praising God. It was a miracle for sure. Later, as I began to process what had just gone down, I realized Buddy, who was an attorney, worked about forty-five minutes away from where Dana lived. When God laid it on him to buy us some groceries, it was a good half hour before we began to pray. God knows what we need long before we ask.

Over the next few weeks Stephen Lawhead sent me a few letters from record companies that had decided to pass on us. Our music was too rock, too preachy, too didactic (I had to look that definition up), or too bluesy. We received letters from Billy Ray Hearn at Sparrow Records and reps from other labels. Even Larry Norman, who had his own label called Solid Rock, turned us down. They all gave different reasons, but had one thing in common; they didn't want us.

One day our telephone rang at home and Susan answered it. She listened for a second and then hung up.

"Who was it?" I asked.

"Some weirdo saying he was Pat Boone."

"Oh."

"I hung up on him."

Pat Boone was a major star in the seventies. He was still making movies, still singing, and was a frequent guest on late night shows like *The Tonight Show with Johnny Carson*. It did not make sense that he would be calling us.

The phone rang again. This time I answered. The voice on the other end said, very quickly, "I'm Pat Boone. Please don't hang up on me. I'm looking for Eddie DeGarmo. Someone sent me a tape with this telephone number written on it. I don't even know who sent it to me. You see, I like this music very much and I think I can help you."

"I'm Eddie!" I screamed.

That is how it happened. I just didn't hang up the telephone the second time. Pat went on to say he owned a small record company called Lamb and Lion with his partner Mike Curb. Pat was the lamb, he joked, and Mike was the lion. He explained Lamb and Lion was a boutique label and really only had a couple of other artists outside of himself and his daughters. Pat also said his youngest daughter, Debby, recorded a solo project they were about to release called "You Light Up My Life."

"I really think I can help you," he said. "Is it okay if I come to Memphis to meet you guys?"

"Are you kidding?" I said. "Just say when."

"How about tomorrow?" he asked.

Lamb and Lion offered us a recording contract in the summer of 1977, and things suddenly took on a more serious tone for Susan and me. I was a senior in college and was very close to graduation. We had two small children, and we were both working every conceivable odd job to make ends meet. It seemed like every month or two our utilities would be shut off because we were late in paying the bill. I'm glad I knew how to pull the meter and turn them back on. Susan and I got together and had a long conversation about our future and what this recording contract and re-starting the band could mean for us.

She looked at me with those big brown eyes and said, "Honey, I feel God has called us to this mission. I was introduced to Jesus through your music and I think it is important to use it to reach the world with God's message of love."

That night Susan and I made an important commitment. We got together and told God we would fully dedicate ourselves to this music venture for four years. We would give it everything we had to help it succeed for that period of time. If, at the end of four years, we couldn't provide for our family adequately, we would take that as a sign from him it was time to move on.

Over time I have come to believe with that commitment, we stumbled upon an important principle for any new business or venture. The U.S. Small Business Administration states that on average it takes at least three years for any new business to stabilize and survive. If you can't plan to make it that long, you probably shouldn't start the business.

Later, as an owner of record and music publishing companies, I shared this "four-year commitment principle" with aspiring artists and songwriters. I told countless young artists they should make a commitment to their dream for a period of years. When we started we chose to commit for four years; I told them they could choose how long they would give it, but it needed to be at least three years. During that period of time they should give it everything they had, come hell or high water. At the end of the time period, if they still couldn't support themselves and their families if they had them, they should give it up. "Don't let your dream become a noose around your neck," I would say. "Don't let it drown you by allowing it to drag you to the bottom of the river."

I've seen creative and talented people drag their families through the muck and mire too many times as they chase their dreams long past their expiration dates. That being said, I encourage young people to follow their dreams. It is much better to know you tried, even if you fail. Failure is part of the success. If someone hasn't failed, it just means he never attempted much. You don't want to look back on your life and wish you'd chased your dream if you were able to. Some people can't chase their dreams for one reason or another. If you can, though, you should—for a time.

Dana and I were ready and willing to do whatever was required of us. We were willing to be bi-vocational. I was fine with holding several jobs until our music could support us. I did all kinds of things to make money during those early D&K years. I built porches, painted houses, did maintenance work, fixed stuff for people, and even mowed lawns. I was able to hire Dana to help me with that work from time to time. We also both continued to work for Youth for Christ part-time.

We often lost money on those early tours. We came home and had to work odd jobs to pay the tour bills off. We often laughed about it. We definitely weren't in it for the money. Pat Boone and Mike Curb were true gentlemen to us during that contract period. Later I discovered our agreement gave them ownership virtually of all of our rights for years to come, including all merchandise and motion picture rights. They never enforced those terms, though. They always treated us very decently. I think they might have been distracted by Debby Boone's "You Light Up My Life," record, seeing it was the biggest selling song in the history of recorded music up to that time. It was also very good for us. It gave Lamb and Lion the capital to invest in our career. I still should have read the contract, though. That is the last time I failed to read and re-read every word of a contract. It was a good lesson to learn. It could have been a nightmare.

There was a rock band in Memphis called Target. They landed a record deal with A&M Records and were on tour with Boston and Black Sabbath. Dana and I liked their sound and noticed their album was produced by Ron Capone. Ron had a legendary career working with many of Memphis's own Stax Recording artists like Sam and Dave, Isaac Hayes, Wilson Pickett, Otis Redding, and The Barkays. He also worked with the rock 'n' roll bands out of our city like Target, Alamo, and others. I mentioned to Dana I thought we should meet with him about producing our album.

Those were exciting days for the recording industry. Ron Capone was on staff at Stax for years before moving to Ardent. He knew how to mix blues, soul, and rock 'n' roll together. It was just what the doctor ordered.

We went into the studio in the summer of 1977. I was twenty-two years old. Dana and I were beside ourselves with excitement to record again at the legendary Ardent Studios in Memphis. We were working in Studio B, which happened to be the same room in which *Led Zeppelin III* was mixed.

Ron Capone was a true Cajun gentleman. He grew up in New Orleans, and the gumbo still dripped off him. He was a silver-haired, short, stocky Southern dude who sounded like he just left the bayou when he would shout, "Who Dat?" He was a good fit for us, but I knew our old friend Lewis Willis was hurt by our decision not to record at Allied Studios. We had a good reason. Allied was still just an eight-track studio, and Ardent was a sixteen-track one. That gave us much more flexibility in the recording process.

DeGarmo and Key was always signed as a duo to our recording, publishing, and management contracts. That meant we always needed to hire a band to back us up. As you can imagine, we were very particular about the musicians we hired. Dana and I strove for excellence in everything we did. We took great pride in the skills we cultivated and intended to constantly push ourselves to new levels of professionalism. But a band is a unit. We needed the musicians we hired to have that same kind of drive and passion. You also spend a lot of time with the members of your band, so it's important they are like-minded and easy to hang out with.

We heard through the grapevine David Spain, the drummer of Target, became a Christian. I was able to look him up. David was a great help to us on our first record, *This Time Thru*. He played drums on about half of the songs. Max Richardson, the drummer who played with "Christian Band" in our early days, played on most of the others as well as contributing as a co-writer on a couple of tunes. The drums on one song, however, were played by the night doorman at the studio. About a year later I had that job (the doorman gig, not the drumming gig).

The title track of the album, "This Time Thru," had a fairly complicated rhythm track. It had a middle section that switched from 4/4 to 5/4 time. Both David and Max had a hard time playing it. Ron Capone bragged about how good the doorman, John Hampton, was as a drummer and suggested we hire him to play on the track.

So we did. He nailed it.

That's how we met the man who would become an integral part of the D&K production team for years to come. He co-produced and engineered many of our albums.

Years later we learned Ron Capone had never even heard Hampton play drums before that day. Ron just took a shot at it. In fact, it was the first time Hampton ever played on any album. You could have fooled me. Well, I guess he *did* fool me.

During our *This Time Thru* era, Dana and I were heavily influenced by what I call the "British Cape Bands." In other words, the music best played while one is wearing a cape. You get the picture. Those were bands like Emerson, Lake, & Palmer, Yes, and Jethro Tull. I think we melded that influence with Jimi Hendrix, ZZ Top, and the Memphis Blues. It was kind of like mixing barbeque with fine wine. It was a little eccentric and unconventional, but it tasted good!

Dana and I met a guy named Kenny Porter years earlier when we were playing with Globe. He was a student, and the student activities leader, at the University of Tennessee campus in Martin, Tennessee. He brought Globe to town from time to time to play for dances and events at the university. He was also an excellent musician and remarkable bass guitar player. Kenny became a Christian at some point, though totally separately from Dana and me. We reached out to him through a mutual friend and asked if he wanted to play bass on our album. That began a great friendship between us. I'm forever appreciative of Kenny's contributions to our band during those early years.

We recorded *This Time Thru* over the late summer and fall of 1977. Dana and I were both college students at the time. We went to classes in the morning and then off to the studio in the afternoons until late in the night.

My folks owned a second rental house out in Whitehaven, not too far from where I grew up. They offered it to Dana and his wife Suzy to live in, rent free, while we were trying to get the band off the ground…hopefully. The fact is, without my folks' help—as well as the help of several others along the way—we may not have survived the early years.

On a very hot and humid August day in 1977, I was driving from our little house on the north side of town out south to where Dana lived in Whitehaven. We had just begun to record our first album and I was going to his house for something.

I needed to stop and buy some gas on Highway 51 just a half mile or so from Graceland. I would stop in those days and buy a dollar's worth of gas. Believe it or not, that would buy you three or four gallons.

While I was stopped there I noticed a fellow putting gas in his chromed-out, tricked-out, custom trike (three-wheeled motorcycle.) As sweltering as it was, this rather large fellow was wearing a powder blue, down-feather winter jacket with matching powder blue down-feather pants. He looked a whole lot like "The Michelin Man" in the advertisements—you know, the cartoon man made out of tires.

As I was buying my dollar's worth, he turned to take a look at me. It was only then I realized I was looking at Elvis himself. There, with a plastic-tipped cigar in his mouth, wearing a down-feather snow suit, the King of rock 'n' roll was putting gas in his motorcycle. Our eyes locked for a moment. There were a few other folks around filling up their cars, but I'm fairly sure I was the only one who recognized him that day. It was probably because he was so large and puffy. I saw him many times while growing up in Whitehaven, so I recognized him.

As I have said, my dad was a real estate man and a homebuilder. When I was a little boy in the early sixties, he took me out on Saturday mornings to visit his job sites. The first stop was always the Gridiron Coffee Shop on Highway 51, just a short distance from our house. It was also just a little ways down from Graceland. They renamed 51 "Elvis Presley Boulevard" years later.

The Gridiron was the old man's favorite hangout. He knew the cook and all the waitresses on a first name basis. The smell of greasy bacon, sausage, and eggs was spectacular. Whitehaven was fairly sparse in those days. A lot of it was still made up of rural homesteads and farmland pastures. The little strip where the Gridiron sat also housed a Rexall drugstore that still had a soda bar.

This particular Saturday morning was clear, blue, and warm. After Dad finished drinking his coffee and flirting with the waitresses a little, and after I had finished my eggs, he paid the bill. He made a couple of wise cracks to the waitress, which she immediately threw right back at him. We left the Gridiron and got into Dad's old Chevy pickup truck and pulled out onto Highway 51 headed south toward Mississippi. Just about as quick as you can imagine anything happening in Old Dixie, a man came running out from the Rexall next to the Gridiron and up onto the highway screaming like a banshee, "Elvis is in there! Elvis is in the Rexall!"

I noticed a sharp looking motorcycle parked by the front door. When that man went to screaming, cars all over the highway just stopped in their tracks. It was like one of those 1950s alien movies when a spaceship shoots everyone with a laser beam that makes all the machines quit working and all the power go out. People just stopped in their tracks and got out of their cars, wherever they were, and proceeded to make haste to the Rexall.

About that time, I noticed a fella with blue-black hair running up from around the back of the building as fast as he could with his legs and elbows flinging into the wind like a crazy man. He ran onto the highway going north toward Graceland. I knew it was Elvis. I'm not sure I ever saw anyone move his legs and elbows as fast as he did that day. As he hightailed it, the crowd of about thirty people saw him make his run and took off after him like a hound dog after a rabbit. Elvis ran all the way back to the gates of Graceland that morning with those folks chasing him. It was just like in the movies.

———————

As I looked at powder-blue Elvis, all those years later, pumping gas, I tipped my head, just like they do in the Western movies. Elvis tipped his head right back at me. It was like he was saying, "Thanks, kid, for not busting my cover with all these people around." I had a flashback to Young Elvis, before he was all big and puffy, running for his life from behind the Rexall on a Saturday morning. It was a truly peculiar comparison of personas.

Elvis Presley died two weeks later from a drug overdose. That was a sad day—especially for us Memphians and this kid who grew up in Whitehaven.

THIRTEEN

ALL THE LOSERS WIN

orking at Ardent was a fantastic experience. We finished the album right before Christmas of 1977. It was released a few weeks later in January of 1978. Only two songs from our initial demos, "Emmanuel" and "Addey," made the record. "Addey" was the song that really turned the heads at Lamb and Lion. Dana wrote that one about a girl we met who was working the streets. It was always interesting to me the song that excited the Christian industry most was about a hooker.

Stephen Lawhead, who enlisted to be our manager by then, and a friend of his named Harold Smith drove from Chicago to Memphis in the spring of 1978. The reason for the trip was twofold. Dana and I were going to have a day of strategic planning with Stephen. We were excited because we'd never had a strategy before. Also, Stephen and his wife Alice bought a new car and decided to give Susan and me their old one. He and Harold towed that car all the way from Chicago to Memphis. It was such a blessing to us at the perfect time.

Harold and Stephen stayed with us for those few days and slept together on a funky pullout sofa in our tiny living room. It's kind of funny, now that I think about it. Stephen became a world-class, best-selling author and Harold became the editor-in-chief and CEO of *Christianity Today* and its host of publications. It was the world's leading Christian magazine group. But back in 1978 we were all crammed into that six hundred square foot house dreaming up an unlikely strategy to make this Jesus rock 'n' roll ministry work. We were all just young people on a great adventure.

We also met with Rick Miller that week. He was a local friend of ours who signed on and became our first booking agent. Rick said he thought there was a lot of excitement about our album and he thought he could cobble together a West Coast tour. We had never played the West Coast before and were eager to go do it. We would have left that night if we could have! Stephen and Rick also told us the "Jesus People" (the commune our friends in Resurrection Band came from) were sponsoring an all-day music event in Chicago, like a mini-festival. It was called "Love Fest" and they invited us to perform there.

Stephen then said something that might not seem like a big deal now, but was pretty radical back then. "You know guys," he began, "When I see all the big mainstream bands play, they all have t-shirts with their names on them for sale."

We went into a deep dive discussion about ego, pride, commercialism, and whether it was appropriate in God's eyes to promote our image with something so crass as a t-shirt with our names plastered across the front of it. Dana wasn't so sure.

The next day I went out and ordered five hundred t-shirts. I was sure. Susan made the design for the shirt, complete with a lightning bolt between the "D" and the "K." What could be better?

We also needed a touring band. David Spain decided he didn't want to start touring again after his years with Target, so we were on the hunt for a full-time drummer. I can't recall how I became aware of Terry Moxley, but I'll definitely never forget him. He had quite a resumé. He spent several years drumming for Charlie Rich. Charlie had some big hit records during those years and was playing in arenas.

When I first called Terry, it was after his Charlie Rich days, and he was playing at a club called The Airport Lounge off Airways Boulevard in Memphis. I knew the place. Terry said he was very interested in playing with a Christian group and was ready to move beyond the club scene. I went out to see him play. I was very impressed with his drumming chops. I hired him on the spot. Kenny Porter, who played bass on our album, decided to join up and go on tour as well.

That Chicago trip was huge for us. It was an all-day music festival with several artists and speakers. I had never been to a Christian music festival before. There was no pot smoke hovering around in the air and no stoned people stumbling around. People's eyes weren't glazed over like I saw at some of the mainstream festivals. It was a great day and an eye-opener as well.

When we played that afternoon the atmosphere was electric. The festival was inside a cavernous building that looked like an airplane hangar. When we took to the stage, the crowd roared and it felt like a real rock show. We played, preached, and shared Jesus to a wildly enthusiastic crowd. But not everyone was enthused.

There was a group of very offended pastors who wanted to talk to us as soon as we walked off the stage. They all seemed to be baring their teeth at us. They were mostly upset about Kenny, our bass player. They thought he gyrated his hips inappropriately as he played his guitar. Sound familiar? That was the very same thing that got Elvis in trouble when he appeared on the *Ed Sullivan Show* in the 1950s. The television network decided it would only show Elvis from the waist up in one of the most famous, and now humorous, rock 'n' roll scandals of all time.

Anyway, Dana and I told Kenny and threatened we would make him play inside a refrigerator box with armholes to hold his bass and a window cut in the front of the box only showing him from the waist-up if he didn't stop gyrating his hips like Elvis. Actually, Kenny got his feelings hurt badly that day. He was just into the music. We heard that kind of stuff a lot in our early days, as bizarre as it sounds.

We also sold out of t-shirts. Dana came around really quickly on that issue.

After the Chicago journey and traveling in an old beat-up wreck of a van, it became clear we desperately needed a permanent travel solution. We had a West Coast tour coming up and needed something sturdy with sufficient room to ride inside and also haul our band equipment. I found a used Ford "Hi-Cube Van." That kind of truck worked for us because the driver's compartment was open to the cargo box on the back. You couldn't pass through standing up, but you could half crawl all bent over from the front to the rear. That truck had a fourteen-foot long cargo box behind the driver's compartment.

After we bought it, we built a wall top to bottom about five feet from the front end of the cargo area, just behind the cab. That gave us a little room for passengers with all of our gear stacked in the back behind the wall. Dana and I did the work in my driveway. Mr. Bill came over from next door to supervise, and Mike the parrot yelled at us every time we went to hammering.

Across the truck, at the bottom of the wall, we built a rough couch facing the back of the driver's and passenger seats so you could sit on it and look out the windshield. It was kind of like *The Beverly Hillbillies*, except we had a roof over us. Above the couch we made two bunk beds with just enough headroom to sit on the couch below. The couch also doubled as a bunk, so you could sleep three people high. We made the sofa bottom and the bunks tilt toward the rear a little bit, so if the driver hit the brakes too hard in the middle of the night, the sleeping band members might not fly out of their bunks. I emphasize the word "might." It worked most of the time. We put a roof vent in the ceiling because the truck didn't have air conditioning. No joke! There was no air conditioning.

Susan made cushions for the couch and mattresses for the bunks and covered the cushions with colorful striped material. We were looking uptown and fashionable at least. She could sew and make anything. She learned how to make her own clothes while growing up with a single mom in the sixties. They couldn't afford store-bought dresses so Susan just made her own. She got so good at it she made wedding dresses, purses, bags, and many other things to make extra money when we needed it early in our marriage.

We knew the truck was a Godsend. In fact, we named it "Happy Truck" because it made us so happy. That was then...

FOURTEEN

ARE YOU READY?

Rick Miller successfully booked three weeks' worth of West Coast shows for us and we could not wait to load up Happy Truck and hit the road. The tour started with a show all the way across America from Memphis in Bakersfield, California. From there we worked our way north, through the San Francisco Bay area, and then on to Portland, Oregon, and Seattle, Washington. Then we did an about face and worked our way back south, ending with a show at the famous Calvary Chapel in Costa Mesa, south of Los Angeles.

My dad asked me privately before we drove away, "How much money have you got, son?"

"About 150 bucks," I replied. "We'll be fine." None of us would have qualified for a credit card at that point, and $150 was all we could scrape together.

"This is for emergencies," he said as he handed me his Master-Card. "Now get outta here." Again, his support was both touching and important. I actually think he would have gone with us had we had enough room in the truck. There were four of us in the band plus our soundman. That meant three guys in the back could sleep and two up front would drive and navigate. Perfect, but full.

It was an adventure for us to drive across the Mississippi River and the flat delta of east Arkansas, to the hills of west Arkansas and then across the Oklahoma plains where the towns had peculiar Native American names. Some of us had never been as far west as New Mexico. We'd not had the pleasure of seeing the stark beauty of the Arizona desert. When we climbed the hills toward Flagstaff though, things started going badly for Happy Truck. It seemed the more you mashed on the gas the slower the truck went—even though the engine was revving high enough to blow sky-high any minute. I had a sick feeling in my stomach the transmission was going out.

We exited the interstate and saw a transmission shop close to the ramp. When we came to the first stop the truck would barely take off again. We needed to make it about a half mile down the road to get to our destination. It was 9:00 pm when Happy Truck finally rolled into the parking lot of the repair shop and came to a stop. The shop was dark and empty as the mechanics had gone home hours earlier. I noticed the "Office Hours" sign on the door and was pleased to see it opened at 7:00 am. We had an extra day to get to Bakersfield, which was still roughly five hundred miles on down the road.

Our plan was to spend the night there in the parking lot, and then get up early for the shop to repair the transmission the next day. Then we would leave in the evening for Bakersfield. We still had the Mojave Desert in front of us and would rather make that drive at night due to not having air conditioning in the truck. It could get pretty stifling in the rear, not to mention smelly from the stink of sweaty bodies (and who knows what else).

As we settled in for the night, we noticed we were in the industrial section of the city. There were zero restaurants anywhere near us.

There wasn't even a gas station with a vending machine or a pay phone close by. Cell phones were a few decades away, too.

So, we just sat in the parking lot of the repair shop and grumbled. Fortunately, Flagstaff is a little higher in elevation, and thankfully it's not as hot as the rest of Arizona can be.

I had never seen the night sky from the high desert before. It was amazing. There were so many more stars than I ever saw through the muggy and humid Memphis night air. It made me feel incredibly small, in the scheme of things. But the idea God took an interest in us also made me feel very important. We were on a mission.

We awoke at daybreak to the clanks of an old wrecker dropping off another car the desert had chewed up and spit out overnight. A few minutes later the shop opened up. We were the first in line. Actually, we were the only ones in line. I explained our situation to the man in charge and that we needed to be in Bakersfield the next night. He was wearing the stereotypical blue mechanic's jumpsuit with his ball cap cocked off to one side and the stub of an unlit cigar in his mouth. He cut his eyes toward me and I can still remember his fateful words.

"Son, we will look at your truck, but it's going to be four days until I can get to it. We are covered up."

I tried another tack and told him we were a Christian band and just had to make it to Bakersfield for a concert. I made it sound like the world would end if we didn't show up.

He stood, looked at me square in the eyes, held up four fingers, and whispered, uncomfortably close to the end of my nose, "Four days."

I went back to the fellas and explained what the man told me. We just sat there in silence for a few minutes when Dana finally asked, "What do you think we ought to do?"

"I think we crank this beast up and go for it," I replied. "No reason to stay here."

Then Dana and Kenny both spoke up, "We ought to pray first."

We got out of that truck, got down on our knees, hung on to the rear bumper, and prayed. There were three or four mechanics peering from just inside the roll-up workshop doors, watching as we prayed. It must have been a peculiar sight. Here were five long-haired hippies who slept in the parking lot the night before, praying God would get them safely across the Mojave Desert with a busted transmission.

In case you don't know, the Mojave happens to rank as the hottest place in the USA. And this was the month of June.

I started Happy Truck up, and we limped out of that shop and back onto I-40 toward the desert. The longer we drove, the stronger the truck got. It did smell kind of funny, though. Maybe it was us. It was hard to tell.

Gosh, it was hot! We stripped out of all unnecessary clothing, which at that point was just about everything we had on, and opened every window and vent. We were nearly buck naked, and hanging out the windows when we passed through Needles, California and on to Bakersfield. That wouldn't be our last run-in with the "Stinkin' Desert," as we called it.

We stopped along the way and I was able to call the church where we were scheduled to play the next night. I explained our situation and asked if we could unload our equipment when we arrived later that afternoon. I also asked if they knew a transmission mechanic. After we played in Bakersfield we were due the very next night in Oakland for another concert.

We rolled into the church parking lot at around 5:00 p.m. that afternoon. They were waiting for us and let me know they set up a delivery time for our truck at an AAMCO Transmission shop that agreed to repair the truck overnight. Exactly what we needed.

We slung the equipment out of the back of the truck and then I left, with a couple fellows from the church following, to take the truck to the repair shop. When we got there I had to stop to turn left across two lanes of traffic, and into the shop's lot. When I stepped on the gas, though, the truck just sat there. It wouldn't budge an inch. A bunch of guys had to help me push the truck across the traffic and into the transmission shop. It was a good reminder that God really got us through the desert and right to the street in front of the shop. It was a cool lesson in faith for me.

The concert that evening was filled to capacity. The band played well. It was one of the first times in our history that, late in the set, Dana preached and invited folks to accept Jesus. Many came forward that night. I led them back to a room and prayed with them to receive Christ. It was a pattern Dana and I repeated for many years to come. He delivered the message, and I managed our counseling efforts. Over the years we saw thousands upon thousands of people ask Jesus to forgive their sins, and then commit their lives to him at our concerts. I still get letters and emails from some of those folks to this day, almost twenty-five years after we retired.

The next morning was beautiful. We got up early to go fetch Happy Truck. A couple of guys from the church picked us up to take us to the shop. The good news was it was ready and repaired. We got the hard news, however, when we arrived at the shop. The repair bill was over $1,500, which was way more cash than I had. We were paid a few hundred dollars by the church for the concert and sold t-shirts and albums. I only had about $600 in my pocket.

But wait! I just remembered dear old Dad gave me his Master-Card for emergencies. I proudly plopped that puppy on the counter and said, "Just charge it, please."

In those days, the shop owner had to call MasterCard on the telephone for an authorization code for a purchase of that size to go through. I smiled and waited. And then waited some more. The attendant looked up at me and said, "Card's no good. It won't go through."

"It must be a mistake," I responded. "My dad gave me the card for emergencies. Would you try it again?"

He shook his head and whispered, "Okay."

He dialed the phone. We waited—and waited—and waited some more. Then the shop manager lifted his head and said, "Same as before. The card is no good."

I didn't know what to say or what to do. I stammered a little bit as I thought out loud. These guys did us a great favor by working on the truck overnight and then this happened! It was so embarrassing.

Right as I was about to begin trading guitars and drums, one of the fellows from the church who drove us that morning stepped forward and said, "I would like to pay the bill. You guys blessed us last night and now I want to bless you."

That was a great moment and just one more of the many miracles we experienced.

We drove all day and night to make it to Oakland in time for our concert the following evening. At the urging of Stephen Lawhead, Lamb and Lion and their distributor Word Distribution coordinated several promotional appearances for us over the next few days in the Bay Area. Thus Oakland became our hub for the following week or so. We figured it would be cheaper to rent a motel room by the week than to get different rooms each night. We found a place not too far from the Bay Bridge and rented one room for the five of us. That's all we could afford. It was two guys per double bed and one on a rollaway.

The promotional events were interesting, to say the least. We made an appearance on a San Francisco morning TV show. I remember the lead act on the show that morning was a local sister duo called "Two Tons of Fun." They were very, very, large twin sisters. They could really sing, though. It was them and us that morning. I can't imagine what the ratings were.

We were also scheduled to do our first in-store autograph party to meet our fans. The place was a mom and pop independent Christian bookstore in downtown Oakland. I remember showing up and awkwardly introducing ourselves to the storeowners. I say "awkwardly" because no one else was there. It was just the elderly couple who owned the store and us. I walked over and thumbed through the record bin, which was in a dusty corner of the store all by itself.

The store was a peculiar mix of books, Bibles, and all sorts of trinkets, with just the one lonely bin of records in the corner. A jewelry case proudly displayed crosses in every size and made out of every possible material you could imagine. The floor was green asphalt tile. It reminded me of my elementary school. Big fluorescent bulbs glowed their eerie ice-blue color overhead.

The elderly couple seemed welcoming and nice, but the store and the vibe was very creepy. It was hard to imagine any somewhat-normal teenager ever walking through the door. We felt about as out of place as cats in a swimming pool, but did everything we could to be friendly and grateful. I recall asking the older lady just how they let kids know we were going to be there.

"Well," she said, "We put a poster in the front window."

"Hmm," I replied.

I thought most teenagers would run past those windows as fast as they could. They'd probably be afraid of being seen by the aliens inside. I also realized this was indicative of where our records were being sold.

"Houston, we have a problem!" I thought. "How are the kinds of people who might like our music going to find it?"

I was pleased to at least find two copies of our record in the store. Eventually a couple of fans showed up to meet us. Those were the only two who came that day. The awesome news was they each bought one of the copies the store had in its record bin. We called it "Our first sell-out!"

We had a great concert at a little venue in downtown Oakland that evening. There was a good crowd that filled the small room perfectly.

FIFTEEN

YOU CAN'T RUN FROM THUNDER

We headed over to Sacramento and up to Redding the next couple of days for nightly concerts. Then we drove north, farther up the coast to Portland and on to Seattle. The people promoting the concert in Portland all lived together in a couple of large, older Victorian homes not far from downtown. We stayed the night with them, and it was my first taste of sleeping overnight in a commune. There were families with small children and several single folks. Everyone got along well, but it was new for me to be in a house with a bunch of people I didn't know too well.

After the concert in Portland we drove three hours to Seattle. I remember waking up in Happy Truck to the sound of our drummer Terry screaming. As he was also the driver at the time, you can probably understand my concern. Terry had a Grape Nehi soda in one hand and an open package of Twinkies in the other. Rock 'n' roll and health food didn't blend in those days. Also, he was navigating the winding mountain roads with his thigh jammed up against the wheel from the bottom.

He was overcome with excitement at the sight of the scenery outside the window. Mount St. Helens was glowing in the moonlight. Terry wanted us all to share in the beauty of it. I remember asking him to set the grape soda down while he tried to eat a Twinkie and wondered aloud if doing either of those things while steering down the side of a mountain with his knees was such a good idea. I think that may have been the night I started driving more than the other guys.

Anyway, if you have never taken the drive from Portland to Seattle, I encourage you to do that. It's one of the prettiest drives in the country. Just save the snacking for later.

The next day was to be an exciting one. Not only were we scheduled to play at a large outdoor stadium in the evening, but we were also booked to do our first live radio interview during afternoon drive time at the local Christian radio station. We were definitely excited about that.

We arrived in Seattle in the early hours of the morning, so we just slept in the truck for a few hours before going over to the stadium to set the equipment up. We were scheduled to be at the radio station at 5:30 in the afternoon. That's right in the middle of the peak radio listening hour during the drive home time.

We arrived at the station, walked in, and introduced ourselves to the receptionist. I was a bit surprised she didn't know who we were. I figured that out because I had to spell my name about three times in a row. We should have listened to Pat Boone when he suggested we call ourselves "Memphis" when he signed us.

"D_E capital G_A_R_M_O," I said slowly.

"Now, what's that again?"

"Geez Louise," I squeezed out of my lips.

Sometimes I would end those episodes of name spelling help with a snarky "D_E capital G_A R_- M_O_U_S_E" like Mickey Mouse to get a laugh, but not that day.

The receptionist said she would be right back and then stepped through a coded door behind her. I think radio stations were very secure to keep crazies from taking over the airways. She came back in a couple of minutes and said so and so would meet us through the door. She buzzed the door and we walked through into the inner sanctum of the broadcast studio.

The DJ who met us was friendly enough, although I noticed he was dressed in conservative double-knit slacks and a starched shirt with a button down collar. He didn't necessarily portray the rock 'n' roll culture. Dana asked him, "Which one of our songs do you guys play?"

"Uh—we don't play your music," he replied.

"Good!" Dana replied.

Dana was always the best for a wise crack at the most opportune time. I was pretty good at it too. We thought we were funny.

I looked at the DJ and said, "I just happen to have one of our records with me. I thought you guys might not have the whole album."

I could tell when I handed him the album it was the first time he ever laid eyes on it.

"So when this song is over," he said, "let's talk for a minute, and then I'll play one of your songs. We are a fairly conservative station, so I would like to play one of your mellower tunes if that's okay."

"Play 'Wayfaring Stranger,'" I suggested. "It's an old hymn we have re-done. I'm sure your audience will be familiar with it."

When the song he was playing was over, he asked us some questions.

"Where are you guys from?"

"Memphis, Tennessee, where Elvis and Johnny Cash came from."

"What brings you to town?"

"We are playing at (so and so) event. Everybody should come out. It's free admission."

After a couple of minutes of Q and A, he asked Dana to introduce "Wayfaring Stranger" to the listeners. Dana explained it was an old hymn born in southern cotton fields. We grew up with it, gave it a new arrangement, and updated it a bit to record.

The DJ put the record on the turntable and cued up the song. They actually played vinyl records in radio stations then. He started the song and jumped a little at the electric piano intro. He was okay through the verse. Then came the electric piano solo. I noticed him twitch a little, and then Dana's guitar lead began with a lick reminiscent of Jimi Hendrix.

That's when it happened. The DJ actually dove over Dana to reach the turntable and hit the record needle and it slid and scratched all the way across the record sounding like a big zipper right there on live radio!

"Well, that's De Marco and Key! Now, a word from our sponsors," the DJ blurted out in a near panic.

He quickly started a commercial and said, "Thanks, guys, for coming in. I hope it goes well. I gotta get to the weather—or the traffic—or the news—or something different—see you later!"

We were escorted back into the lobby and were busy thanking the receptionist and saying goodbye when the coded door opened. It was the DJ.

"Oh," he said breathlessly. "I forgot to give back your album. Didn't want you to leave without it."

That was our first live radio interview. It turned out pretty well I think.

That evening's concert was at a fairly large, open air football stadium. That can be a little tricky in Seattle, where it rains about every fifteen minutes. When it's clear, though, Seattle is pristine, and we were fortunate because that evening Seattle was clear. There was no rain at all. It was summertime, so the sky was still somewhat light well past 9:00 p.m.

We made it over to the stadium around 7:00 p.m. A local band started its set at 8:00 p.m., then we followed them at 8:45. After our set the pastor of the church sponsoring the event was slated to speak and bring a message to the audience. One of the elements that made this concert a little different was they rented a lighting system for the stage. As hard as it is to imagine, in the beginning days of Christian music most of us played under the house lights. The kind of stage lighting we are so accustomed to today wasn't available back then. That night was different. There were trees of red, blue, yellow, and green stage lights along with a couple of spotlights. We were excited about playing under the "Big Lights."

The stands at the stadium filled to capacity on the side we faced from the track and field. There must have been a couple thousand people there. We played our songs and shared a few words in between a couple of songs. We talked about who we were and where we were from. Occasionally we threw in a spiritual anecdote. We were to leave the preaching to the pastor.

We had a good time playing. The crowd went nuts over our southern blues and our drawl. After we "warmed 'em up" the pastor spoke for about forty-five minutes about every reason possible to get right with God. It was a good message, but, truth be told, a little too long.

As we were meeting people at the foot of the stage at the end of the night, I noticed over to the side there were about fifty people gathered. They seemed to be waiting until there was a clear path to us so they could meet us as a group. None of them looked too happy, either.

A bit of a line formed with this big bulge of people inching closer every minute. When they finally reached us, a woman from the group took the lead and walked up closer to us.

"How dare you?" she snarled.

"How dare you use flashing lights? I could see the demons rising up from the smoke and lights while the devil's rock music was blaring!"

I thought to myself, *that was probably Terry, our drummer, actually*. I was glad I didn't say it out loud. She might have hit me. She was pretty upset and ready to wrestle and she had the snarl to prove it.

While she was cranking up for more, several of the others in her group chimed in.

"The beat is of Satan himself!"

"You guys are doing the devil's bidding!"

Had it been a century earlier, they probably would have tried to burn us at the stake.

I was just grateful that they didn't throw stuff. We have had people throw stuff at us before. That had been in the Deep South, though. Down there they figure they'll get your attention better if they hit you upside the head with something.

We knew better than to get into a public rock 'n' roll justification debate with these folks. We politely asked them to pray for us and then reminded them "God loves you," to pour some hot coals on their heads just in case.

It wasn't uncommon for us to stir up anti-rock protests when we came to town back then. It was a hot topic in those years. Even highly respectable pastors and speakers would sometimes preach against the "Jungle Beat." A few times we generated enough controversy with the opposition that they hosted "record burnings" outside our concerts. I always thought it was a bizarre phenomenon, but it happened and the press loved it. People have loved seeing Christians dancing around fires for centuries.

Often times, when we were booked to come to a city to perform, the local papers would write a story about whether or not it was acceptable to play rock music about Jesus. I guess that was sensational. Years later someone found a huge file of old D&K newspaper and magazine articles in Capitol Christian Music Group's archives when I worked there long after D&K. They thought I might want them. As I thumbed through the various articles and newspaper stories, I was amazed at how many of them were about the controversy around whether Jesus liked rock music. Did Jesus Rock even have a moral right to exist?

As I look back, I realize the controversy was the press and publicity engine God used to get our music out there. With the exception of a few small but loyal radio shows that played rock music, the majority of Christian radio and TV broadcasters wouldn't touch rock music in those days. Those scandalized articles were sometimes the only PR we got.

SIXTEEN

EVERY DAY A CELEBRATION

After the concert in Seattle we drove back down through California. We had a concert scheduled south of Fresno and then the tour finale at Calvary Chapel in Costa Mesa. Many people considered Calvary Chapel to be the Jesus Movement's Ground Zero. It certainly was the epicenter of the Jesus Music culture. Stories of the packed Saturday Night Concerts made it all the way back to Memphis. We also knew the show would be broadcast live on "Maranatha Radio" and on local TV. We were very excited and honored for the opportunity. There could be no better place to close out our first West Coast tour. Also, after feeling like strangers in a strange land, we were really looking forward to being with like-minded folks.

A few miles north of Fresno I began to hear a squeaky sound from the rear of Happy Truck. It kind of sounded like a hamster spinning on a wheel. As we drove the noise grew louder and louder. Eventually we decided to find a repair shop. Fortunately, we made it into the north side of Fresno.

The mechanic at the garage took the truck for a drive around the block. When he got back he advised us that he thought we had "spun" a wheel bearing on the rear axle. Of course, the replacement part was nowhere to be found in Fresno, and he would have to order it. It would take a day or two to get it, maybe more.

I asked the mechanic to take us to a motel to wait it out. He graciously agreed and dropped us in front of a Motel 6 on a major boulevard. There were even restaurants around that time. I had a little bit of cash from t-shirt sales and booked us a single room for all five of us again. We were used to cramped quarters by then. It was kind of like being in an Army barracks or camping out.

We had a couple of days to kill before our next concert and four days before we were due at Calvary Chapel. We ended up spending that whole time in the Motel 6. We made the most of it, though. The motel manager greeted us each morning with a knock on our door and a demand to be paid in cash before we could stay another night. One morning we returned from an early breakfast to find all of our stuff sitting outside the door on the balcony. No cash, no room. I guess I understand that, actually. We were a ragged looking bunch of longhairs carrying guitars around and all piled up in one room together like savages.

One nice discovery in Fresno was a sizeable Christian book and music store called Fresno Bible House. It was walking distance from our motel, so we darkened their doors several times. I practically haunted the place. I had never seen a store like that before. It was very professional looking and well stocked. The owners, Stan Jantz and his son Dan, were extremely kind to us. They gave us a grand tour of the store and treated us like real friends. I must have asked them a million questions over those few days.

I wanted to know everything. Who orders the product? How did they manage promotions and advertising? Where did the merchandise come from? The Jantz family gave me my first crash course in Christian retailing. That education proved invaluable to me in the years that followed. I'm sure I must have worn them out showing up day after day with all of my questions, but they were never anything but kind. That meant a lot to me.

On the second day of breakdown number two, we were scheduled to play a concert about a hundred miles from Fresno. It fell to me to call the pastor of the church to inform him of our predicament. "Sir," I said over the hotel phone, "I realize we are supposed to be at your church to play a concert tonight, but unfortunately we have broken down in Fresno and don't have enough money to rent a truck to get over to you. I'm very sorry."

"Where are you guys staying?" he asked.

"We are at a Motel 6 in Fresno waiting on the part to fix our truck. We hope we have enough money to pay the repair bill, but we don't have enough to do that and rent a truck to get to you."

Then the pastor said something remarkable I'll never forget.

"If you guys can't come to us," he said cheerily, "we'll just have to come to you. See you in a few hours." Then he hung up the telephone.

I went back to the guys and relayed the conversation.

"I guess a few of them are coming to see us," I said, astonished.

At around 7:00 p.m., two big vans and a small church bus pulled into the Motel 6 parking lot. I ran downstairs to greet them.

The pastor, who looked as big as an NFL lineman, came toward me with a huge smile on his face. "We came here tonight to praise the Lord and to hear you guys play!" he shouted. He then bear-hugged me so hard I couldn't breathe.

That night we crammed about fifty or sixty people into our motel room. We got out our guitars and played and sang for them. When we were done they prayed over us and anointed us with oil. Being raised Southern Baptist, I was never anointed with any oil that hadn't come out of an old hot rod in our driveway as a kid. It was a powerful experience.

I'll never forget that night. As the folks were piling into their vans to leave, the pastor handed me an envelope full of cash.

"What's this for?" I asked.

"We agreed to pay you guys for a concert and that's the money."

"You don't owe us anything," I protested. "We couldn't even set up our equipment and play properly for you."

With great authority and grace the pastor said, "You guys have blessed us tonight, and now it's our turn to bless you. Take the money. Besides, it looks like you could use it more than us."

In many ways I think that unplugged Motel 6 set was one of our best concerts ever. And yes, the money came in handy. It turned out our truck would not be ready to drive to Calvary Chapel, which was about five hours away. But because of that church's generosity we were able to rent a van, load our essential equipment up, and hightail it down to Costa Mesa for another unforgettable evening playing in front of 4,000 people. That was the grand finale of our first real, extended tour.

We picked up Happy Truck the next day in Fresno and started back across the "Stinking Desert." Our soundman, Madison, fell asleep on the floor with his head crammed between the driver and passenger's seat tilted toward me while I was driving. I got bored during the endless night and found a felt-tipped marker on the dash. Slowly and carefully I drew a mustache on him while he slept. Every time I drew a line, he flicked at it like he was flicking away a gnat. It took me two hundred miles to get that mustache on him. The long, squiggly lines looked more like rat whiskers than a mustache, but I was proud of my work nonetheless.

In the morning, when we stopped for breakfast, I got out and began to fill the truck with gas. The other guys slowly rolled out and made their way to the adjacent restaurant. When Madison came in the rest of us had a good belly laugh at his expense. He didn't know what was going on. The waitress came by and had a good laugh too. Then he thought he'd better go take a look in a mirror. He wasn't too happy about what he saw, mainly because you have to almost scrub the skin off to remove magic marker. He got over it after another hundred miles or so and we all had a good laugh. It was a good way to end the tour.

After we got home and paid our guys, Dana and I had to get a job painting a house to pay off the rest of the tour bills. That was the early days of Christian music. It was great—and it was work!

It remains a mystery why my dad's MasterCard was declined at the transmission shop. We never really got to the bottom of it. Who knows? As I've pondered for years that gracious man paying our bill, I've come to realize that is just how God works. He meets us in our time of need. We certainly needed his help that day. He chose to deliver us through an act of kindness from a stranger. It wouldn't have been the same blessing for any of us had the charge card worked. That's the best answer.

SEVENTEEN

ACTIVATE

The little house Susan and I lived in proved to be a real blessing for our family. As I mentioned, my folks owned it and offered it to us rent-free as long as I went to college. Now, the problem with that was I dropped out of college my senior year to go on tour. My folks understood my decision, but didn't necessarily like it at all when I quit school. I promised my mother I would finish someday. We soon got so busy, and I was so driven to succeed beyond what is normal for most people, I never looked back.

We began to pay rent to my folks, which was good. We also began to slowly climb out of the need for government welfare and food stamps. The lessons I learned from that journey are immeasurable. Firstly, a government safety net for people who can't take care of themselves is a wonderful and necessary service of society. However, I do believe help should come with responsibility from the recipient and commitment to learn how to better his or her situation and also work to serve the community in return. Government assistance should not be a way of life for anyone except those who are elderly or disabled to the point of not being able to help themselves.

The second thing I learned about government assistance was I never intended to go back to it if it was at all in my power. Susan and I desperately wanted to provide for our family with every ounce of life we had. To say we were driven is an understatement. There was no plan B. I've come to believe that is a very important building block of starting a business. There really can't be a viable plan B, or when the going gets tough, plan B will be the easy fall back.

That doesn't at all mean one shouldn't be flexible. I was flexible in every way I knew how to be while working bi-vocationally or even tri-vocationally, meaning I always had two or three ways to make money while getting the band and our calling off the ground. While we lived in the little house on the rougher side of town, we saw God's miracles many times in our lives.

One summer morning, I rose from bed, put on some shorts, and went outside to mow our yard. There wasn't much I hated more than mowing the grass. I'm sure that aversion took hold of me as a kid. My dad always had me out mowing the lawns at his construction sites. He bought a beast of a lawnmower, so it would cut the tall Johnson grass. It was one with big wheels on the rear, so I could push it easier and sweat a little less. Nothing could stop that monster from chewing up a yard littered with various junk and litter thrown around by construction workers building a house. Dad paid me a little money to do it. It was good training on how to hate mowing grass as an adult. Come to think of it, I never saw my dad mowing grass while I was growing up. He knew better.

I got up that morning, made myself a cup of coffee, and stumbled outside. Susan came outside about five minutes after I started mowing. She shouted to me over the noise of the mower, saying she and the girls were going to the grocery store. I watched all three of them load into our canary yellow Volkswagen Squareback and head down the street, waving goodbye. After I finished mowing the front yard, I wheeled the beast around to the side of the house.

There was a big overgrown bush on the side of the house that was around ten feet tall and eight feet in diameter. I looked at it a thousand times, knowing I needed to prune it, but I just never got around to it. I don't know what kind of bush it was, but I knew it wasn't prickly, so I could get close to its waxy leaves with the lawnmower.

I skipped a few weeks mowing the yard while being away on tour somewhere, and the grass had grown tall and thick around the base of the bush where its branches met the ground. I learned from mowing those gol-darned construction lots of my dad's that when you need to mow tall grass, one effective maneuver is to tilt the mower back on its rear wheels, roll forward slowly, and then let the mower lower over the grass a few inches at a time. That will let you chop it off little by little without stalling out the mower.

I reared that mower back on its rear wheels and pushed it up toward that big shrub. But just as soon as I moved forward I heard a loud voice shout at me.

"Stop!" the voice said sternly. "Breckon is in there!"

The voice startled me so badly I stopped and turned around to see who was screaming at me. I clearly heard a man's voice, but when I turned around, there was no one there! It was just sticky, dusty air. "That's weird," I thought to myself. I reared back the mower again to cut the tall grass, but an overwhelming feeling I should not move forward came over me. I shut down the mower's engine, walked a couple of steps to the bush, and spread back the branches to peer inside. There, hiding in the bush, was sweet little Breckon, our daughter, just smiling and looking up at me with her big brown eyes.

"Hey, Daddy," she said playfully, "I stayed home to surprise you and be with you!" She had no idea what almost happened.

I grabbed her and hugged her so tight she probably thought I was going to break her in half. My mind raced, imagining the tragedy that would have happened had I rolled forward with that blasted lawnmower. I went and settled on the front porch, holding our little girl in awe until Susan got back home.

When she drove up she could see the shock on my face. I explained to her what happened and described the commanding voice that prevented a disaster. Susan squeaked in shock. "As we left, Breckon said she wanted to stay home with you. So I drove around the block and dropped her off in the driveway. I thought you saw us!"

That is the only time in my life I have ever heard an audible voice from an invisible source...or force. I'm convinced it was my guardian angel. Breckon was only three years old. Another miracle.

By the way, I still hate mowing grass.

EIGHTEEN

LONG DISTANCE RUNNER

When we got home from the West Coast adventures of our first big tour, it was back to "real life" in a hurry. Dana and I continued to work various jobs to make ends meet. The joy and thrill of our music and ministry calling, however, made all the menial labor worthwhile and meaningful even though we hoped one day soon we could be full time musicians. It was like holding down three jobs at a time.

Out behind our little ramshackle house stood an old, rickety, single-car garage. It was leaning to one side, and the bottom row of siding had all but rotted away. Several of the supporting studs were completely gone. It was a disaster waiting to happen, but in my mind's eye, and with a little TLC, I saw the perfect band rehearsal room. I pointed it out to Dana, and he agreed. So, we went to work re-constructing that old garage.

We poured a new concrete floor high enough to keep the water out. Then we replaced all the rotted wood and applied new siding on the outside. Inside we double insulated it, removed the large garage door, and installed a normal-sized door in its place. We installed brown sheathing board on the inside walls and ceiling and covered every square inch of it with salvage shag carpet I was able to get from the apartment complex where I did part time maintenance. It looked like Elvis's jungle room—or at least our cheap imitation of it.

Our neighbor, Mr. Bill, came over from next door to help several times during the project. I think he thought the rock music might drive him, Mrs. Katy, and Mike the parrot crazy, so he worked hard to help us soundproof it. It worked perfectly well and became our rehearsal room during the *Straight On* and *This Ain't Hollywood* albums. It was also where we rehearsed countless hours in preparation for our work with Amy Grant. But we'll get to that later.

We wrote the songs for *Straight On*, our second album, in our new rehearsal room. There was a Pentecostal Holiness Church bordering our back yard. It often seemed their band was competing with us to see who could be louder. Despite the soundproofing, the walls were thumping pretty hard. There was a lot of music going on.

Terry Moxley was on drums and Kenny Porter played bass, but Dana and I wrote all the songs for the album. We had various ways of writing together. Many times one of us would have a piece of a song like a chorus line or musical riff, and then the other one would fill in the blank. That happened on "Jericho" and "Long Distance Runner." Dana wrote part of the lyrics on each of those, and I contributed the music and worked on the melodies. Sometimes we wrote songs almost entirely on our own. I did that on "Livin' on the Edge of Dyin.'" Dana wrote "Mary" alone. Both "Bad Livin'" and "Let Him Help You Today" were older jam songs built on Dana's guitar riffs born years earlier during our "Christian Band" era.

From the beginning of DeGarmo and Key, Dana and I decided to share all of our songwriting credits and the corresponding publishing royalties fifty-fifty, right down the middle. We really didn't want competition between us to get our songs on the albums. We just wanted the best song to win out, bottom line. By taking the financial gain, and credit, out of the equation, the competition was neutralized between us somewhat.

As a result, on some albums I might have written six songs with Dana writing four or five. Then the reverse would happen. We worked on each other's ideas together, but rarely did we sit in the same room, at the same time, and write together from scratch. I think some of the songs we wrote individually would surprise some folks. We each contributed rock and pop radio songs. We also each wrote ballads. As I step through the albums, I'll point out some of our individual contributions.

When we were recording *This Time Thru* I met a young producer at Ardent named Joe Hardy. He was an interesting combination of things. Joe was an intellectual sort of guy and well read. He dressed very business-casual-like and wore his hair shorter, but at heart Joe was a music and art aficionado. He just didn't look the part.

At that point most of the recording work Joe did was on his own solo work, but it sounded fantastic. I went to Dana and told him about Joe and how impressed I was with the sonics and the modern production techniques he employed. I thought Dana and I should meet with him to see if he might be interested in co-producing our next album.

Dana and I wanted more of a voice in the album production process, so the decision was made we would co-produce our records going forward. Both of us practically grew up in the recording studio with Lewis Willis at Allied Recording Studios and felt we had the chops to co-produce. But a third, objective voice could be a good thing.

I set up a time for Dana and I to meet with Joe Hardy. Joe played us all the demos he self-produced. They were fantastic. The three of us hit it off with our shared philosophy of music. We decided that day Joe was a perfect fit for us.

The recording of *Straight On* was an effort in experimentation for all of us. We set up Terry Moxley's drums in the center of the big room, rather than the small drum isolation booth. We felt like the expanse of the high ceilings allowed the sound of his drums to reverberate, giving them a more natural sound. Kenny Porter wired his bass guitar up through an amplifier and used a direct signal simultaneously to give more of a "live" sound. I played Ardent's Hammond organ (which was the same one Booker T. played on the MG's legendary albums, including *Green Onions*). Dana switched from a Marshall amplifier to a Lab L-5 to allow his guitar to have more diverse tones.

It took about a week to track the album. That means we had drum tracks, bass tracks, rhythm guitar tracks, and keyboard tracks at the end of the week. We also recorded scratch vocals, which were replaced later.

Interestingly, backing up to the control room wall of Studio A, which was the larger studio at Ardent where we were recording by now, was the Mercury Records A&R (artists and repertoire) office in Memphis. Jud Phillips, who was the nephew of legendary Sam Phillips—who discovered Elvis, Johnny Cash, Jerry Lewis, and Carl Perkins among many others—ran the Mercury operation in Memphis.

Jud knocked on the studio door and asked to come in and listen from time to time. He asked questions about what we wanted to accomplish with our music. He was keenly interested in our faith as well. Jud was convinced that at least a couple of songs on *Straight On* could be mainstream radio hits. He fell in love with "Long Distance Runner" and "Livin' on the Edge of Dyin'" in particular.

After a few more visits and conversations, he asked if and how he could get in touch with our label (Lamb and Lion) and Pat Boone. He felt we would be a great fit for Mercury Records and wanted to research whether there was a way they could partner with Lamb and Lion on us. Jud flew out to Hollywood to meet with Pat and the gang, and on one occasion, the Lamb and Lion execs came to Memphis to meet with Mercury.

At the end of the day, though, it was to no avail. It seemed Lamb and Lion and Mercury couldn't come to terms on markets, owner-ship, royalties—you name it. Dana and I were very disappointed at first. We wanted a crack at the mainstream market, and Mercury, at least in the beginning, was willing to take us un-censored. That was very different from the experience we had with Hi Records and Lon-don Records when we became Christians while in Globe. They didn't know what to do with our overt lyrics about God and faith. That didn't seem to be a barrier this time. It was unfortunate Mercury and Lamb and Lion couldn't get together. It might have been a great experiment for all of us.

Straight On was released in 1979 to rave reviews and much critical acclaim. It seemed to really strike a chord with our audience. The larger Christian radio audience was still elusive, as Christian radio just wouldn't play our music very much. They said it was too aggressive for them and complained that Dana's voice was too bluesy, and they couldn't understand the words he sang well enough.

"That's only rock 'n' roll!" I say to that.

We did get a smattering of national airplay on our song "Mary," which was about Mary looking for Jesus in the garden following the crucifixion. He wasn't there. He had risen! Though few in number, loyal Christian rock stations played our music endlessly and with fervor. We appreciated them and their work to get our music heard on the airwaves. There just weren't many of them around.

In the early days of Jesus rock, our music was mostly played on college radio stations and on one or two-hour specialty shows on mainstream radio stations programmed in the late night hours, or perhaps on Sunday mornings. Those radio DJs who liked Christian rock got permission from their mainstream stations to program shows centered on Christian rock to fulfill their station's criteria for public service broadcasting. Those shows sprang up on major mainstream rock and pop stations around the country during the seventies and eighties.

That was really the only way we could achieve mass media radio for Jesus rock music then. There were a few diehard Christian rock stations around, but very few. The majority of Christian radio was middle of the road music in the adult contemporary format. Ironically, it still is today. Actually, Christian radio is still a far cry softer in its format and sound than radio that appeals to most young people in my opinion. The reason is their format is geared for and largely reaches out to soccer moms and thirty-somethings. That is perfectly fine. It just makes it tough on artists who have a more aggressive sound. In my day that was Jesus rock music. Today it is hip-hop, and some rock and pop music.

We began to tour the country playing the new music from *Straight On*. Our concert audiences were all over the spectrum. Some nights we played to a couple hundred people. Other nights it would be a couple thousand folks. There didn't seem to be enough places for us to play. Or, to clarify, there weren't enough places that would pay us an honorarium to play a concert. Most places and promoters loved to have us play, but it would have to be for free. That was great for the ministry and we saw many lives changed in those concerts. It was a tough way to make a living though.

One night we played a show at a stately, secular, Southern university in Mississippi, where the sidewalks were lined with magnolias and live oaks and moss hung from giant limbs over lush lawns edged with azaleas. We played that night to a shockingly wild group of "mainstream" college students. It was not billed as a "Christian" event so we had all kinds of students attending. We learned to thrive in those conditions and enjoyed presenting our music, and God's message, in a neutral setting.

At the end of the concert I noticed a very attractive female student hanging out by the stage where my keyboards were. I went over to speak with her and she began to ask me very personal questions about my life and so forth. Her questions were a bit too personal, if you know what I mean. I answered some of her questions and made some small talk to distract from the rest. Then she asked me where we were staying for the night. I certainly did not want to tell her, so I called our bass player, Kenny, over to save me. He walked over, and I gave him the eye. He saw what was happening and called me away. Later, after we packed everything up in our truck, we got a bite to eat at a late night restaurant and then proceeded to our motel.

How this next part happened is something, to this day, that remains a mystery to me. The inn was one of those old style motels where the second floor doors all opened up onto a long balcony with a rail overlooking the parking lot. When I placed the key in the door and opened it, I was first startled to see the lamp was on, but when my eyes focused, I freaked out. The attractive girl from the university was lying on one of the beds reading the Gideons Bible. As I said, we roomed two guys to a room, so Kenny was close behind me and also saw the girl in there.

After I recovered my wits, I said, "You've got to get out of here. Right now!"

She wanted to talk about it.

I said, "No more conversation. Get out now!" She got up and left while Kenny and I sat there bewildered by what just happened. And then I made a big mistake. "Kenny," I said. "I'm really worried about what Susan may think of all this craziness. I don't want her thinking about stuff like this happening to us on the road. I think it's better we don't tell our wives. No need to have them worrying about us."

Famous last words.

A few days later we were having band practice in our rehearsal room behind the house. It was customary for us to rehearse for an hour or so and then take a coffee break for a few minutes. We would all go into our little house through the back door and into the kitchen area. Susan and the girls would usually be around to join in on the conversation and catch up on the goings on of the band members and their families.

That day was no different. The four of us went inside for a break. Susan and Dana were having a conversation about who knows what when I heard a knock on the front door. I walked over, opened it, and met the stare of a florist holding a long stem rose in a vase.

"Is Eddie DeGarmo here?" he asked. "I have a delivery for him."

"That's me."

The deliveryman handed me the goods, smiling. "Then this is for you."

I walked back inside and found all eyes focused on me.

"Is that for you?" Susan asked. "What is it?" She looked to be in shock. Her face tightened. "Who is it from?" she snarled.

I opened the note card and it simply said, "Next time you can stay with me, Eddie." It was signed "Love from Mississippi."

Susan then asked me what was written on the card. Either I couldn't think of the answer, or my mouth momentarily forgot how to form any words at all. Either way, I was dead.

"I promise, baby," I began desperately, "This is not what it seems. I swear! Nothing happened! Just ask Kenny. He was there! There was this—this crazy college girl was chasing me. I swear, nothing happened!" I said that last "I swear" while sinking to my knees to the floor in front of her. Next up: full-blown groveling.

All the band guys were in shock like me. I think they were all either about to drop to their knees and beg for my life with me, or to turn and run. Either was possible. At that point Susan couldn't contain it any longer. She suddenly burst into laughter.

She pointed her finger directly toward the end of my nose and said, "Don't you ever withhold anything from me again. You tell me everything that happens while you are on tour. It's not right to keep stuff like that from me. You see, I'll always find out. I sent the flowers!"

"What?" I gasped.

"Yes!" she continued, in utter victory. "Kenny told his wife. She told me. I sent you the flowers to teach you a lesson!" She then turned to the band members, who at that moment were trying to sneak out of the back door.

"That goes for you guys too!" she hollered.

That taught me a good lesson. I married a wild and spirited woman who is not to be messed with. She can be pretty funny, too.

Thankfully, I never heard from that Mississippi girl again. I learned through these shenanigans, though, something about the strange way some people relate to people they see as celebrities. Fortunately, that story ended well. Susan made fun of me and also made a strong point at the same time. Those living in the public eye or enjoying a little celebrity of sorts, even if it's in the Christian realm, can attract this kind of unwanted attention. In fact, sometimes the Christian element just makes it weirder. These moments can begin as amusing or flattering, and usually they involve nothing more than an awkward conversation. But they can turn really scary.

For example, a few years later, after the release of our *Mission of Mercy* album, our popularity rose to a new level. We enjoyed a few big hits by then. I was working in the studio producing Farrell and Farrell's *Choices* album while off the road between tours. Oddly,

I began to receive small gifts in my home mailbox with simple, hand-written notes to me. They were weird things like stuffed animals and various trinkets. Over a period of a week I found a few of those things. I showed them to Susan and it weirded us out a little bit for sure.

One night we were home watching TV, and Susan noticed a person watching us through our window from a car parked on the street in front of our house. She got up, opened the front door, and the car immediately started up and sped away. Then it happened again a few nights later. Our phone rang a lot, too. We noticed that if Susan answered, the caller would hang up. A few minutes later it would ring again. If I answered it, I would hear the cheery voice of a girl who worked in the Nashville office of a company D&K hired to provide press, publicity, and promotional work for us. I started to put two and two together. It takes me a minute, sometimes.

She called one night and I thought I was smart enough to talk some sense into her. That was a big mistake. Susan didn't like it at all so she just walked over and unplugged the phone from the wall.

"You can't talk any sense into her!" she shouted. "My gosh, she's driving down here from Nashville at all hours of the night and stalking our house. There is something wrong with her."

Susan was right.

A few days later, I was driving to Ardent in the morning to work with Bob Farrell and stopped to get a cup of coffee at a convenience store. When I came out, I noticed the same girl from Nashville sitting in her car staring at me. She even waved. I nervously waved back in a state of disbelief and got in my car and drove away. *She lives over 200 miles away*, I thought to myself. That really disturbed me.

After a long day at Ardent I left to go home at around 6:00 p.m. I walked out of the building and there she was, waiting for me right outside the studio door.

"I just gotta talk to you, Eddie," she said. "I know we are supposed to be together. God told me so!"

"Well, He didn't tell me that," I insisted. "What in the world are you doing? Please leave. You need to go home."

She blocked my path as I tried to walk away. "Why won't you talk to me?"

"Because this can't go anywhere! I'm going home to my wife. You gotta leave me alone." I seethed while I spoke.

She just smiled. Then it dawned on me she got what she came for; attention from me. Any attention. It didn't matter if it was positive or negative. The really scary thing was she was not crying, screaming, or even upset. She spoke calmly and seemed rational—other than she was CRAZY!

The next day when I came to the studio she was still there. I think she slept in her car. I had no choice but to call the police. They told me they couldn't do anything without an order from a judge about stalking. Hopefully those laws have changed. By then I was thinking about Clint Eastwood in *Play Misty for Me* or the ending of *Fatal Attraction*. Neither one ended well. Those guys crossed the line of decency in those movies. I did nothing improper, but I was really freaking out, thinking this girl could still shoot me.

Bob Farrell offered to go out to her car and talk to her. He actually got her to leave.

Unfortunately, when we came out in the dark at the end of the day to go home, she was back!

I ran inside and had no choice but to call the folks she worked for to hopefully get a contact for someone in her family who could help her. I tried not to do that because I knew it would probably mean she would get fired. Finally, I was able to get her parents' phone number and I called them immediately. Her father answered the phone.

"Hello sir, my name is Eddie DeGarmo and I'm calling about your daughter."

Before I could get another word out he said, "I know all about you. I know what you've done to my daughter. She's told me everything. You should be ashamed!"

I said, "Look, I absolutely haven't done anything to your daughter, but you can believe what you want to believe. I can't change your mind about that for now. But, your daughter is living in her car, as we speak, in a recording studio parking lot in Memphis, Tennessee. She's been there for a few days. You need to come help her and take her home."

He began to settle down after I said that. He drove a few hundred miles that night to Memphis and rescued his daughter. Thank God.

It can be difficult to know how to act as a public person while maintaining a private life. You want to be friendly and open. I didn't want to put boundaries around me and be removed from "real life" in terms of friends, neighbors, or church. I also needed to be accountable to those around me and those who love me. It's not always easy to know where to draw the line. It's a balance. But sometimes, well, things can definitely get weird.

NINETEEN

SPECIAL KIND OF LOVE

One of the tours we mounted in support of the *Straight On* album took us east to Washington, DC and on up to Maine. I was driving one afternoon on a beautiful two-lane road through the Shenandoah Valley in Virginia on our way to our first show in our nation's capital. Happy Truck suddenly began to shake violently. It felt as if the truck was acting like a Hawaiian hula dancer while barreling down the road. I had to stop immediately.

When all five of us sweaty bodies rolled out of there to assess the problem, we discovered the right dual rear wheels appeared very loose and oddly tilted to one side. Upon closer inspection we found six of the eight lug bolts designed to hold the rear wheels in place on the axle had sheared off. The wheels were only being held by the two remaining lug bolts. We were very lucky the wheels didn't come flying off at full speed.

We were parked on the side of the two lane road down below a gorgeous antebellum mansion sitting proudly on a gentle rise about a hundred yards or so above us. The house was surrounded by acres of manicured, fenced, pastureland and huge oak trees. There were several horses roaming freely near an impressive looking barn that was nicer than most of my friends' houses. I decided I would hike up the hill to the mansion and ask if I could use their telephone to call a repair shop. Kenny Porter, our bass player on the tour, decided he would accompany me up the hill.

The genteel old house was indeed an imposing looking edifice—a throwback to the Old South. I could easily visualize southern gentlemen smoking cigars on the front steps while women in hoop skirts drank mint juleps served by servants in tails and white gloves. It was that kind of place. Spooky. I was intimidated by the surroundings, and the thought of knocking on its massive oak doors made me nervous. When we reached the front porch with its tall Greek columns, I was taken aback by the beauty of the place. The tall porch ceiling was painted robin's egg blue, which I later learned deterred the wasps from building nests because they were fooled into thinking it was the blue sky. I kind of got that same feeling when I was fortunate enough to be able to look out of the windshield riding in the back of Happy Truck.

I gathered myself and knocked on the door. After a few moments it opened slowly, and a beautiful lady appeared. Although it was the middle of the afternoon, she was wearing a long red evening gown. She whispered in a low and breathy voice, "May I help you?" I was probably blushing so much my face matched her dress, but I got it together and quickly explained our situation. I told her we were a music group headed to DC for a concert and pointed to our broken down truck below on the road.

"Would it be possible to use your telephone to call a repair shop?" I asked.

"It's possible," she said languidly. "The telephone is at the top of the stairs." She turned around and pointed the way up a curved stairway rivaling anything in *Gone With the Wind*.

I proceeded slowly up the stairs while she and Kenny followed a couple of stairs behind. As I climbed the staircase I thought I heard laughter from the left, beyond the balcony. I continued up, cautiously. When I reached the top balcony I looked to the left and saw the entire second floor of the large house was converted into one big room. I also noticed rows of twin-size beds lining both sides of the room. There were easily eight to ten beds up there. It was like the most elegant Army barracks you could imagine. I also became instantly aware of the fact that upon most of the beds sat a beautiful woman; some more dressed than others, if you get my point. My eyes were popping out!

Nobody said a word. The ladies were all just staring at me. I stood speechless as I was on my honeymoon. Just as I was about to completely lose it, scream, and bolt down the stairs, a door opened at the far end of the room that looked to be a bathroom. A topless lady walked out into the large room. Upon closer examination of the situation, however, I noticed something bizarre indeed. The woman had no breasts! She was as flat-chested as a man.

At that moment, I looked at the lady who met us at the front door and blurted out, "Okay. The joke's on me. What's going on?"

The room burst out into laughter and all the "girls" were cracking up. Some were clapping their hands. Then the lady (more on that later) said, "Oh honey, we are all transvestites. We are a band of musicians, too."

It turned out they were a show band of female impersonators living together in the mansion. They were just a normal group of traveling troubadour transvestites. That was something we saw every day in Memphis—not!

Whispering, I asked if it was still okay to use the phone. "Sure," she—or he—said, "But the closest town is about ten miles away. What's wrong with your truck anyway, honey? We have a couple of 'girls' who can work on those beastly things."

They walked down and assessed our situation, drove to town to get the necessary parts, came back, jacked up our truck, and fixed it. Some of them stayed in drag, wearing dresses the whole time while working on the truck. They had to remove the wheels, slide under and take out the broken lug bolts, and then replace them with new ones. It was honestly one of the strangest things I have ever seen, but they were really nice to help us out like that.

That afternoon, as we got to know each other, they showed us promo pictures of them on stage, decked out in their best evening drag and playing their musical instruments. We showed them our pictures too. They discussed what they were all about, and we shared with them what we were all about. We told them about how God changed our lives and we were spreading the Gospel of Jesus through rock 'n' roll. Truth be told, I'm not sure who thought the other was more strange or weird.

It was great to experience how God works despite such vast and different backgrounds in this world. We don't always have to agree on everything to work on some things together, do we? And, we are told to take the Gospel into ALL the world.

TWENTY

PREACHER, I'LL NEED A FRIEND

few months after we released *Straight On* cracks began to form in the foundation of Dana and Suzy's marriage. I don't know if I'll ever completely understand it. They were high school sweethearts and grew up dating and going steady. Perhaps the communal life was more than Suzy could handle. Dana was a stubborn one, for sure. He could have a "my way or the highway" type of personality. You had to know how to handle him. I only partially learned how. Maybe Suzy didn't. Dana was also a wonderful guy with an undying heart for God. He was still a stubborn cuss, though.

Somehow their marriage fell apart. We were all in a state of shock about it, especially Dana. When they divorced, Dana moved out of the communal house and was able to buy an old house in mid-town Memphis in much need of repair. It was on Morrison Street, about a hundred yards from Ardent Studios. Oddly, it was the same house in which Susan's mother grew up. That was a strange coincidence for sure.

After Dana bought that old house, I went over from time to time to help him fix it up. He was going through a really tough time with the divorce, and I wanted to be with him as much as I could. Dana went to Bible College and really wanted to be a pastor someday. He felt like damaged goods because of the divorce, though. He thought he would never be asked to pastor a church.

It became obvious to us both it was going to take more time for our band to be able to support us financially. Dana, living down the street from Ardent, began to hang around the studio quite a bit. Over the course of a couple months, the studio offered him a job answering the door and telephone at night. A few weeks after he started to work there he called me and said John Fry, the studio owner, wanted to offer me the same job. That was a real Godsend for both of us. John Fry was quite the peculiar character. He grew up in a prestigious Memphis family and he still carried that sophisticated air around him. His voice sounded exactly like Jimmy Stewart's in *It's a Wonderful Life,* and he spoke with the same disarming stammer. He also seemed to wear the same outfit every single day, but upon further inspection, he just owned thirty pairs of beige khaki pants and thirty powder blue cotton twill, button-down, ivy league dress shirts hanging in his closet. He really took a liking to us, but he was eccentric.

I started the night job at Ardent in the fall of 1979. Dana and I swapped nights. The job had bizarre hours. We clocked in at 5:00 p.m. and often wouldn't clock out until after the sun came up the next morning. Sometimes the clientele in the studio were legendary artists. Other times we were dealing with free-spirited local artists who just hung out until the wee hours of the morning. I met a ton of very talented and interesting characters during those long nights at Ardent. There was a lot of late night storytelling and even some amazing spiritual conversations. I'm sure some of those people were under the influence of serious drugs or alcohol, but I was used to that, having grown up around the music scene.

John Fry threw Dana and me a major lifeline. We came to an agreement that while we worked there, it would be okay for us to take a few weeks off in the spring and fall to tour. That was not only extremely accommodating; it also kept Lamb and Lion happy that we could promote our records.

I was doing odd jobs during the days while working at Ardent three or four nights a week. Dana and I came to a very tough decision during that season. DeGarmo and Key couldn't tour enough to support us, so we needed to set our band free to pursue other things to survive. That was a tough call. We met with Kenny Porter and Terry Moxley to let them know we took full time jobs with Ardent, and we planned to consolidate our touring to a few weeks in the spring and fall combined with a smattering of summertime events. It wasn't enough activity to support a full time band. We understood we would probably lose those guys for good. They were going to need to go to a full time band or take jobs elsewhere. That was tough on all of us.

Shortly after I began to work at Ardent, John Fry seemed to notice I had a deeper interest in the business side of things. He began to groom me to take over Joe Hardy's position as studio manager. That's right. Not only had Joe Hardy co-produced *Straight On*, he also performed all of the daily tasks of a studio manager. Ardent was bustling with activity then. There were two recording studios, a mastering lab, and a video room under construction. There were about thirty-five employees. That was a lot to manage.

One night, after a few weeks of being the "night guy," there was an occasion when one of the staff recording engineers became ill and couldn't make it to a session. Joe and John asked me if I could fill in as the engineer. Now, I had recorded a couple of albums with D&K at Ardent by then and knew my way around, but I had never engineered a session for someone else. They seemed confident in me, though.

John said, "Go set up a radio on the studio floor, put a microphone on it, and experiment with the patch-bay for a couple of hours. You'll be fine."

That is how I began my recording engineer career at Ardent. Dana was on the same engineering track and both of us became staff engineers. That proved invaluable to me as we began to produce albums for other artists throughout the late seventies and into the eighties. John also promoted me to studio manager around that time. I booked all the sessions, negotiated the rates, collected the payments, and kept the financial books. It was a great experience for sure. I learned a lot and was pretty good at the job.

In many ways it seems I have always been somewhat torn between the creative, the technical, and the financial aspects of the music business. It's a tension that has existed at the center of most of my career. I always loved writing, recording, and performing, but I was also the guy who had to think about how we were going to buy a tank of gas in the next town. Some creative types seem to hate the money side. Not me. I've always been fascinated by how things work and how I might be able to make them work better. Being the studio manager at Ardent was definitely one more way of being bi-vocational in the early days of the band, but it was more than that. I can see now, unlike repairing apartment buildings or painting houses, the work at Ardent built skills in me that would come in very handy down the road in a different sort of way.

DeGarmo and Key was definitely a ministry. But it was also a business. It would have to be operated as such if we wanted it to survive and wanted to support our families with it. Ardent was helping me learn how to do just that.

TWENTY-ONE

RISE UP

Like I said, I met some pretty eccentric characters during my days as studio manager at Ardent. Take Allen Jones, for instance. Allen was a part of the Stax Records scene and wrote some big hits in the sixties. He became a notable record producer and managed several disco artists in the late seventies and early eighties. One of his acts was the platinum selling disco/funk band The Bar-Kays. They were at Ardent recording an album for several months and Allen and I became friends over that time.

Allen was convinced he came from a planet called "Motah." I thought maybe he was just referring to Detroit, aka "Motor City," with a thick accent. But he was convinced he was an alien of sorts. I kinda agreed with him, actually. He was definitely a cultural leader in the black music scene in Memphis. He had a very magnetic personality and a larger than life persona. He spoke with an animated, street-wise, husky voice.

At around 9:00 one morning, Allen came storming into my office, shouting. "Eddie," he hollered. "Eddie! All this time I thought you was different! Turns out you just the same. Same as every other white SOB 'round this damn place. You a racist, man. You a racist!"

I stood up and asked him, "What's wrong with you, Allen? What are you talking about? You're acting nuts—like you must've stayed out all night!"

Allen ranted on, "Come out here with me! I wanna show you sumthin.'"

We walked out the front door and around the side of the building to the parking lot. Ardent had just built an additional recording studio for the facility. It was a room attached to the back end of the building. As a result of the new space, though, we lost some parking spaces.

Parking at Ardent was always at a premium. The first people to arrive each day would park in proper spaces, but later arrivals tended to just pull in and park along the side of the building in a way that prevented the other cars from being able to back up. So, when we had to have the parking lot resurfaced after the construction, we decided to paint "No Parking" several times along the side of the building on the new asphalt in the area where the problem parking tended to happen.

As Allen and I stared at the parking lot, he screamed, "Jus' look at that. Look at that! That's what I mean! You're a racist, talking about us like that."

As I looked at the parking lot I couldn't believe my eyes. I saw the words "NO-PARKING" stenciled four or five times on the asphalt along the side of the building, just as we had requested. The problem was, however, that the parking lot painter misspelled it. By reversing the "i" and the "n" the words read "NO-PARKNIG"! Allen took that as a racial slur against black people.

I immediately looked in his eyes and promised him it was a mistake that didn't mean anything. Thank God the parking lot painter was still there. Also, thank God he was a black man—a very, very old black gentleman who just goofed up.

Needless to say, Allen settled down when he realized the truth and we both had a good belly laugh about it. "You want me to leave it this way?" I joked. He hit me and ran away. We fixed it immediately.

Joe Hardy, Dana, and I forged a strong working alliance when we made the *Straight On* album. It got some good attention from people in the industry due to its sound and production quality. Frankly, at that point few Christian albums had very good "production." Making good records required a conducive space with certain acoustical properties, good technical equipment for recording the sounds, and people who knew how to use it all. There was also value in knowing what music should and could sound like, and how to identify, or craft, the best possible songs. Between the three of us we had all of those skills, and we enjoyed working together. I thought it might be possible for us to expand our impact by inviting other like-minded artists to Ardent to record, with us as their production team.

A producer is in charge of just about everything that goes into the making of a record or an album. The number one task of a producer is to assist the artist in accomplishing his or her best possible work. A good producer helps a solo artist or band achieve peak performance and creativity. The producer also assists artists in finding the best songs to record. If the artist is a songwriter, the producer should act as a sounding board for the artist to to improve his or her craft and make the best possible decisions about the songs. The producer should also help artists find a unique sound they can own, and then help them stay true to that vision. The artist has to be the originator of the work, but the producer helps sculpt and craft it with him or her. It's an intricate, sensitive, and sometimes very challenging creative process.

At times the producer's job is also very practical. He or she will help find and hire the best musicians for the style and the best recording facilities and engineers the artist's budget will allow. The producer will also manage the budget, deliver the project in a timely fashion, and act as a go-between for the record label and the artist.

Joe, Dana, and I felt we could provide those services to other Christian artists. We liked the idea of bringing a creative and sonic lift for artists in our budding genre. Ardent was a world-class studio and we believed that with our combined skills and talents, we could raise the creative bar for Christian music. In fact, we believed we could help it compete sonically and artistically with the best mainstream music out there.

I went to Joe and Dana with my dream of starting a production company. They both thought it was a great idea. We came up with the name "Mint Productions." In our insider cool slang, if something was "mint" it was top notch and of the highest quality. John Fry was into the idea of new clients coming to work at Ardent, so we were ready to go.

My first call was to Myrrh Records. Myrrh, then based out of Waco, Texas, was arguably the hottest Christian music label at that point. It had a large and talented roster of artists. The head of A&R was a fellow named Mike Blanton. I introduced myself to Mike over the phone and invited him to Memphis to tour Ardent and to talk about production. Mike was familiar with DeGarmo and Key and was already a fan of our work. I explained to him we formed a production company and would like to see if we could help with any of Myrrh's artists. We hit it off over the phone, and he agreed to visit Memphis. That was a big moment for us all. Mike came the next week. We gave him a tour of Ardent and spent several hours discussing the various ways we might be able to work together.

Mike called me a few weeks later and said he would be coming to town in a few days with a young Myrrh artist named Amy Grant. Amy was scheduled to perform at Ellis Auditorium down by the river.

Mike invited Susan and me to come out, see the concert, and meet Amy.

I was aware of Amy, but not overly familiar with her music. Word Records was the parent company of Myrrh. Word was also the distributor of Lamb and Lion's records to the Christian bookstore world. In 1978 Word launched a marketing plan designed to simultaneously promote twelve "contemporary Christian" artists. It was called "Bringin' a New Song" and it included the release of a compilation LP of the same name and some corresponding print and in-store advertising. Amy Grant was one of the artists in that campaign, as was DeGarmo and Key, and Farrell and Farrell (more about them later). That was my first introduction to Amy and her music.

Amy had just released her second album, *My Father's Eyes*, which was becoming a big success on Christian radio and in sales. Her music was in a different wheelhouse and not really in the same stylistic world as ours. She was more inspired by singer songwriters and light pop artists, which was a bit of a foreign realm to me coming from rock 'n' roll. I spent the next few days listening to her first two albums and getting to know them. There was plenty to like in her sweet, gentle, sound.

Susan and I went to that show at Ellis Auditorium in 1979. Amy was still just a teenager. A lone guitar player by the name of Gary Chapman accompanied her on stage. They were very good as an act, playing off of each other constantly and adding a nice blend of humor, charm, and poignancy to her songs. Also, the auditorium was packed. It certainly was a different crowd than we would see at a typical DeGarmo and Key show. There were more adults, for one thing, and there were a lot more people in general. Mike brought us backstage after the concert and introduced us to Amy and Gary. Amy's manager, Dan Harrell, was also there.

I learned a lot that night.

Mike called me at Ardent a few weeks later and told me he resigned from his role at Myrrh Records and was forming a management company with Dan Harrell. He also let me know they would be managing Gary Chapman, and Gary was going to record an album. He asked me if Mint Productions would be interested in taking a meeting about the possibility of producing it. We met with Gary shortly after and we had a great connection. He was a really charismatic and rambunctious guy. He was also very talented. So Gary made his way to Memphis, and we got busy making his first album.

Mint Productions went into Ardent Studios with Gary Chapman and emerged two months later with his debut LP, *Sincerely Yours*. Gary is a wonderful songwriter, so it was easy to produce a great project for him. It was the beginning of a very different kind of career for DeGarmo and Key, too.

TWENTY-TWO

JESUS IS COMING

first met Dan Brock in 1979. I knew of him and his Nashville-based management and booking agency, called The Tame Agency, for a while before I met him. Dan was the manager of the Christian rock band Petra. Even though Petra formed the same year Dana and I formed our "Christian Band," they got established much more quickly than we did. Their first album came out in 1974, four full years before *This Time Thru*. By 1978 they were on their third album and touring quite a bit. We felt like we were still just getting started.

I invited Dan to come see us perform in 1978. We were playing a concert in Memphis at our home church and I thought it would be good for Dan to see us in action. He said he'd come and I was excited to see what he thought of us. I was pretty sure we needed some additional partners in the music business to help us get to the next level, especially in terms of touring. Unfortunately, he stood us up that night.

I was determined to meet with him, though. I talked Dana into driving to Nashville, unannounced, to just show up on his agency's doorstep. It was a brazen move, and could have backfired big-time, but I thought it was a risk worth taking. So that's what we did. We drove to Music Row in Nashville and waltzed right through the front door of The Tame Agency. We asked the receptionist, Darlene, if we could see Dan Brock.

"Do you have an appointment?" she asked politely.

I told the truth. "No we don't," I said. "We were just driving through town and thought we'd drop in."

Darlene, who later became Mrs. Dan Brock, got up from her chair, went into Dan's office, and closed the door. A couple of seconds later his door opened and Dan came out. "Hello guys," he said, inviting us in. "Glad you could drop by. Have a seat."

Dan was a tall drink of water. He towered over us at six foot six inches, but we had him on the weight. One of my legs probably weighed more than him. He wore long dirty-blonde hair down past his shoulders parted down the middle and had a goatee about four inches long. He kind of looked like Greg Allman.

We've laughed about that meeting many times over the years. Dan once told me, "I figured I had better meet with you just to keep you from breaking down my door."

He was right. I was one determined fella in those days. I guess it was hard to tell me "no." Maybe I just have a hard time hearing that word. Dana was always less forward and aggressive about our business dealings. He was fine to let me take the lead in those areas. When it came to ministry work, however, he definitely grabbed the reigns. I was cool with that, too.

When we met with Dan Brock in Nashville that day, I must have asked him a thousand questions about how things worked with Petra. It was a great learning experience for Dana and me. Petra was more developed than us, but they had their own challenges, too. Before we left that day Dan agreed to work with us as our booking agent for a "trial period" to see how it would go. We didn't talk about management issues, as Stephen Lawhead was still working with us in that capacity, but The Tame Agency would take us on as clients. We were ecstatic. Things were definitely about to hit a new gear for us. I could feel it.

As we were preparing for whatever would come next for the band, however, we continued to dial in the Mint Productions project. One day, when I was at Ardent, I received an out-of-the-blue phone call from Mylon Lefevre. Mylon was a member of the Atlanta Rhythm Section, and did a string of solo albums for Mercury. But I only knew of him from a set he did with his band "Holy Smoke" opening for the group Mountain in their heyday of *Mississippi Queen*. I actually wasn't even at that show, which took place at the Overton Park Shell in Memphis in 1972, but Dana was and he told me all about it.

"This guy, Mylon, was wild," he told me. "He had a huge white cross painted on the back of his leather jacket. He turned around to show it off and told the crowd he followed Jesus. I was completely in awe and impressed." Now, Mylon was definitely a mainstream artist. He wasn't really doing Jesus rock like we were, but the fact he would make such a bold statement for Christ at a big time rock show was very cool and real to us.

I was a new Christian at that point. I had never seen or heard anything like that before. I was inspired by the story and the fact someone else from the rock 'n' roll world accepted Christ. Maybe we weren't as alone as it sometimes felt in Memphis.

So, Mylon calling me was a big deal. He asked if I was Eddie DeGarmo and said he'd heard our song "Long Distance Runner" on the radio while driving in Atlanta. He said he was so struck by it he had to pull his car off the road to take it in.

"I've spent the last three weeks trying to track you down," he said. "I want to meet you!"

A short time later I flew to Atlanta to meet him. I'll never forget him picking me up at the airport. He showed up in a red Mercedes convertible. His long, jet-black hair was halfway down his back. He wore big Elvis-looking sunglasses. In fact, I'm pretty sure he thought that he was Elvis. He looked a bit more Native American than Elvis, though—like a handsome Indian brave.

I spent three great days with Mylon and his family at their home in Atlanta. We talked a lot about Jesus and music. Although later he would become a major Christian artist, in the late seventies he was still deep in the vestiges of his mainstream rock 'n' roll glory. He had recently kicked a long-term drug habit, and was deepening in his understanding of the Gospel, but he was definitely still a creature of rock. He would stay up all night, go to bed at 5:00 a.m., and wake up around 1:00 in the afternoon. He was like Elvis in more ways than one. I later learned Elvis recorded one of Mylon's songs. How many people get to say that?

Over the next few months Mylon made many trips to Memphis. Dana was single then, so Mylon stayed with him at his house. We started working together at Ardent, crafting and tracking songs. Mylon was still under contract with Mercury Records. He owed them a new album and invited Mint Productions to produce it. We were extremely honored to be working with him.

The first recording sessions were wild. I mean, like, "Monkeys In The Zoo" wild. Although standard practice at the time was to record the instruments in the band individually first and then to add the vocals at the end, Mylon was his best and most comfortable when he was surrounded by musicians in the studio. He wanted the recording process to feel and truly be like a live show. So we set his vocal mic in the center of the studio with some sound baffles around him. Then, we positioned the band all around him in a loose semi-circle. We flew in a couple of his musician buddies to be in the band with us.

One of the players was a percussionist from Jamaica named Jamal. He wore a sock on his head, sandals, and traditional Jamaican garb. One day, as we prayed to start the session, Mylon closed us out by giving thanks to "The Most High." Without missing a beat, Jamal jovially quipped, "I think I qualify as the 'most high' in the studio today!" He was so right! We set up his congas and assorted percussion instruments in a small drum isolation booth in the corner and often couldn't even make out his shape through the glass walls because the ganga smoke swirling around in his booth was so thick.

It was a fun way to record. The chemistry between the band members, though at times feeling almost totally out of control, was actually pretty amazing. The interaction was electric and zany at the same time. We wrote and recorded the songs as a group. Then we went back later and over-dubbed individual parts to get the sound perfect. The record we made was never released in its entirety. Mylon really wanted out of his mainstream contract with Mercury in order to work with people who understood the spiritual side of his new music. That's ironic in today's music world. These days most artists would die to be with a major mainstream label. A few years later, in 1982, some of the songs we made with him were included on his first completely Christian album, *Brand New Start*.

Even later, when D&K were flourishing in the eighties, I always made time to produce albums for others. Usually those projects, like the records I made for Farrell and Farrell, happened between our tours. I always felt that working with other artists helped me stay well rounded and fresh for our music. It's possible my next major transition came a little more naturally because of all that.

TWENTY-THREE

NOBODY LOVES ME LIKE YOU DO

Over the course of the next several months, Dan Brock and The Tame Agency were able to book D&K a two-week East Coast tour with shows from southern Florida all the way up to Boston. The only problem was we didn't have a band. It was time for us to find a new bass player and drummer.

Larry Raspberry was a local Memphis music boy who made good. In the 1960s his band The Gentrys scored a huge top ten hit with "Keep On Dancing." They appeared on all the national TV shows and became an inspiration to a lot of us kids trying to make it big. Larry was a local hero ever since.

By 1979 The Gentrys were old history, but Larry formed a popular local band with a major label deal called Larry Raspberry and The Highsteppers. They happened to be recording their first album at Ardent. Dana and I became good friends with Larry and his band. His drummer was an eighteen-year-old kid named Greg Morrow whose drumming was over the moon. He and I bonded by talking music in the studio lounge for hours on end. He was interested in the DeGarmo and Key story and liked our music.

One day, sitting by the coffee pot outside Ardent's central garden patio, staring at the largest crepe myrtle tree in Memphis, I asked Greg if he would be interested in playing drums with us on our two-week tour. I explained our plans were to tour for a couple of weeks in the spring and a couple of weeks in the fall, and we were looking to find a high quality drummer and bass player to work with us. Greg was elated to be asked, but said he couldn't do anything to interfere with The Highsteppers' plans. He would need to speak with Larry before committing to anything. I asked Greg if he knew of a bass player who might be available as well.

"If I am able to go," he said, "it only makes sense that Mike Brignardello, The Highsteppers' bass player, would be free to go as well. Do you want me to ask him?"

"Yes! Talk to him." I was elated. I didn't know Mike as well as I knew Greg, but I trusted Greg's judgment.

Greg called me the next day and said, "It looks like your tour is a perfect fit for Larry's schedule. I can go. Also, I spoke with Mike, our bass man, about it. You should meet him. He's interested, but doesn't know anything about Christian music and what you guys do. He wants to know more."

"That's great news!" I exclaimed. "It also makes perfect sense that Mike wants to know more and may be a little skittish about the Christian music world. At the end of the day, you guys are just going to play our music. That is all there is to it."

A day or two later I sat down with Mike Brignardello and explained to him what our concerts were like. I could tell he had some apprehension about Christian music, and religion in general, but by the end of our talk he agreed he was game to go along.

Dana and I were thrilled. Both Greg and Mike were great musicians. We were a bit apprehensive about whether these guys would be accepting of our faith. But we thought it was a good thing to be with them regardless. Perhaps we could introduce them to something good.

The tour came up in a couple of months and it went extremely well. Both Greg and Mike were awesome additions. Greg grew up in church so he walked alongside us in our Christian faith very quickly. Mike was a little slower to warm up, but he asked a million questions, and I truly believe he had a spiritual awakening on that tour. When we got home, he shared with his wife Kay everything he saw and experienced. Kay was firmly planted in the hipster and chic crowd in Memphis. She founded and owned a boutique called "Chelsea." Her shop was located in the geographic and cultural hub of the local scene at Overton Square, and it was the coolest and most influential boutique in all of Memphis.

At some point over the next few weeks, Kay had a lightning bolt experience with God and pronounced to the entire community Jesus changed her life.

That message had a ripple effect through our Ardent friends. Kay was very close to all members of the local music community in Memphis. She dressed most of them in their rock 'n' roll clothes. Kay and Mike began holding Bible studies and gatherings in the Chelsea boutique. People's lives were being changed. Sadly, a few years later, Kay Brignardello was hit and killed by a car while walking their dogs on a suburban Memphis street. What a sad day that was for all of us, especially Mike. It was devastating. She lives on in our memories to this day.

That first tour was the only tour Mike played bass with D&K. He went on to become one of the top go-to session players in Nashville. Greg, however, stayed with us for almost ten years. Because we played together for so long he will always be known as the Drummer of Record for D&K. Today Greg and Mike both still play with Amy Grant. I'll explain more about that later.

A few months after *Straight On* was released and we completed that first tour, Lamb and Lion named a new president. Dan Raines was his name, and neither Dana nor I knew much about him. Our contact at Lamb and Lion was Doug Corbin, who left to do other things. It wasn't too long before I got a call from Dan Raines.

Dan came to visit us at Ardent shortly after, and we spent an entire day together. He was interested in our story and our mission. He also wanted to figure out how to boost the sales of our albums. They weren't selling badly, mind you, but there was room for improvement.

Dan was intrigued by the production business we built with Mint Productions and how our relationship with Mike Blanton and Dan Harrell seemed to be good for all involved. He was also anxious to hear our side of the story on the lost opportunity with Mercury Records and how frustrating that was to us personally.

Toward the end of the day he asked if we had ever thought about having Blanton and Harrell "executive produce" our next album. Both of them had seen some real success in the music business. They also seemed to have a bead on what kinds of songs would work on Christian radio. It was an interesting idea that could work well, he thought.

The role of executive producer on an album is different than the role of producer. An executive producer is much more about casting a musical vision and establishing a high level overview related to finances, marketing, and more. The producer's job is very hands on and "in the room" with the artist at all times. The executive producer comes and goes and helps the artists reach their audiences. Dana and I talked it over and told Dan Raines that we thought it was a good idea to get more input into our process. We would be happy to approach Blanton and Harrell about helping. We called them, and they were ecstatic to come on board with us.

Another challenge for us when we began *This Ain't Hollywood* was the fact we didn't really have a band for recording. That was a major departure from our earlier records. Instead of us working the arrangements up as a band in a rehearsal room as we always did before, Dana and I worked them up alone and then brought them into the studio for the guys to learn. It was a different dynamic. Our band for *This Ain't Hollywood* was Joe Hardy on bass and John Hampton on drums. We even used their pictures on the back cover with us. Both of these guys were staff producers and engineers at Ardent. I was the studio manager and Dana was engineering rental sessions. We were an Ardent family.

Mike Blanton and Dan Harrell did a good job educating us about the parameters of Christian radio acceptance. That was a good learning experience for Dana and me. We were big fans of The Doobie Brothers and Steely Dan. I think some of the pop and jazz influence on *This Ain't Hollywood* rubbed off on us from those two groups.

We wrote the songs in the same fashion that worked for us in the past. Dana came up with the lyrics for "Stella, This Ain't Hollywood." I supplied the music and melody. "When He Comes Back" was a song I wrote the music and chorus for, and then Dana supplied the lyrics to the verses. I wrote "You Gave Me All" and "Love Is All You Need" by myself. Dana wrote "Never Be the Same" and "All Night" by himself. We wrote, "Light of the World" and "Over and Over" together.

Shortly into the tracking process Mike Blanton came to Memphis to ask me if we would be interested in having Amy Grant appear on the album. He said they wanted her image to have a bit more edge, and he and Dan Harrell thought that having her sing on our album might help that. My only concern was we'd never done any male/female duets before. It could be a challenge to find the right song and we were already in tracking mode.

"Mike, we don't have a song that fits a duet at all," I offered.

He looked back at me and said, "Go write one."

If it were only that simple, I thought to myself.

That night I went home and wrote "Nobody Loves Me Like You Do." I played it for Dana the next day.

"Wow," he said, sincerely. "That's different than anything you have ever written before!"

"Different good or different bad?" I asked.

"Uh…" he eeked out slowly. "Different good, I think."

I only had a verse and a chorus so I asked Dana if he would write the second verse. We went into the studio that night and recorded it. I had Dana sing both parts of the duet on the demo and mailed a copy to Mike Blanton overnight. Mike called me the next day astonished.

"That's the perfect song for Amy!" he marveled. "How did you do it so fast?"

I didn't have a good answer. "We got excited," I offered.

Amy came to Memphis with Mike Blanton and Dan Harrell a week later to record her vocals on the duet. It turned out fantastic, but it was definitely an artistic stretch for both D&K and Amy to come together on that song. It would have been a stretch for any song, actually. It worked, but we all would soon understand it would create a bit of a stir and backlash from her fans and ours.

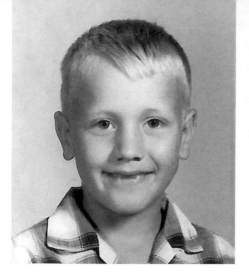

1963: Eddie DeGarmo, nine years old

1965: The Chants—Buddy Bass, Larry DeGarmo, Eddie DeGarmo, Tom Byars

1971: Globe—Eddie DeGarmo, Dunk Carter, Dana Key, Mary Perry, Doug Gill, Mark Heffington, Paul Roberts

1972: Prom Night, Eddie DeGarmo

1973: Christian Band
setting up in a parking lot

1973: John Hagerman,
Mitzi Hagerman,
Susan DeGarmo, Eddie
DeGarmo, Marguerite
DeGarmo, Clifton
DeGarmo

1974: Jim Dickinson
and Eddie

1978: Kenny Porter, Eddie,
Dana, Terry Moxley

1980: Eddie and Dana

1987: Susan DeGarmo

1987: Eddie and Susan

1984: Larry and Eddie DeGarmo

1985: Clifton and Marguerite DeGarmo

1987: Russ Taff, Breckon DeGarmo, Shannon DeGarmo, Eddie

1989: Bill Gaither, Ron Griffin, Bobby Roberts, Mark Farner, Eddie, Russ Taff, Dan Brock, Larry Howard

1990: Eddie

1990: Eddie and Dana

1987: Breckon, Susan, and Shannon
DeGarmo

1987: Susan and Eddie

1990: DeGarmo
family portrait

1990: D&K—Steve Taylor, Eddie, Tommy Cathey, Greg Morrow, Dana

1987: CCM *Magazine* cover

1991: Easter, DeGarmo family

1986: In Africa with Mission Aviation Fellowship

1992: Australia—
Doug Jones, Mark
Pogue, Tommy
Cathey, Dana, Eddie,
Kevin Rodell

1990: At the White
House—Gary Jines,
Eddie, Tommy Cathey,
Steve Taylor, Dana,
Paul Lameroux,
Dan Brock, Chuck
Reynolds

1993: Hard Rock
Cafe D&K retirement
party—Ken Pennell,
Jerry Park, Eddie,
K-Max, TobyMac,
Michael Tait, Amy
Grant, Jayne Farrell,
Gary Chapman, Bob
Farrell, Dana, Rob
Michaels

1992: *Heat It Up* release party at Hard Rock—Eddie, Jerry Park, manager of Hard Rock, Dana

1994: Audio Adrenaline video shoot

1995: Eddie and Rebecca St. James

1995: Eddie with Skillet—Trey McClurkin, Ken Steorts, John Cooper

1996: Big Tent Revival with John Tesh and Eddie

1993: ForeFront partners—Dan Brock, Eddie, Ron Griffin

1996: EMI adds ForeFront label

VOLUME 10 ISSUE #27　　JULY 8, 1996

The CCM Update

#1

EMI Adds ForeFront Label to Its Growing Roster

EMI CHRISTIAN MUSIC GROUP made its anticipated announcement last week that it had acquired ForeFront Communications Group for an undisclosed amount. The announcement was made by EMI Music President/CEO Jim Fifield, EMI Christian Music Group President/CEO Bill Hearn, ForeFront Communications Group President/CEO Dan Brock and ForeFront Executive Vice President Eddie DeGarmo.

ForeFront will operate as a separate label within the EMI CMG umbrella, with Brock reporting directly to Hearn. ForeFront, which has grown into one of the Christian music industry's most successful independent labels, plans to maintain its creative autonomy while taking advantage of EMI CMG's worldwide publishing, marketing and distribution network.

"We are very proud to partner with Dan

New label partners (l-r) Dan Brock, Bill Hearn and Eddie DeGarmo.

and Eddie, their talented staff and remarkable roster of cutting edge artists," Hearn said in a prepared statement. "We share a common vision for the future of Christian music. We aim to bring the positive messages of Christian music to an ever increasing audience both here in the United States and around the world. I am extremely excited to be working with Dan and Eddie, who have already accomplished so much for Christian music. Together I know we can build a bright and meaningful future not only for EMI Christian Music Group and our artists, but for our industry as well."

"I'm already seeing aspects of [EMI's] vision on where this thing can go," Brock told THE CCM UPDATE. "The uniqueness of this situation is that we've been able to see this company in and out, worldwide over the last year and a half with our distribution through the Chordant system. We've been able to get a real understanding of what they can do for us in the foreign territories, in being better *(continued on page 2)*

(continued on page 2)

Christian Hit Radio
"All Fall Down"
Sarah Masen • re:think

Inspirational
"Walkin' With My Lord"
Larnelle Harris • Benson

Adult Contemporary
"I'll Be Around"
Michael W. Smith • Reunion

Mainstream Album Sales
Jars of Clay
Jars of Clay • Essential/Silvertone

Christian Album Sales
The Message
4HIM • Benson

Southern Baptist Convention vs. Disney

"NIGHT OF JOY" need not despair. The Christian music festival scheduled for Sept. 6-7 and 13 in the Magic Kingdom at Walt Disney World, near Orlando, hasn't been

Disney theme parks and purchase Disney products. That is, if Disney keeps making entertainment in what the SBC views as an "anti-Christian and anti-family trend."

SCOTT KRIPPAYNE
hope has a way

1998: Steven Curtis Chapman, Twila Paris, Dallas Holm, Eddie

2003: Les Moir, Eddie, John Paculabo, Brenton Brown, Jeremy Ash, Matt Ewald, Dan K. Keen

2005: unknown, Eddie, John Foreman (Switchfoot)

2006 ASCAP Awards: Eddie, Jeremy Camp, Connie Bradley

2007: At the Grammys—Jon Hornyak, unknown, TobyMac, Dan Pitts, Eddie

2007: Dan Keen, Peter Furler (Newsboys), Eddie

2007: Susan and Eddie

2006: Louie Giglio, Chris Tomlin, Eddie, Shelley Giglio

2005: Eddie, Shelley Giglio, David Crowder

2007: D&K reunite at ASCAP Awards—Dan Keen, Tommy Cathey, Greg Morrow, Dana, Connie Bradley, Eddie

2010: Eddie and Stephen Lawhead

2003: *!Hero: The Rock Opera*

1992: Dana and Eddie

2005: Meaux Music acquisition by EMI— Richard Green, Susan DeGarmo, Bill Hearn, Eddie, Rick Horne, Kent Draughn

1985: Eddie and Dad (Clifton DeGarmo)

1990: Eddie and Dana at the White House

2017: Pat Boone and Eddie

2017: Mike Huckabee and Eddie

2017: Michael Carpino, Shannon Carpino, Edison Carpino, Paisley Carpino, Stella Pennell, Oscar Pennell, Breckon Pennell, Marcelo Pennell, Susan, Eddie, Louie Carpino (front in the middle)

TWENTY-FOUR

TEMPORARY THINGS

D an Brock booked a string of concert dates on the West Coast to support the release of *This Ain't Hollywood*. We needed to add a guitar player to support Dana for the music on that album. We were fortunate enough to land Jack Holder, another notable Memphis musician, for that tour. Jack played guitar with Black Oak Arkansas, one of the biggest bands ever to come out of our area. He was one of those guys who could play anything. If I needed help re-creating the numerous keyboard parts live, he could help with that too. He was an amazing addition. He was also a bit of a character.

Additionally, since Mike Brignardello decided to focus on session work instead of touring, we found ourselves in need of a new bass player. The rumor around town said Target, the epic mainstream rock band I mentioned earlier, was about to break up. Despite major label support, and opening tours for Black Sabbath, Boston, Robin Trower, Bob Segar, and a host of other well-known mainstream acts, Target just never caught on nationwide. Jimi

Jamison, their lead singer, did some background vocals on *This Ain't Hollywood*, for us. I checked with him and he confirmed the rumors. Interestingly, after Target, Jimi went on to become the lead singer for the group Survivor on some of their biggest hits.

I had been a big fan of Target's bass player, Tommy Cathey, from the time I was in high school. He was part of several very good and respected Memphis bands I saw play around town. I wondered if he might be interested in playing with us. After letting Dana know about my idea, I found Tommy's number and called him. To my surprise he was excited to meet with me.

When I met with Tommy that afternoon he shared with me he was looking for something deeper and more purposeful in his life. He'd experienced the highs (or lows, depending on your perspective) of rock 'n' roll madness and debauchery and found it lacking.

"I'm ready for something different," he said. "I'd love to give it a shot and play with you guys."

I was thrilled. On the other hand, I wondered what Tommy would think when he came to our improvised little practice shack behind our tiny little ramshackle house with the exterior paint all chipping away and a dude named Gator living across the street.

Tommy stayed with us for fourteen years. He became a big part of our personality and sound. He was the "coolest of cool" and became known as the gangster persona in our shows with his white fedora and black pinstriped zoot suit. Without Tommy Cathey and Greg Morrow, it's hard to imagine D&K in the eighties.

That West Coast leg of the *This Ain't Hollywood* tour took us through Oklahoma, Arizona, and California. The final date was at Knott's Berry Farm in Anaheim, California. For those unacquainted with Knott's Berry Farm, it's a theme park and a close cousin of Six Flags or Disneyland. Knott's was the first of the major theme parks to sponsor a Christian Music Day. They sold out every year. We performed there a few times over our career. This particular time was unforgettable for several reasons.

First, Pat Boone and his wife Shirley were planning to see us perform. It was the first time Pat saw us play, so it was a big deal for us. We were to play three, repeated, one-hour sets in a very nice theater in the park that had excellent sound and lighting. We were happy to have that much control over the environment. Concerts in amusement parks can often be disrupted by the noise of the rollercoasters, rides, screams, kids getting sick, and other chaos. At least we wouldn't have to deal with all that.

Pat, Shirley, and the whole Boone family were coming to the second show. That was good news. We should be able to work any bugs out during the first performance.

The stage had a large, curved, curtain across the front. We would be on stage, behind the curtain, while being introduced. Then the curtain would open as we started our first song. Very dramatic. We even made an intro tape. Humble as we were, we chose to play John Williams' "Theme from Superman" as our walk-on music. Nothing wrong with that. It fit who we thought we were at least. We had issues with that from time to time. We thought we were a bigger someone else.

As the fanfare began we were behind the curtain, dressed cool and holding our rock 'n' roll poses. As the intro ended the curtains opened and we jumped into our first song. It was epic fun. We played that first show to a packed house. It went well.

As the curtain began to open for the second set I could see Pat and the whole Boone family sitting in the second row. Remember, Pat was one of the owners of our label, Lamb and Lion. It was a bit unnerving to see the whole Boone clan sitting together watching us, but the set went extremely well. Afterward we were scheduled to see Pat and his family backstage in the green room. We had a wonderful time. We knew Pat, of course, but it was the first time we met Shirley and their four beautiful daughters.

Pat needed to visit the men's room, so he got up, excused himself, and went to find it. While he was gone we continued our conversation with Shirley and the girls. Shirley began by saying, "Pat's travel schedule is so hard on him. He is always away working on the weekends, so he almost never is able to attend our church with us."

Then Shirley looked straight at Jack Holder, our new guitar player, formerly of the loud and rowdy Black Oak Arkansas band, and asked him, "Jack, just how do you guys get fed when you are on the road for so long, away from church?"

Jack raised his head. "At a lot of truck stops, Mrs. Boone," he said honestly. "But occasionally Eddie will take us to MacDonald's or even a better restaurant."

You could see by the confused look on her face the wheels in Shirley Boone's head were grinding to a halt. Of course, that was not what her question meant. In Christian jargon she was asking about how we got fed spiritually. But Jack didn't know that language. He called it like he saw it. Fortunately, Pat showed back up in the nick of time to save us.

The second highlight of that day was I was able to meet Keith Green after our concert. I was a fan of Keith's and respected his stand for Jesus. He was wearing farmer's overalls when we met that day. He was very gracious.

The third thing I recall about that night at Knott's Berry Farm happened after we packed up and left. We made a bet with Petra, who was also playing at the park, that we could beat them on the way back to Tennessee to a big truck stop in Fort Smith, Arkansas on I-40. Whoever got there first had to buy the other group's dinner. Of course, it was 1,400 miles to Fort Smith, so we both had to stop several times along the way.

Our first stop was just a few miles outside the park at a Howard Johnson's restaurant. They were known as HoJo's back then, and they were open twenty-four hours a day. It was around one in the morning when we pulled into HoJo's parking lot in Anaheim. It was nicer than many others in the chain, probably because of its proximity to Knott's Berry Farm and Disneyland. There were a few cars in the parking lot. When we entered the front door I noticed an elderly couple sitting in a booth along the plate glass windows. I thought to myself it was peculiar to see people as old as them out so late at night.

In those days Howard Johnson's had a long counter with round swivel stools bolted to the floor, like a vintage ice cream shop. Farther around the corner of the bar was a dining room with booths lining the walls and larger round tables in the middle. I also noticed the dining room was carpeted, and the chairs around the round tables had wheels on the chair legs. Very swanky, and, it turned out, quite useful.

As our band was seated at one of the round tables I put my brief case next to me on the floor and pulled it up close to my chair. It was full of the cash from our merchandise sales and checks from concert promoters we collected on the entire tour. We didn't dare leave it in Happy Truck since it didn't have a safe.

Suddenly, from behind me, I heard two screams! The first was a man screaming at the top of his lungs, "Open the register! Open the f—-king register!"

I remember realizing he had a pronounced Brooklyn accent, which was completely out of place in southern California. Then I heard a woman screaming at the top of her lungs. She didn't say any words. Her wailing and screaming didn't stop. I looked over my shoulder, past the soda bar to the cash register, where the ordeal was happening. I saw the man had a very big handgun trained on the waitress, with the barrel actually touching her forehead.

Back in the days of mechanical cash registers, waitresses would often have the register key on a retractable clasp with a cord hanging on their belts or dress pockets. It wound up like a yo-yo into a silver reel. This waitress had one of those gadgets and the robber was freaking out at her, demanding she open the register. The only problem was, she couldn't. She was in a state of shock with that pistol barrel on her forehead. You can't blame her. Her only response was to scream uncontrollably with her eyes bulging out like Marty Feldman's in *Young Frankenstein*.

After a second or two she reflexively began to back up from the pistol and through the double swinging doors behind her that led into the kitchen. I really thought the guy was going to blow her away, and then start shooting all of us witnesses who were left. That's what happens in these situations, right? As this crazy drama was playing out, about thirty feet from us and just a little around the corner at the bar, I decided to take my chances. I reached down, placed my brief case on my lap, and began to drive that chair backward away from the table like a sports car wheelchair, through the restaurant and toward the bathroom in the rear.

In just a few feet I would be completely around the corner and out of the sight of the robber. Instead of looking forward, my eyes were trained over my shoulder to avoid crashing into all of the other tables and making noise. Because the floor was carpeted, my escape was quiet. I then turned my head and looked in front of me to see our whole band also driving their chairs, winding through the tables, backward, following me. It was like a surreal picture of the old video game "Centipede" playing out in Howard Johnson's in real-life color.

I finally got to the bathroom and only let the others in one by one after they convinced me through the door the robber hadn't taken them hostage and was on the other side of the door with his gun to their heads. You gotta make sure, right? I let the entire band into the men's room with me, and we waited for a few minutes until it was all clear outside.

Fortunately, the robber ran away as fast as he arrived and nobody got hurt. That was a miracle. The waitress got her wits back and the cook called the police. They asked us if we would stay until the police arrived to give an eyewitness account. Of course we would. But in the back of my mind I thought about Petra racing ahead of us to Fort Smith. It was a premonition of things to come, as we seemed to race them one way or another for our entire career. Needless to say, they won the race to Fort Smith and we had to buy dinner.

Remember the elderly couple sitting in the booth by the plate glass windows? They never moved throughout the entire ordeal. I don't think they missed a bite that night. They just kept on sipping their coffee, too. Only in California.

Much to our surprise and delight, *This Ain't Hollywood* was nominated for a Grammy Award. It was the first time a rock band was ever nominated in the Gospel category. The other four nominees included The Imperials, The Archers, Cynthia Clawson, and our good friend Amy Grant. It was such a big deal for us to be nominated, my parents, Dana's parents, Susan, and Dana's sister, all went to the awards in Hollywood. Pat Boone kissed my mother on the cheek that night. I thought she was going to faint and melt on the floor. We didn't win, which was a bummer, but it really was an honor to be nominated. It was also cool to make a little history.

Life was really busy in those days. I was managing Ardent Studios full time, while also occasionally producing other artists' records for Mint Productions and traveling to play significant one-off D&K shows and short tours. We dug ourselves out of needing government assistance and Susan was saving every spare nickel in hopes of making a down payment on a house someday. I was so busy she came to me one day to talk about her goals. "Eddie," she said. "I love staying home with our babies, but with you gone so much I think it's important for me to make a life decision for myself, too. I want to attend art college and really study art and graphic design."

Susan was always the creative one in her family. From a very young age she could draw, paint, sew, or make anything that came to her imagination. She was voted "Most Creative" in her high school. When it came time for college, however, her folks were unwilling to help her go. They were divorced and never once tried to help her attend college. She had long wanted to study art, though. We just got married and started having kids so fast she sort of missed her window.

When Susan made the decision to attend art college I was committed to help her any way that I could. I wanted her dream to become a reality. She enrolled full-time in the prestigious Memphis College of Art in the fall of 1979. She qualified for a few scholarships and grants and we were able to get loans to cover the rest of the costs. It was a great investment.

The amount of work she had to do to earn that degree was mind blowing. After our girls went to bed, Susan stayed up into the wee hours working on homework or studying for tests. It took almost five years, but she graduated Summa Cum Laude with a Bachelor's of Fine Arts in Advertising and Design. My parents, our girls, and I, were so proud to see her walk for her graduation. It was an especially incredible accomplishment since she was left home alone most of those years, raising two little girls, while I was gone so much. I'm very proud of her for sticking it out through the tough times.

I was also thrilled to see her graduate because it meant no more Life Drawing and anatomy practice sketches around the house. I was sick of seeing drawings of naked men and women lying around. "Geesh!" I'd sometimes complain. "We have little kids here!"

TWENTY-FIVE

SHE BELIEVES

We did a string of dates in the Midwest later that year. The final show was for a roaring crowd in Chicago with Resurrection (Rez) Band. It was a great way to end the weekend. That's what I thought, anyway. The weekend was not quite over.

The next morning I was driving Happy Truck and Dana was riding shotgun. It was around 5:30 am and the dawn was breaking on a new day. I recall a beautiful sunrise with the light bouncing off the bottom of the clouds, refracting shades of purple and orange. Dana and I were discussing how great the previous night's show had been. Traveling southbound on I-65, about thirty-five miles north of Nashville, all was well with the world when the "Demonic Hamster Squeaky Nightmare Noise" began.

We'd heard that noise before, but this time it got very loud, very quickly. Suddenly all sound was drowned out by a massive crashing noise. All I saw through the windshield was that beautiful sunrise sky as I was facing almost straight up. It was like the truck was doing a wheelie. Dana began to scream and bodies were flying everywhere out of the rear bunks! Looking left, toward the median of the interstate, I saw Happy Truck's entire rear axle and differential, with all four tires still on it, careening past us on fire. It was like a parade in hell.

The rear end of the truck was scraping on the pavement. It's remarkable how fast a truck can come to a complete stop from seventy miles per hour using that particular technique. It wasn't pretty. Two or three truckers immediately stopped to help. It seemed the rear end of our beloved Happy Truck was in flames too! Yikes! All of our equipment was in there. We rolled up the rear door, which was flapping like a window shade, and began heaving equipment out onto the highway while the truckers were battling the flames with fire extinguishers.

I learned a couple of things that day.

Number one: it's pretty hard to throw a Hammond B3 organ, but it can be done. Number two: we shouldn't have put out that damned fire. We had insurance on the truck, but because we put out the fire and managed to somewhat salvage the gear, the insurance company considered it to be a repair job instead of a fire loss. And of course, we had no coverage for repairs. Despite our ability to stomp out the fire, I am sad to report Happy Truck never recovered. She was put out of her misery.

Following the demise and disintegration of Happy Truck, we bought a Dodge Lark RV from my dad. It was an ugly Winnebago looking thing that had been my father's prized possession for years. How I arm-wrestled it away from him, I'm not completely sure. Seems like we rented it for a time and when we brought it back and he saw the condition, he didn't want it anymore. Imagine that. A rock band can screw up and break anything, including a ball bearing.

Riding in the Lark was only a trifle better than riding in Happy Truck. It had air conditioning—sort of. It had a rooftop unit powered by a generator engine that never worked right. It had heat, too—sort of. The heat came from the kind of butane furnace a travel trailer was meant to have. When we lit the furnace and drove down the road at night passing drivers could see flames shooting out of the side of the RV into the darkness. It kind of looked like we mounted a jet after-burner to the side of our camper. Truckers honked at us as they passed, and reported the fire to us over the CB radio. Over and over. Constantly.

One night, while touring in Canada, the temperature dropped to forty degrees below zero. I remember seeing Dana driving the Lark with a blanket over his head and draped over his shoulders. I was behind him looking at his hooded silhouette lit up by the dashboard lights. The rest of us were huddled together in a pile of bodies on the floor trying to stay warm. I actually had ice form in my mustache from breathing because it was so cold in the Lark. I could see the large side mirror to Dana's left, and in that mirror I saw the reflection of long flames shooting out of the butane heater, spewing down the side of the RV. It was as if the Grim Reaper was driving us down the highway to hell.

The Lark wasn't all bad, though. We could at least stretch out a bit. It had a bunk bed that lowered on a scissor-like mechanism from the ceiling across the rear of the RV. We called it "Acid Bunk" because when you tried to sleep in it, you felt like you were tripping on LSD. We used to flip for that bunk. If you lost, you had the opportunity to have a nightmare in "Acid Bunk." That was the Lark. That was life on the road.

This Ain't Hollywood was the last album we made for Pat Boone. Lamb and Lion had moved their distribution from Word to Benson Distribution before that album was released, and they were not happy about how things were going. Most of their frustration surrounded the first Debby Boone album Benson distributed. "You Light Up My

Life" sold millions of copies. Her meteoric rise to fame created its own set of problems. It would be difficult, if not impossible, for anyone to maintain that kind of breakout success. It also seemed Benson was failing the test in Lamb and Lion's eyes, so the two companies began to look for a way to end their business relationship.

Bob MacKenzie and Wayne Ericson were the savvy business executives saddled with the task of running The Benson Company. Benson was the oldest music publisher in the city of Nashville, and it was expanding rapidly into record label and distribution work. As the company negotiated a settlement for the exit of Lamb and Lion, MacKenzie decided he wanted to keep "that little rock band," DeGarmo and Key. "I kinda like them," he reportedly said. "I think they have a lot of potential."

MacKenzie was like a little dynamo. He was of modest size—just like Napoleon. His tank was full of unbridled energy and passion. He had a voice that blasted like a trumpet. Ericson was the quiet New Jersey power guy of few words.

That's how D&K ended up recording for The Benson Company. We stayed with them, in one way or another, for the rest of our career.

Because our relationship with Lamb and Lion ended, *This Ain't Hollywood* was also the only album we had the opportunity to make with Dan Raines. After his time with Lamb and Lion, Dan went on to form Creative Trust, one of the most successful and effective artist management companies in the industry. In the future, during my tenure with EMI Christian Music Publishing, which later became Capitol CMG Publishing, I was honored to serve Steven Curtis Chapman, Third Day, and several other artists and writers Dan managed at Creative Trust. We enjoyed working together for many years.

Going back to the early eighties, Mike Blanton, then with the newly formed Blanton/Harrell management, called me at Ardent one day. He asked if he and Dan (Harrell) could come to Memphis to meet with us about an idea. They came a few days later and told us they were going to record a live album with Amy Grant and wanted it to include a full band. She had never toured with a complete band before, and they thought DeGarmo and Key might be a good fit. "You're both pretty studio savvy," Mike said. "We think it might be a good blend. It seems like a good artistic stretch for Amy, and maybe for you guys too."

"What an interesting combination," I thought to myself as he spoke. It might be comparable to pairing Aerosmith and Ariana Grande today.

Dana and I thought about it for about five seconds, and enthusiastically said, "Yes!"

Mind you, we didn't completely understand what we were in for. Dana and I came from a purely rock 'n' roll background, so mashing us together with Amy Grant was as much a stretch for us musically as it was for her. When it was done, however, I think it was a challenge worth accepting. Mike sent us a song list and a box of her records. I made tape copies of the songs for Dana, Tommy Cathey, and Greg Morrow. I have to say, we dug into her material and learned it completely. We stayed pretty true to the recorded style, but probably rocked it up just a bit. That would be like us to do that. The first time Amy came to Memphis to rehearse with our band I think she was pretty impressed with the quality with which we played her music. Brown Bannister, her producer, was impressed as well. He was awesome to work with. He helped to dial in slight changes in the arrangements of the songs, but we had done our homework. It sounded very natural.

Memphis didn't have any music rehearsal spaces like Nashville did, so the only place I could find for us was an old soul studio in the ghetto. The carpet looked like it may have actually seen battle action during World War II, and the bathroom didn't work. Even if it had worked, no one wanted to go in there. It was gross. That scene was sort of natural to me. I grew up making music in those funky kinds of places. In retrospect, I shouldn't have chosen that place, though. It probably scared Amy half to death.

The full band ended up being a pretty interesting combo. Tommy Cathey fell ill and was forced to sit out the recording of the live albums. Fortunately, Mike Brignardello heeded my emergency request and stepped in on short notice. He did a fantastic job, as usual. Tommy was able to rejoin us for the majority of the tour that happened after the two live albums were released. Dave Durham, Bonnie Keen, Gary Pigg, and Jan Harris, four very strong background singers, were added to the mix, as was Amy's new acoustic guitarist, Billy Sprague. Although we all obviously came from wildly different musical backgrounds, that diversity was ultimately part of the magic. It was the beauty of it. When we blended all our pop, folk, and rock 'n' roll influences, it sounded fabulous.

After a few rehearsals, we traveled to Oklahoma to record two shows. The first was in Tulsa at the Mabee Center on the campus of Oral Roberts University. The second was in Norman, Oklahoma at the University of Oklahoma Sports Arena. Everything went off without a hitch. The band played well and the recording technology worked perfectly. But none of us were ready for the pushback we got from the audience.

There were plenty of raised eyebrows and lots of deep concern among Amy's most vocal fans. They wondered why in the world she had been paired with a rock band. Instead of seeing it as an evolution of her sound they seemed to take great offense. Our fans weren't much better. There was a chorus of disapproval of us for "selling out" for this "easy listening" artist. We got it from both sides!

The music itself, however, was quite good.

Brown marveled at how well the recording came out. It was so good, Myrrh made two different albums and released them back-to-back. The first of the two albums was nominated for a Grammy Award in the same year *This Ain't Hollywood* was nominated. We were involved with two of the five nominees that year. But it definitely took some time for certain elements of Amy's fan base to come around. I think some of D&K's fans are still mad at us.

After the release of the album, Mike and Dan asked us if we would consider doing a full tour as Amy's band. We were also invited to play a set of our D&K material as part of the show. It made a lot of sense, actually. Amy sang on our record, and we played on hers. Obviously it meant we would have to step away from our studio work and odd jobs, but we were definitely okay with that.

The tour with Amy was a learning experience for all. Someone dubbed it the "Bambi versus Godzilla" show. Sure, there was a certain amount of culture blending and boundary pushing, but no one expected the kind of outrageous and vocal criticism Amy received from some of her fans. It was downright mean-spirited at times. Fortunately, I learned to control my temper better or I would have been ready to fight some of them. The tour went very well and the majority of her fans were happy, but the amount and intensity of the criticism was weird and unsettling for Amy's camp as well as ours. Our fans saw it as a compromise. Her fans thought she had lost her mind.

The last show of the tour was at the Christian Music Seminar in the Rockies, a well-known annual gathering of artists, music industry executives, and fans held in Estes Park, Colorado. We had never been invited to perform there before, as we were perceived as being too extreme and on the fringe for the very conservative core of the Christian music scene. It seemed like the entire industry was there, though.

As we took the stage with Amy, I saw what looked like frowns of physical pain in the faces of the audience members. It was really bizarre. We rocked the first number. Ironically, it was a song called "Beautiful Music." At the end, though, there was absolutely no applause. You could hear a pin drop. All I could see was a large room full of people with their arms crossed, looking like they had severe indigestion and needed to pass gas.

Amy began to cry.

She passionately poured her heart out to the audience. She explained she wanted make a difference in the lives of young people. Since young people liked more energetic music, she chose to ask a rock band to help her reach them. It was a completely bizarre moment, to say the least, and definitely a defining one for me. I was moved by what Amy said, but I was confused by what happened. I was raised on The Beatles, the Rolling Stones, Jimi Hendrix, Sly and the Family Stone, Santana, Otis Redding, and Sam and Dave. I assumed most of the people in the audience were too. What planet did they come from? Besides, it's not like we were playing heavy metal. It was upbeat pop music. I was very perplexed.

During that tour Dan Brock began to court us heavily. He really wanted to be our manager. We liked Dan, and I really thought he was the right fit for us, but out of respect for Blanton and Harrell, who also expressed a desire to manage us, I didn't think it was prudent to make the decision public while we were on tour with Amy. It was a good spot to be in, but it was also important for us to play it out respectfully for all involved.

One of the most important business principles I have learned along this journey is it is important to always be honorable and respectful to everyone when at all possible. First, we're supposed to be that way as Christians, anyway. I'm not sure why so many Christian business people seem to miss that. On the other hand, one never knows when you may need to call in a favor from someone. You don't want that call to be to a person you have dishonored or disrespected.

I've heard it said, "The ones you pass on the way up are the very same ones you pass on the way down." That is so true.

The Amy Grant tour was also the official end of the *This Ain't Hollywood* tour and it was time to re-set. We officially hired Dan Brock to be our manager. Stephen Lawhead and D&K parted amicably and we remain close friends to this very day. Stephen's destiny was to become a best-selling author and not the manager of some crazy rock 'n' roll band from Memphis. We couldn't have done it without the help of Stephen and his wife Alice.

That tour took the better part of 1981 to complete. It was a big deal for us. It was the catalyst and launching pad that helped us end our bi-or-tri-vocational lives and the beginning of our career as full-time artists. It also wrapped up almost four years to the day after we signed with Lamb and Lion. Susan and I made a four-year "make or break it" commitment to God regarding the band, and it took every second of that time. We had finally arrived at a place where we could provide for our family.

Susan saved every penny from my royalties, producer payments, and residual checks. We finally saved enough money to place a down payment on a modest house. We had been off government assistance for a couple of years and it felt really good to be able to stand on our own feet again. Of course, I had to borrow a little money from Dana. He was still single, though, so he had extra.

TWENTY-SIX

I HAVE DECIDED

Dan Brock and D&K began to dialogue about what our next album should be. What would excite us creatively? What would our fans want? What was best for our new relationship with The Benson Company? There were a lot of factors to consider, and having just come off such a great opportunity with Amy we wanted to make the most of every moment.

Ultimately, we decided we wanted to showcase our live performance. We were always a great live band. I pride myself on that. It's where the rubber meets the road for musical artists. Can they pull it off live? We could, and we wanted to showcase that. Benson agreed.

Of course, we couldn't do just one record. That would be too easy. This had to be a "Double Live" album; eighty-nine minutes of rock 'n' roll glory. We recorded *No Turning Back /Live* in November of 1981 at concerts in Tulsa and Oklahoma City. That's actually how our song "Oklahoma Blues" was born. Ironically, those were the same cities where we recorded Amy's live albums.

I'm not sure if that was coincidence or planned magic, but it worked out that way.

Dan Brock moved from Nashville to Oklahoma City to work with a large, progressive church that hosted concerts and events in Edmond, Oklahoma. While he was working with them, along with his wife Darlene, he also began to promote concerts on his own in Oklahoma City while managing D&K. We all did whatever we could to eke out a living.

No Turning Back/Live was the first time Greg Morrow and Tommy Cathey recorded with us. Tony Pilcher was back as our second guitarist after many years away. He had played in "Christian Band" and was the one who brought Susan to our band practice at Lewis's studio in the downtown Memphis ghetto. It was great to have Tony back with us. The band was really a tight unit at that point. We were definitely firing on all cylinders.

Through recording the Amy Grant *In Concert* albums and a Gary Chapman live record called *Happenin'*, which Mint Productions produced, I became quite the live album recording expert. I knew all about cutting the tracks, splicing tape, and fixing mishaps that happen during recording. We hired Malcom Harper to engineer and his old remote recording bus called "Reelsound Recording" to record the shows at the auditoriums. Afterward, in the recording studio, I took the mantle and engineered and mixed *No Turning Back/Live* with Dana helping me. It was a great tutorial for other things to come.

There were a few new songs on that album we added to the best of the tracks from the first three LPs. In addition to "Oklahoma Blues," which was definitely a jam tune, Dana wrote a very powerful song about a young man's confession to God, called, "Preacher, I'll Need a Friend." Dana also wrote "Matter of Time" and "Love One Another," which bubbled a bit on Christian radio. That song got more airplay than we ever received before, even though it was scattered.

We closed the album with our version of the Gospel standard "I Have Decided (To Follow Jesus)," which became a standard closer for us for years to come. It was a simple acoustic version Dana and I led the audience in every night as people came forward to publically proclaim their decision to follow Christ. It was moving and effective even though it was written over a hundred years earlier by a Christian convert in India. I probably played that song a thousand times and witnessed a hundred thousand tears of repentance as I did. Folks of all ages walked forward and gave their lives to Jesus in our concerts. It was powerful beyond words.

I still believe that album captured our performance, and who we were, better than anything before. I often have fans tell me it is still one of their favorites.

D&K toured heavily to support *No Turning Back/Live*. With the band getting our full-time attention, and Dan Brock managing us, we had a shared vision to do nothing less than change the world. That might sound grandiose and egocentric, but our vision was simply to carry the Gospel of Christ into places it might not have gone before. We saw ourselves as sub-culture missionaries. We were all about carrying out the ministry we knew God called us to.

One leg of the *No Turning Back Tour* took us to Western Canada. Canada was always a hot spot for us. The audiences were large and crazy with enthusiasm. That tour was no exception.

"May I speak to Brenda?"

It was then I heard the most frightening words I have ever heard spoken in any language.

By that time D&K was very popular across Canada. We spent a lot of time up there. The Canadian audiences were energetic and awesome to play for, but we always seemed to tour there in early spring or late fall, when the snowy weather was either coming or going. This particular tour was in March. At that time of year Canada could be beautiful or rocked by blizzards. We were traveling overnight from Saskatoon, Saskatchewan to Winnipeg, Manitoba. Most of the larger cities in Canada are fairly spread out from one another. The two cities are around five hundred miles apart, which is about as far as you can travel overnight.

We rented a bus for the tour, which was a first for us. A semi-truck travelled with us carrying the sound, lighting, instruments, and stage equipment. For a band to upgrade from a van or motor home to a tour bus was a significant career milestone. Any band will tell you that. The bus was equipped with bunk beds, TVs, a galley kitchen, and it came with a professional driver instead of me spending each night behind the wheel. We were in hog heaven.

We drove away from Saskatoon at around midnight after playing to a sold-out house and were headed for Winnipeg, where we had another capacity crowd awaiting us the next night. On this particular tour we welcomed a new artist named Carman to open for us at some of the concerts. He was scheduled to appear in Winnipeg with us. We got on our comfy tour bus and headed out into the darkness. There was snow in the forecast—no big deal in Canada.

The next morning I woke up early, rolled out of my bunk and headed up to the galley to make coffee. I noticed the bus wasn't moving. I could hear the constant hum of the diesel power generator though, which was a normal feature of most mornings.

Oftentimes, we'd wake up in the parking lots of the auditoriums we were to play in that night. If the auditoriums had shower facilities, we might forego the hotels. Most days were filled with promotional obligations, record store appearances, or radio and TV interviews, and it was just too much trouble to get back and forth from the venue to a hotel. We would just clean up at the venue. There was always catering there as well.

This particular morning however, as I gazed out the bus windshield, all I could see was snow as far as the eye could see. Not just a little snow, mind you, but several feet of it in all directions. It wasn't falling, but was piled up high around the bus.

Through the windshield, far out in the distance, I saw a lone figure slogging through the snow toward the bus. It looked like Nanook of the North, toboggan on his head, and scarf blowing in the breeze. I then recognized him as our bus driver, Bobby. He came in through the bus door shivering, looked at me, and said, "Bad news. We're broken down. I've just come from a roadside café about a mile up the road. Good news; the equipment truck kept going and has made it to Winnipeg. I called the auditorium."

"How far are we away from Winnipeg?" I asked.

"Almost three hundred miles."

About that time Charles Gilliland, our road manager, came through the bunkroom door wiping the sleep from his face. We brought him up to speed. One by one Dana and the other band members stumbled in. Fortunately, our crew was also ahead of us with the truck, so there were only six of us left there, plus Bobby. It was about 8:00 a.m. We quickly decided to walk to the café (as this was in the age before cell phones) to use the pay phone to try to arrange for emergency transportation. The sky was a clear ice blue with full sun and a zero degree wind blowing.

Bobby told us there had been whiteout conditions throughout the night, with the wind chill dropping to forty below. "The wind was blowing like a hurricane," he said. "The bus engine shut itself down." Turns out the direct drive shaft running the cooling fan failed and the bus had, believe it or not, overheated in a minus-40-degree wind chill. It was a repair that required a specialized part and would take days to arrive.

So, we took off for the café. We must have been a sight walking single file through several feet of snow wearing our rock 'n' roll clothes. We made it to the café in what seemed like an hour, and Charles went immediately over to the pay phone and started making calls. The restaurant was a time capsule. It could have been any roadside café on Route 66 back in the fifties. The pay phone was at the end of a typical counter lined with bar stools. Checkered tablecloths covered about ten square tables already crowded with local regulars. This little diner was obviously the only place to buy a cup of coffee, eggs, and toast for a million miles. The smell of smoke and frying grease filled the air, but the food was good and hot.

A local mentioned that the closest town of any size was almost eighty miles away in either direction and that until the snow plows did their work they would be impossible to reach. He said the plows would be by anytime. This was a national Canadian highway we were on, by golly, and they kept it clear of snow as much as was humanly possible. In the meantime, Charles tried everything. He tried to rent a car; too far away. He tried to rent an airplane; no airport close by. He tried to rent a helicopter; couldn't find one. Our anxiety increased with every relentless tick of the second hand. Nine o'clock turned into 10:00. Then noon came and then it was 2:00. Things were getting desperate. For the first time in our career we were about to miss a gig and it was a sold-out show. We tried everything we could think of while our manager, Dan Brock, and his staff down in Oklahoma City did their best as well. Nothing was working.

Suddenly I felt the need to visit the men's room. Now as any guy will explain, there's a time you can stand up, and there's a time for a guy to take a seat. This particular time I needed to take a seat, so I went into the stall inside the restroom and closed the door. I was deep in thought, considering our predicament. We prayed all morning that God would show us the way. About that moment I looked at the funky green wall of the restroom stall and saw scrawled across it in black magic marker ...

"For a good time, call Brenda."

Below that seedy promise was written a local telephone number. As I thought about it, a strange thought crossed my mind. "Well, God," I said in a sort of prayer, "I've tried everything else. I'll call Brenda and see if she has any ideas." I finished my business, wrote down the number from the stall, and went back out to the pay phone. I noticed the guys in the band looking my way, but I didn't want to try to explain what I was doing at that moment. I dialed the number. The phone rang a few times and then was picked up. On the other end a low, gruff, decidedly male voice semi-growled, "Hello?"

"May I speak to Brenda?" I blurted out before losing my nerve.

And those frightening words that I'll never forget?

"This is she," the gruff voice replied with a mild chuckle.

Embarrassed, I immediately blurted out our story as fast as I could get the words from my mouth. "Sir, you don't know me," I began. "My name is Eddie DeGarmo and I'm down here at the 'so and so' café, stranded with our band. We're a Christian rock band from Memphis, Tennessee, and our tour bus broke down on the side of the road. We walked a cold mile through the snow to make it here to the café. We have a sold-out concert in Winnipeg tonight, and we are desperately trying to figure out how to get to the 'so and so' theater there. We've tried everything from renting a car to an airplane to helicopters. You name it and we've tried it. We can't find anything that will work. I confess I saw this name and a number written inside the men's bathroom stall at the café with a magic marker. We've tried everything else, so I figured I would call you and see if you have any ideas."

I could feel the pitch of my quivering voice rise with each sentence until it faded out with the wounded whimper of defeat.

"Well, I guess I can take you," he offered. "I'm not doing nuttin."

"Really?" I screamed. "I'll pay you whatever it takes." We settled on a price of a few hundred dollars and discussed some other details.

"I'll be there in twenty minutes," he said, and hung up.

A few minutes later a sprawling, full sized Oldsmobile pulled up to the café and a young man about as big as a lumberjack got out and came into the café. "Is Eddie here?" he bellowed.

A few of the locals, whom he obviously knew, called out greetings to him. I figured at that point the whole phone number on the wall thing was probably a prank. I didn't dare ask. There are some things in life you just don't want to know.

We gathered up our stuff, piled all six of our bodies into "Brenda's" Olds, and drove back to the bus to get our stage clothes. Fortunately, the roads were plowed by then, so once our rock gear was secured we made flight for Winnipeg. I call it "flight" because Brenda drove about one hundred miles an hour to get us to the theater. We left the café at 4:15 p.m., and pulled into the parking lot of the theater in Winnipeg right at 7:30. Show time. We made almost three hundred miles in three hours and fifteen minutes. Carman had already started.

Judging from the salty vocabulary Brenda used often and liberally, I didn't think he was necessarily God's angel. He cussed like a pirate. I liked him, though. He was a good talker and we chatted the whole way. He asked about us being Christians and playing in a rock band. We were able to share our stories with him while I kept one eye on the road, scared beyond belief. He politely asked if he could stay for the show. "Of course," I said, "And I'll get Charles to pay you."

"No hurry," he shrugged. "See you after."

He stayed for the whole concert, watching every move and listening to every word. Dana shared the Gospel at the end of the show, and we gave the invitation to accept Jesus. Brenda even sat through that. I went up to him after the concert and asked him what he thought of it all.

"Man, that was unbelievable," he said. "I'm glad I came."

I asked if Charles paid him. He said, "You know, you don't owe me anything. I don't want to be paid for this. It was my pleasure. I needed this tonight."

I learned that day God definitely moves in mysterious ways. Even when you think there is no way out, he can provide one from the most unlikely places. Just don't forget to read the writing on the wall.

We chose to headline the *No Turning Back* tour for almost two years. Dan Brock encouraged us to do that. He felt we needed to firmly establish ourselves as a headline act, especially coming off a high visibility tour like Amy's. He encouraged us to build our audience, even if it was just a few people at a time. That was good counsel. Over the course of our career we always enjoyed the unwavering support of our core audience. We always drew more people to our concerts than our record sales reflected. That investment in our fans allowed us to be able to book and control most of our tours for years.

No Turning Back/Live was our biggest success to that point in our career. That being said, we knew that in order to crest the next hill we needed more media exposure. That meant radio. It was the primary driver for an artist to accumulate an audience on a mass scale. But Christian radio had already levied a judgment on our music. They screamed that we sounded "too mainstream" and that Dana's voice was "too bluesy" for most stations. We believed we needed to win radio over in order to have the kind of impact and sustainability we desired. That would probably mean a musical compromise for us. But like Amy's tour, we suspected it was a compromise worth making.

TWENTY-SEVEN

LET THE WHOLE WORLD SING

A s the *No Turning Back/Live* tour came in for a landing we knew
it was time to get back to the drawing board creatively. The long
tour was effective at building our fan base, but we were still seen
as being too "out there" for Christian radio. The Christian music
industry was growing, and radio was a huge piece of that puzzle.
It was the best mass media the industry could offer. We definitely
saw significantly better sales for the live album, but it was still not
enough to sustain our vision. I felt we really needed to reach for the
next level musically and creatively. We needed to make some
changes. Some of them weren't so much a natural fit for us at first.

Dan Brock introduced me, or actually re-introduced me, to a
singer, songwriter, and producer named Bob Farrell. He was one
half of the very successful Christian pop group Farrell and Farrell.
His wife Jayne made up the other, much prettier, half of the group.
I say, "re-introduced" because I met Bob way back in 1973. He
played in Memphis with his band, Dove, at a large city-wide crusade
Susan and I worked at on our wedding night (yes, that's true). Dana

and I helped Dove move their equipment around between high school assemblies the week before the big crusade night. Talk about strange coincidences. I was just getting started with our "Christian Band" and Bob was very encouraging. Here we were, nearly a decade later, and Dan was managing both of us. It definitely felt like a divine appointment.

One afternoon, at a sound check in Albuquerque, New Mexico, I began playing a hooky little riff on my keyboard that had just flown into my brain. The band immediately fell into the groove. Brock came up to me after sound check and asked me what it was.

"Just something I came up with on the spur of the moment," I replied.

Dan told me not to forget it.

A month or so later, I invited Bob Farrell to write with Dana and me at my house in Memphis. That was different for us. We never really wrote with others, especially for D&K. But this was part of the stretching process. Bob was an excellent pop writer who really understood what worked at radio. We thought maybe he could help us find something true to our own Memphis-shaped musical DNA, but was also accessible to a wider audience.

I began to play that riff from Albuquerque, and we turned it into a song. I still remember Dana singing out the chorus. Right there, in the room, we had a feeling we tapped into something special. It was another defining moment for us as a band. "Let the Whole World Sing" was way outside our comfort zone, but it became a huge number one hit for us across all Christian radio formats in 1983. That song, and the album it appeared on, opened us up to a whole new, and much larger, audience.

It also opened us up to a wave of criticism from many fans of our brand of bluesy, Southern rock 'n' roll. Just like the pushback to our tour with Amy, many screamed we "sold out." As I look back on it, I think there is some truth to that.

To compromise one's work for commercial success is always an uncomfortable stretch for an artist. But, I firmly believe the moment artists decide to sell their art for money, they begin to make that compromise. When your livelihood depends on selling your art, you had better have art someone wants to buy. It might seem crass, but it's true. The challenge is to manage that compromise so you maintain your integrity.

Sometimes, you're better off sticking with what you're good at. Some artistic compromises don't work at all. All artists find themselves facing this dilemma.

"Let the Whole World Sing" began a long and fruitful creative relationship with Bob Farrell.

As we continued to write songs for our next record we were taking note of some changes happening in mainstream music. Groups like Men at Work and Human League were climbing the charts with hooky, synth-driven pop. At the same time, one of the big taboos in Christian music was the dang electric guitar—especially the bluesy rock guitar style Dana played so well. Between those two facts we saw an opportunity. We decided to attempt to craft a new sound that would overcome our barrier at Christian radio by leaning heavily on the keyboard sounds we were hearing on mainstream radio. Synths were a huge part of our sound from the very beginning, obviously, so this wasn't completely out of left field, but taking Dana's guitar out of the mix was definitely a departure. Many of our fans were not thrilled. Many others, however, started to hear us for the first time.

We began to record the album that eventually became *Mission of Mercy* long before we had the album title. We wanted to go into the studio and experiment with new sounds and the new direction. We decided to demo the entire album so Dan could take some songs to MacKenzie and the rest of the staff at Benson. Demos are basically rough sketches of songs designed to get the ball rolling, but without all the bells and whistles of final masters.

No Turning Back/Live officially fulfilled the last album of our first recording contract with Lamb and Lion. We were now out of contract and wanted these demos to demonstrate where we were headed musically so Benson would hopefully catch the vision and get on board. We rented Crosstown Studios in central Memphis for recording. Howard Craft and his son James built the studio and Greg Morrow was close friends with James for many years. Actually, a few years later they became partners and upgraded the studio. I recorded my first solo album, *Feels Good To Be Forgiven*, there. ForeFront also recorded the first dcTalk album and several other albums at Crosstown. It was the ForeFront hangout in the early years.

Crosstown felt familiar and comfortable to me in many ways. It was located in the shadow of the gargantuan Sears and Roebuck store downtown. The Sears building was the size of a couple of city blocks and was several stories tall. It was one of the star attractions of the mid-south in its day. I spent many Saturday afternoons there with my family shopping when I was a kid. In 1983, however, it was vacant; a home to the homeless. Its ghostly presence arched over that entire part of the city, hearkening gloomily to its long-dead glory days.

That neighborhood had also been the home of the Crosstown Movie Theater, and the Crosstown Pharmacy next door to it. My older brother and I often rode the city bus to the Crosstown Theater on Saturdays, back when movie houses were grand temples to the glory and glamour of Hollywood. We saw *Spartacus* and *Cleopatra* at the Crosstown. In high school our music teacher took the whole class to see *Fiddler on the Roof* there. I remember that day well because Larry Brown licked his "Dots" candy, making them extra sticky, and threw them at the movie screen. They stuck to the screen and gave Tevye's daughters zits.

The theater was also where I took Susan to see the movie version of *Jesus Christ Superstar* the very night I proposed to her. That was right before our gourmet meal at IHOP. At least I thought I was being romantic …

So I felt right at home at Crosstown Recorders when we set up. Greg, Tommy, and I laid the basic tracks down, and then I added track after track of synthesizer overdubs. I worked 24-7 for the first three days. Poor old James Craft hung right in there with me as I experimented with different sounds, effects, and arrangements. I was determined to find a new sound for our music. I knew what was at stake for us.

Those sessions produced "Ready or Not," "Special Kind of Love," "Let the Whole World Sing," "You Can't Run from Thunder," "When It's Over," and "All the Losers Win." As you might guess, I wrote several of the new songs. Dana contributed "Ready or Not" and "All the Losers Win," which still stand as some of the best songs he ever composed.

I had been up the better part of four days and was borderline delirious when Dan and Dana walked through the studio door on the morning of day four to hear what we came up with. James, Greg, and I stayed up all night mixing the demos and giving them their final touches. I believed our entire future and destiny just might depend on our work. James was convinced I had lost my mind. Maybe I had. Maybe Dana had too. But it was time to play the songs for our manager to see just how crazy we were. He was going to be flying the tapes to Nashville to play them for Mac and the Benson folks later that day.

I played the songs for Dan Brock from top to bottom. As the final song ended he looked at me, with all seriousness, and gave us his opinion.

"Eddie," he said, "This changes everything."

He took the tape and went to Nashville.

Dana and I were on pins and needles at my house by the time the phone rang later that afternoon. It was Dan and the meeting was over. "Guys," he said, "Bob MacKenzie was dancing around the room, laughing and shouting like a Pentecostal preacher. He loves it! In fact, Benson wants to release these demos as your record!"

We were elated and, maybe for the first time in a week, breathed a huge sigh of relief. We felt even though it involved a compromise of sorts, we made a significant turn in our career. We thanked God for the favor we found with Benson, but we weren't ready to release the demos as our record. We knew we could make it better.

Mission of Mercy was the first studio recording Dana and I produced without the help of a co-producer. We did ask Ron W. Griffin to help produce our background vocals, though. Ron was a trained Southern Baptist choir director and also a rock 'n' roll aficionado. He was a little bit of an odd blend of things in a good way. We played at Cumberland College when he was their student activities director. Dana and I also signed songwriter contracts at Paragon/ Benson Publishing when Ron was managing that business. We believed he could help us achieve a new sing-along quality to our vocals. We were fans of groups with iconic vocal sounds like Three Dog Night, Queen, The Beatles, and The Cars. We wanted to see if we could capture that sound on the record. Ron helped us immensely.

In addition to the new sound, we felt it was important to craft a fresh visual image as well. I started an exercise and running regime to get physically fit. Married life, eating junk food, and late nights in the studio all took a toll on my body. I made a commitment to get into shape.

During my years as an artist, and into my years as an industry executive, I've come to realize how important it is for an artist, or any public personality, to maintain his or her physical fitness. I preached to my artists many times, "If you are going to play on the field, under the lights, you should be in shape."

"When you show up for practice out of shape, don't expect to play much."

Dan, Dana, and I asked Susan to help us craft our new image. She had been designing our t-shirts and merchandise for years and was about to graduate from art college. She had a new level of expertise in her bag of tricks. She designed the set for the photo shoot and picked out the wardrobe we wore on the album cover. We were happy with the results. The photos fit the music. The critics hit us pretty hard on both the music and the image, though. Even the album art was too "pop" for a lot of our diehard fans at first.

We've been criticized for our stylistic shift on *Mission of Mercy*, and I accept that some of the criticism is justified. What I don't accept, however, is the notion we didn't make great music. The music on *Mission of Mercy* is solid. I believe that with all my heart.

I can't emphasize enough that once an artist makes a decision to sell his or her art, it's virtually impossible for that artist not to recognize the audience that is attracted to his or her work. When something works, whether that means a good audience response to a show, record sales, or spins on the radio, the artist will be impacted. Most of us want to be successful. That's human nature. We just have to be careful not to lose ourselves in the pursuit of that success.

Vincent Van Gogh only sold one painting while he was alive. You heard me right. That's amazing. He lived in poverty and took his own life at the age of thirty-seven. Now he is recognized as one of the most brilliant painters of all time. Was he a success? That's a tough question. While he was still on earth and breathing, he was certainly not a commercial success at all. What if he had hung in there? Would the market have come around to him in time? Who knows? Today, he still might have a hard time getting signed.

It's a conundrum that has haunted artists for ages. How should we properly handle the commercial exploitation of our work? Do I recognize what the audience has to say and how the marketplace reacts to my art with integrity—or not? And where does ministry fit into the whole thing?

Again, it all comes down to the difficult concept of artistic integrity. The clever and effective artists journey through these murky waters as they experience the natural tension between their creative instincts and the needs of their audience. That is the stream DeGarmo and Key decided to traverse. I hope we passed the audition.

Sure, some of our most devoted fans were upset about the changes we unveiled on *Mission of Mercy*, but most of them eventually came around. When they did, they definitely must have noticed a lot more fans singing along.

Bob MacKenzie had little time for esoteric questions about artistic integrity.

"Nobody liked it but the people!" he proclaimed. That proved absolutely true.

TWENTY-EIGHT

DON'T STOP THE MUSIC

On the eve of the release of *Mission of Mercy* and a few days before the release of the "Let the Whole World Sing" single to radio, D&K were invited to participate in "Gospel Music Week" in Nashville. It was a weeklong gathering of the whole Christian music industry under the auspices of the Gospel Music Association. The week eventually came to be known simply as GMA. Being from another world and culture, it was our first time at GMA.

The Benson Company encouraged us to attend. In fact, they were slated to host an evening showcase at the Tennessee Performing Arts Center (TPAC) in downtown Nashville and invited us to perform three songs in a premier time slot. That kind of opportunity had never come our way previously.

The showcase went well. Then the next day Bob MacKenzie hosted a reception for key radio people from all over the country. He held his private gathering on a balcony at Benson's offices with the singular purpose of introducing the new DeGarmo and Key, and our new music, to the entire Christian radio world in one fell swoop. He wanted to play them some of the new songs, but even more importantly, he wanted us to share our hearts and our mission with the radio folks. We experienced such an uphill climb over the years to gain acceptance from radio, but Bob and Dan Brock thought a private audience with programmers and station managers could make a real difference for us. They were right.

That evening the balcony was packed with radio programmers, DJs, and station managers from all over the country. We played a few songs from *Mission of Mercy* to a very warm response and then we addressed the radio folks, sharing our personal stories of faith. We described our mission to take the message of Christ around the world. We explained we understood radio played a crucial role in allowing us to fulfill that mission. Dana did most of the talking—he was better at that than me—but we both shared our hearts.

That night was another major milestone for DeGarmo and Key. From then on radio fully embraced us. "Let the Whole World Sing" was the first of a long string of our songs that raced up the radio charts. It was a new day.

Mission of Mercy sold like gangbusters. "Let the Whole World Sing" climbed up the charts and held the number one position on virtually every Christian radio chart for an amazingly long time. The album produced seven number one hits in various formats and outsold any of our other albums by a margin of four to one.

It finally seemed the Christian music world was making room for our little band from Memphis.

A short time earlier, while we were recording *Mission of Mercy* at Ardent, the mainstream music industry came knocking on our door again. This time it was through legendary manager and producer Bill Ham. ZZ Top was at Ardent recording their massive hit album *Eliminator* in Studio A while we were recording in Studio C. I got to know Ham fairly well during my tenure at Ardent. All of the groups he managed recorded there and at that point ZZ Top made all of their records there.

He would ask me from time to time how our record was coming. He also met Dan Brock when he came to town several times while we were recording. Dan played Ham some of the rough mixes from our project and he loved what he heard. He thought "Special Kind Of Love" and "You Can't Run from Thunder" had a lot of mainstream radio potential. He thought they could be hits. He and Brock began to have conversations about co-managing D&K with Ham helping us secure a mainstream record partner for promotion and distribution. He even discussed wanting to see us on tour with ZZ Top.

Brock made a trip or two to Texas to Ham's management office to discuss the relationship and to move it forward. Bill had never seen us perform, and he wanted to do that. We were scheduled to play a show in Memphis at a popular mainstream rock club named Poet's Music Hall. That seemed the perfect place for him to come see us play.

We played that night to a packed house and, true to form, we didn't hold back any of who we were spiritually. We shared how Christ changed our lives. We also rocked the house.

I saw Bill Ham sitting with Dan Brock intently watching the whole show. I could also see how visibly uncomfortable Bill Ham was acting. He was squirming in his seat.

The next day the two of them met at the studio. Ham was careful to be respectful when he spoke. "I don't know how this can work with these guys talking about Jesus so much," he said. "They would have to tone that down to fit with the mainstream world."

He was right. It wouldn't work and we weren't going to tone it down. That was the end of that.

TWENTY-NINE

HOLY HUSTLE

L ife definitely got a lot busier with the release and touring of *Mission of Mercy*. You don't ever want to stop when you're on a roll. We completed a very successful, but demanding, ninety-city tour with the band Servant. No sooner had we wrapped the tour then I was asked to help produce Farrell and Farrell's next studio album, *Choices*. Plus, once the record was done they wanted us to go on tour with them, too.

We recorded the entire record at Ardent in Memphis. One of the songs Bob and I wrote together was the quirky, new wave, pop single "Get Right or Get Left." I saw the slogan painted in graffiti on the side of a railroad boxcar and thought it would make a great song. We wrote the lyrics at my house. It was a fun song with an underlying serious message fans really seemed to love.

Sometimes Bob and I went to one of the piano rehearsal spaces at Memphis State University to write together. That's where we wrote "People In A Box," another quirky synth pop song that came out on their *Jump To Conclusions* album a couple of years later. I knew those rehearsal spaces well. I studied music there for about fifteen minutes years earlier.

My professor met with me one day and suggested, "Don't quit your daytime job." He was certain I would never make it in music. He was right, actually. I began to study classical music way too late in life. I could play rock 'n' roll and the blues, though. That was different, probably because I started so young and loved it.

Bob and Jayne stayed with us during the recording of *Choices*. Jayne traveled back and forth between Oklahoma City and Memphis every few days while Bob stayed for the duration. He and I became good friends during the recording of that album and we remain close to this day.

Star Song, their record label, wanted us to mix the *Choices* album at their Dawntreader Studios outside Houston so they could be close by to check mixes and hear the progress. That worked out pretty well, but it kept me away from home more. We spent eight straight days mixing there and just a couple of days after we finished we left for a three week long Farrell and Farrell/DeGarmo and Key tour of Europe. The Farrells toured Europe previously and had an audience there, but that was D&K's first time across the pond. Dan Brock and Associates also managed Farrell and Farrell, so it made the business of the tour easy to put together.

Touring Europe was definitely a different experience for us. Our music was better known there than we expected. We enjoyed fairly packed auditoriums wherever we played, although the rooms were smaller than the venues in North America.

At that point, communication from Europe to the U.S. was clumsy, at best. When I called home, Susan and I had to say "over" at the end of each sentence like soldiers did in WWII movies when they were talking on walkie-talkies. Susan couldn't join us on the tour because it was her last semester of college. Dana had just remarried to a wonderful girl named Anita and they were able to be together on the tour. Dana and Anita made a great pair.

When I got home from that tour I was beyond happy to see everyone. I was away for almost a month in Europe, and worked on Bob and Jayne's record just before, so it seemed like I had been gone forever. I walked in the front door, grabbed the girls, and jumped on the sofa tickling them. After a few minutes with hugging all around I sat back on the sofa, extended my feet, and rested them on our coffee table.

Susan stared at me. "Eddie," she said sternly. "Kindly get your feet off my coffee table."

Shannon, our youngest, protested, "Mommy, can't he do what he wants? He's company."

"Ouch!" I thought to myself. I realized right then and there I had been working too hard. I was going to have to change that.

THIRTY

SIX, SIX, SIX

Our reset with *Mission of Mercy* was more successful than we could have imagined, so when we began to dream up our next album we wanted to ride the momentum. We wanted to bring the guitar back a bit, though. Both Dana and I missed it.

I wrote, "It's a Shame" and "Perfect Reflection" and Dana wrote "Rejoice" and "Every Day a Celebration." As usual, we both contributed to each other's songs in one way or another—iron sharpening iron.

The biggest story from *Communication* was about an apocalyptic song called "Six, Six, Six." Dana wrote the slightly dark tale about how the end-times prophecy concerning the antichrist might have looked in 1984. It sounded very cool to us, but we were really concerned about how the newer additions to our audience would receive it. We were so worried, in fact, we tried to "soften" it a bit by having some little kids, including my own daughters, read verses from the Book of Revelation to start the song. I'm not sure how we thought that would help. Sweet little kids reading about the

211

antichrist just made the whole song creepier. Stephen King writes children into his stories sometimes to make them feel more creepy. What were we thinking?

The real explosion of the song, however, was centered on the music video we made for it. Music videos were a relatively new medium at the time. MTV had become extremely popular and was a highly effective way to get a song out to the younger audiences. Even some of the major networks were hosting music video shows. It was an exciting and creative new thing for sure. I give Dan Brock the credit for pushing us to create music videos early on.

We felt "Six, Six, Six" was our best shot for a compelling "mainstream" video. Ardent launched a film and video production facility just a few years earlier. Marius Penczner, the head of Ardent Video, directed several concept videos, including some for ZZ Top and other notable rock bands. We met with Marius and asked him to develop a treatment for our little ditty about the antichrist. He came back with the idea to visualize the story in the song as a young man's dream, more or less. First it's a dream, anyway, but then he is being stalked by the antichrist.

Marius showed us a storyboard of the shots, including a scene with the antichrist totally engulfed in flames. The idea was he was showing the world he was invincible and couldn't be harmed or destroyed. We loved it. We asked him to make a video that would be consistent with MTV's style, format, and production quality. We wanted to make an impact on young people's lives and felt MTV was the right place to reach them. If we had a video that fit their format, maybe they would play it. D&K's presence in the "Six, Six, Six" video was really secondary to the story being told in graphic detail. That was fine with us.

The filming of that brief "burning man" scene was a big deal. It took place on a humid spring night in the parking lot at Ardent. The city was abuzz! Our families were there to watch, as was the whole band and several of our friends. There were even local newspapers and TV reporters on hand to capture the drama. The Memphis Fire Department had a truck parked on site, and there were three or four firemen with extinguishers and asbestos blankets ready to quench the flames.

The scene was not synchronized to the track, so there was no music playing, just a parking lot crammed full of media and civilians watching a stunt guy get suited up and torched. They painted his suit with a sticky, paste-like substance and wired him with a simple igniter to use when the time came. He was going to light himself like a matchstick and then walk menacingly across the parking lot, being as scary as possible. They called "Action!" and he did exactly that. After a few steps he fell to the ground and a bunch of guys put out the flames with fire extinguishers. It went off without a hitch. It was exciting to see how it worked. Pretty cool, I must say.

The local hype and attention was fun. I guess the notion of a Christian band filming a man being burned alive was pretty radical. But that was nothing, it turned out, compared to what was about to happen.

When the video was finished we knew we created something very special. Cindy Dupree, the head of marketing at The Benson Company, began to distribute it to the Christian television broadcasters and virtually all of them began to air it. She also sent it to the programmers at MTV for consideration. It actually made it on air a few times, much to our delight.

As a result, we were officially the first Christian music group to have a video played on that famous, or infamous, network. We were thrilled and waited to see what kind of impact it might have when, just as suddenly as it played the video, MTV dropped it like a hot potato. We called and asked why they pulled it. They said it was too violent.

Too violent?!

Right as we heard the news the *Wall Street Journal* ran a feature story on how ironic it was for MTV to ban a video from a Christian band while religious TV networks all over the country were heavily airing the same video. Soon after that article got out the story was picked up by CBS Evening News and *The Today Show.*

The headline was the same wherever the story was told. "Christian Band Deemed Too Violent for MTV." Several international news agencies even picked it up and re-ran the *WSJ* article all over the world.

It was the biggest publicity bonanza that D&K ever experienced. It seemed everyone wanted to talk about D&K and our video being banned from MTV. When the story hit the proverbial fan, Cindy Dupree and Dan Brock were finally able to get through to MTV to find out what happened. They explained they were under extreme pressure from Congress to reign in on-screen violence and to remove it from the airways, or face censorship and fines.

Our burning of the antichrist was suddenly "over the line" for them. They did say if we re-edited the scene to remove the burning man, they would place the video back into rotation. Marius went back into the editing room and replaced the burning man with a crystal ball showing a nuclear mushroom cloud explosion and other scenes of horror. That did the trick with MTV. Somehow the nuclear holocaust wasn't as violent as a dude in a burning suit. A little strange, don't you think? Scarecrow even had a burning scene in *The Wizard of Oz.*

It's ironic indeed that the biggest headline of our entire career was "Christian Band Banned From MTV."

"Six, Six, Six" made a huge difference in our name recognition. I only had to spell my name once for people, instead of several times. Kidding aside, the popularity of the video was a big moment in our timeline. I still get asked about it to this very day. The "Six, Six, Six" video was also the only time D&K ever won a Dove Award. It was before videos were an official Dove Award category, so we got a "Certificate of Merit," instead of an actual statue, but it was something. D&K went on to be nominated thirty or more times for Dove Awards, but never took one home. We did get inducted into their Hall of Fame eventually, but that came much later.

We made a second video from the *Communication* album, for the song "Alleluia, Christ Is Coming." It was a much more standard clip of us performing the song in front of a church choir dressed in robes. To spice it up we issued black sunglasses to all the choir members. It was a little tongue in cheek nod to our rock 'n' roll roots. It was pretty funny to see that big ole' choir all wearing dark glasses like Ray Charles or gangsta rappers.

When we were on the *Communication* tour, we were booked to appear in-store at a Christian bookstore in Minneapolis for an "autograph party." We did a slew of those types of appearances throughout our career. They improved greatly from that strange first one I told you about in Oakland. In-store appearances were a good promotional tool. They were designed to let us meet the fans and support the stores where our music was sold. The stores would be jam-packed with people. This particular autograph signing was in a large store inside a shopping mall. The store was thoroughly modern and even had several large television monitors around the store playing music videos.

The crowd was big that day, and I remember seeing an elderly couple way back in a line of mostly young folks wanting to meet us. When they finally got to the front of the line they were staring behind us at a large TV on which our video of "Alleluia, Christ Is Coming" was playing. The old woman leaned over to her husband, and I heard her say, "Henry, where do you think they got all those blind people from to sing in that choir?"

No joke! That is what she said. I laughed out loud.

Susan was the art designer for the *Communication* album cover. She came up with the concept to put us on the video monitor and then take a photo of the monitor. It was Dan Brock's gloved fingers coming into the frame from the right and adjusting the knobs. The cover concept fit the music well and projected our new music video image.

We toured *Communication* as a four-piece band. I used a sequencer to play additional keyboard tracks to beef up the sound the way we sometimes did with an extra guitarist. Greg wore headphones and played to a click track like a metronome, so he could keep us all in sync with the sequenced keyboard parts.

I was in the final stages of co-producing Farrell and Farrell's *Jump To Conclusions* album after the *Communication* tour. Bob and I co-wrote several of the songs on the album. Our standout was that crazy new wave song I mentioned writing at Memphis State called "People In A Box." I came up with the title and was saving it for a while. I shared it with Bob, and we wrote the song. As peculiar as the song is, it turned out to be a big hit for them. I think the satirical lyrics about TV personalities may even be more fitting today with the twenty-four-hour news channels and reality shows we have.

An instrument I began to experiment with during the making of that album was a relatively new "sampling computer" called the Fairlight. It was basically a piano keyboard interfaced with a computer. Ardent purchased one of those extremely expensive, state-of-the-art machines and I first got a taste of it with Carl Marsh, the guy I hired to do the music programming on *Jump To Conclusions*. It was a game changer in many ways.

Despite my love of the studio, though, Farrell and Farrell's *Jump To Conclusions* album would be my last non-D&K album I ever produced while the band was together. We were so busy with the band

I needed more time to focus on my family. I didn't want my little girls to refer to me as "company" ever again.

THIRTY-ONE

DESTINED TO WIN

ommunication became our best-selling record to date. It seemed all the hoopla surrounding MTV banning our video really worked out positively for us. In that story, the controversy worked to our advantage. We seemed to be hitting on all cylinders for the first time in our career.

In 1985, after wrapping the Farrell and Farrell record, it was time to craft the seventh DeGarmo and Key album. There was a certain rhythm to things by that point. Our audience continued to grow and we figured out the radio piece, which helped immensely. Now, we had the video, press, and publicity pieces working overtime together in sync, and we definitely knew how to tour to top it off. We knew what worked, but we never wanted to repeat ourselves from album to album. In many ways our group was a finely tuned machine. In some ways the next album really reflected that.

Commander Sozo and the Charge of the Light Brigade was unlike any other album we ever made. That was due, in large part, to my infatuation with the Fairlight. The album had very little actual drums or bass on it. It was mostly samples and sequencers. That being said, Greg Morrow still played a major role. He sat for endless hours with John Hampton and me, programming the Fairlight to play the drums exactly like he would have played them. The sounds, however, were completely controlled by the computer. Greg then tracked live cymbal parts over the Fairlight tracks to give it more of a live sound.

The same was true of Tommy's bass guitar. Most of it was programmed into the Fairlight, although Tommy did play on "Destined to Win," "Temporary Things," and "Charge of the Light Brigade." I played Moog synthesizer bass on "Casual Christian" and "Activate." All in all, I believe the decision to record the album this way gave it a much more mechanized "feel." You can really hear that, and even feel it, on the song "Competition." It started with a lyric Dana gave me one day. I put music to it, we worked together on the melody, and then built the thing from the ground up with the Fairlight. I believe we really captured the futuristic "Mad Max" type of attitude we were going for.

The corresponding video for "Competition" hits that same theme. With some pretty sophisticated visuals, Marius Penczner displayed the craziness of a death match fight. In the end the champion fighter is not willing to go through with it and make the kill. The video also earned a rotation slot on MTV. That was exciting.

Truth be known, Dana wasn't actually a big fan of the record's biggest song, "Destined to Win" before we recorded it. It often took a while for things to grow on Dana. He had to sit and ruminate sometimes. I found this true time and again throughout our career together. In fact, we had a huge argument about the album title. I wanted it to be called *Destined to Win*. So did Dan Brock. Dana wanted a more eclectic title. We hammered on it for hours and eventually settled on the crazy long and confusing, *Commander Sozo and the Charge of the Light Brigade.* "Sozo" is a Greek word that means "to save, deliver, or heal." "The Charge of the Light Brigade" was a nod to the iconic English poem with a play on the word "Light." God's children are indeed children of the "Light."

All I knew was the title was way too long and weird to market properly and was difficult to explain to anybody. That is what we ended up with, though. Even though the album sold well, I still believe it would have done even better had it been *Destined to Win.* That was a good "remember-able" title. Dana and I would often debate things like that for days on end. Sometimes he would give in. Sometimes I would. We always seemed to work it out, but we fought like brothers, or dogs and alley cats, to get it done. More often than not, the tension brought out the best in us. We had been fighting like that since the first grade you know, so we had experience.

We followed a singer named Jessy Dixon a couple of times at music festivals and knew first-hand how electric a performer he could be. Following soul gospel performers is not the smartest thing to do. They don't warm up an audience, they wear them out. Jessy was a really impressive performer.

Dan Brock and the folks at Benson recommended we give Jessy a shot at singing the song with Dana, and we were game to try. "Destined to Win" turned out really well. It was amazing, actually. It became a legacy song for us—one of the biggest of our career. It was big for Jessy, too. He and Dana sang it until the day they departed the earth. It feels good to have been part of something like that.

We spent a few months building the sets and assembling all the sound and lighting components. The big *Sozo* tour was coming just over the horizon. With the support of The Benson Company we embarked on a ninety-city tour. It takes around 140 to 150 days to play ninety concerts if you perform five nights a week. That's about the physical limitations for rock 'n' roll. If you don't have a couple days off each week your voice begins to wear out or you get sick. You can burn out if you are not careful to rest up a little.

Dan and Darlene Brock did an amazing job coordinating all the details with Benson. They became our national tour promoters and managed all the local people involved in the shows, including on-site promoters, radio, retail, press and publicity, and church relationships. It was a huge undertaking for all of us as we were centralizing so much of the promotion. Jessy Dixon was booked to open the entire tour, and he traveled along with us on our tour bus. Dana and I decided we wanted to perform the show as a four-piece band again. We rehearsed incessantly for the tour and were at the top of our game. Off we went.

The most remarkable concert we played during the *Sozo* tour definitely wasn't memorable for its grandeur. It was very humbling. We were booked to perform in the small town of Cottonwood, Arizona. We pulled up to an old theater in downtown Cottonwood at the normal 8:00 a.m. Our tour bus and our tractor-trailer took up almost the whole city block on the street in front of the theater. Cottonwood only had around ten thousand residents. We were part of many well-attended and very special concerts in small towns across America for years. The size of the town didn't concern me. Sometimes concerts in smaller towns can be even better than the big city concerts because there is not nearly as much competition—unless it's a Friday night during high school football season, that is. Friday night lights can kill a rock band.

As the crew was getting everything set up, I met with the concert promoter and asked him how ticket sales were going. It was a standard question. He told me the concert was general admission, so there were no advance ticket sales, but interest was high. The only competition was the local high school football game. He was bullish. *Yeah*, I thought.

The crew took the rest of the day getting the massive sound and lighting systems set up just right in that antiquated, well-worn theater. They had to sit a lot of the larger pieces of our equipment across the front of the base of the stage on the floor where the audience would sit because the stage was too small.

As I mentioned before, it was normal for lines and crowds to begin to form outside the front doors several hours before show time at general admission shows. The folks who showed up first got the best seats. Often times I would go out to the back of the auditorium and circle around to sneak a peek at the fans in line. That night was definitely different. When I came around the side of the building there were only three people in line.

Uh oh!

You heard me right. There were only three people in line. I went back around to the rear of the auditorium and explained what I saw to Dana and the band. Dana and I immediately went to the promoter to discuss what was going on. He acknowledged the problem, but said he had tried his best to turn out a crowd. It must be the Friday night high school football. *Yeah*, I thought.

Feeling pretty bummed out, I prayed to God that I would have a good attitude. Then I went to give a pep talk to the band.

"Guys," I started. "I know this is a real disappointment, but we have to remember these people bought a ticket just the same as if the theater was jam-packed. We owe it to them to give it our best and to put on a real show. Who knows? I'm trusting God has the people here he wants here tonight!"

Christians say those kinds of things, but on the inside I was freaking out. I was hoping God wanted more people there so when we took the stage we would be pleasantly surprised. Well, God didn't let us down. When we ran on stage and started to play I counted seven people all in the front row. From a certain point of view, our audience more than doubled in size from the three folks I saw outside earlier.

We played our hearts out that night as if the place had fans hanging from the rafters. More importantly, when Dana shared the Gospel and we gave an invitation to accept Christ, one lone guy got up and came forward. It turned out he was the local town scoundrel and bad-boy. He got saved that night. Isn't that just how God works? So much for us acting like rock stars.

Another highlight of the tour was being invited to perform at "Family Values Day" in Washington, DC, in front of joint members of Congress. That was such an honor for us. The Staple Singers played that day too. I was able to meet Pops Staples and have a conversation with him. Wow! Barbara Billingsley, who played the mom from *Leave It to Beaver*, was also part of the day. So that was interesting; meeting Pops Staples and June Cleaver in the same day.

A lot of growth happened for us during the *Sozo* tour. Our touring became much more strategic and organized. Our concerts were more professional and impressive. We now owned and enjoyed our own new tour bus. Gone were the days of Happy Truck, the Lark, or the 1964 funky bus. We felt more like real humans for a change. We had arrived. Yep, we were a fine-tuned machine. Something was telling me, though, that maybe we needed to rough it all up a bit. Maybe we'd gotten a bit too smooth.

THIRTY-TWO

EVERY MOMENT

With the exception of 1981, when we spent the year on the road with Amy Grant, D&K released a new album every year since our first album came out in 1978. In 1986, as the *Commander Sozo* juggernaut came to a close, we immediately started thinking about some changes. Like I said before, we always wanted to keep our sound fresh—for both our fans' sakes and our own. *Sozo* tested the extremes of mechanized programming, sampling, and computerized music. So, when we got ready to head back into the studio we wanted the pendulum to swing back toward our rock 'n' roll roots. It's good to be reminded of who you are sometimes.

One of the real benefits of commercial and radio success is it allows you to take risks artists trying to break into the scene cannot take. We were grateful for the favor we found with the industry helping us reach our audience. It gave us a sense of freedom and the license to unleash musically a bit, I think. Our goal for the album that came to be known as *Streetlight* was to lose the programming and to really craft a pure rock 'n' roll project from the ground up.

One of the first decisions we made was to track the whole band playing as a unit. All four of us played on the studio floor at the same time. We wanted a truly live sound and that was the best way to get it. Plus, we had a really good band. We made a rule we would get "keeper" tracks of the drums, bass, rhythm guitar, and rhythm keys for every song. Then, we went back and overdubbed vocals and lead instruments. It was back to the old school for us, and we were excited.

We also decided to bring John Hampton back as our co-producer. He was a huge help to me, particularly as our engineer on the previous three albums. John engineered our basic tracks, and then I engineered most of the overdub process. Then Hampton mixed the records. We believed we could use a fresh production perspective, and Hampton was ideal to be involved beginning to end. He knew us inside and out.

We set Greg's drums up in the center of the large room at Ardent's Studio C. Tommy, Dana, and I set up around him. Our amps were cordoned off in isolation rooms to reduce noise bleeding onto the drum tracks. We gave ourselves six days to record the tracks for *Streetlight*, which basically came to two tracks per day. Once we got started, though, we caught fire. We recorded all eleven tracks in just two days. I've seen some impressive musicians in my day, but Greg and Tommy blew my mind. Not many players are able to lay down that many tracks—all of which sounded amazing—in such a short amount of time. I think you can hear the chemistry and the energy in the project.

One of the standout tracks on *Streetlight* was definitely the first single, "Every Moment." It was sort of a different sound for us. I wrote it after seeing Bruce Springsteen's *Born in the USA* tour. Musically there is no denying "Every Moment" was a bit of a tip of the hat from us to The Boss. We made it our own, though. Dana sang it so passionately. It was our first single released from *Streetlight*.

We had Marius Pencnzer make the video for "Every Moment" a tribute to missionary pilots who fly supplies into the most remote places on earth imaginable. The video was aired on almost every mainstream and Christian music video outlet and became a huge hit for us. To make it, we flew to Zaire (now known as Congo) in Central Africa, as part of a larger effort called The Air Care Project, which was the name for our next long form video release. We became familiar with a non-profit called Mission Aviation Fellowship (M.A.F.) through our friend Jon Roberson at Celebration Concerts in California. Jon's company promoted many D&K shows up and down the West Coast.

Dana and I took an immediate liking to Mission Aviation Fellowship and their purpose. Many of their staff were commercial pilots who took furlough from their jobs to help folks by flying for M.A.F. They used small planes to transport missionaries, doctors, medical supplies, patients, and more to all parts of the remote world. They often faced impossible conditions with grace and courage. They are a crucial lifeline for mission work around the globe, but receive very little publicity or recognition for their massive contributions. We hoped to help raise their visibility a bit.

Along with Marius and his video crew, we set off to the jungles of Zaire in May of 1986. The goal was to film the M.A.F. in action, and to get behind the scenes footage of them at work to use in the "Every Moment" video as well as The Air Care Project. It was an eye-opening experience in more ways than one.

Over the next three weeks we experienced the third world, its poverty, its challenges, and its miracles, firsthand. The M.A.F. missionaries were incredible people and impressive professionals. They flew us, in tiny planes, to villages so remote it looked like they were out of a Tarzan movie. We landed on airstrips carved out of steep jungle mountainsides. The local people were wonderful and oh, could they sing! They sang beautiful harmonies to us a capella. We visited several hospitals and saw the plight of the poor and sick firsthand. We experienced the awesome work of the missionaries and the local doctors and nurses firsthand as well. It was truly amazing and inspiring.

During the trip we were able to play an open-air concert on a town square in Kinshasa to several thousand folks. Our guys brought their guitars, and the locals were able to round up a little electric piano and a set of drums as well as a small sound system. I'll never forget the smile on the locals' faces while we played. I don't know if they knew exactly what to make of our appearance and garb, but they seemed to enjoy the music. Music really is the universal language. I sometimes wonder what kind of music God likes. That's some deep water.

Marius was able to use the Africa footage, as well as some performance footage of us, to create an excellent video for "Every Moment." It was an honor to be involved with Mission Aviation Fellowship. The video was received extremely well by mainstream and Christian video channels and got heavy airplay. It was great to be able to use our music and platform to provide a boost for those deserving servants.

Back home we were about to experience another look from the mainstream music world. Benson and Dan Brock made a deal to license *Streetlight* to Capitol Records. Capitol was known as one of the pillars of the mainstream record business. They were home to The Beatles and The Beach Boys when I was a kid, and Queen, Heart, Duran Duran, and many others in the eighties. This was a big deal. Capitol released *Streetlight* to the general marketplace and their radio team began to promote "Every Moment" to mainstream rock radio with some immediate success. D&K earned a lot of publicity from the "Six, Six Six" controversy. Capitol could ride that buzz, add their own marketing and promotions to it, and take "Every Moment" up the charts.

That was the plan, anyway.

It really felt like we were riding a wave, of sorts. The Capitol Records team achieved a lot of success early on with "Every Moment," especially within the AOR (Album Oriented Rock) format. The song even got to number one in a few large cities. Coincidentally, we were scheduled to play a concert in Anaheim, California, at a venue called Melodyland right as the song was climbing the mainstream charts. Capitol informed us their entire Hollywood-based promo team would be at the concert that evening. Dan Brock, Dana, and I had a serious conversation in our dressing room before the concert.

"Dana," I started. "I've been giving a lot of thought to the concert tonight because of Capitol being here. If you decide to preach and we give an invitation for people to accept Jesus, I feel it's likely to freak the Capitol execs out. They may not understand. I just want you to consider all of the possible ramifications of that."

I didn't try to sway him one way or the other. Our band was known for our faith and our evangelistic intentions. We were always up front about what we stood for and how Jesus changed us. I just wanted us all to think carefully about it that night. All of us worked so hard to get this kind of mainstream exposure, and I knew that show could be a "make it or break it" move. The repercussions could be significant. There were both ministry and career implications to consider.

Dana came to me a few minutes later and said, "Eddie, I've thought about it and if I don't preach, and we don't give an invitation tonight, I'm afraid I won't be able to live with myself—Capitol or not."

I totally understood what he was saying, but I also had my suspicions of what it could mean for our new relationship with Capitol and the mainstream crowd.

The show was sold out that night and we were in fine form. The crowd had a great time. I'm sure the Capitol folks must have been surprised to see a band like ours performing at that level. And yes, when the time came, Dana preached his heart out and we both gave an "altar call." Several people came forward to accept Christ. It was awesome.

The next day Capitol Records dropped us like a hot potato.

I understand the desire many Christian artists have to "cross over" into the mainstream world. I know it personally. Most artists just want as many people to be exposed to their work as possible. The Christian market could definitely feel stifling at times from a creative or even spiritual perspective. So yes, I can personally relate to Christian artists who want mainstream audiences. Sometimes, however, the mainstream just doesn't want them back.

Sometimes it works. A few Christian artists have achieved excellent mainstream success over the years. It's not an exact science. It usually comes down to some combination of the artist, the song, the skill level, the cultural moment, and a thousand other intangible elements. Ultimately, it's probably up to God.

That was another defining moment for D&K. It was the last time we attempted to cross over with a mainstream record company. It wouldn't have worked for us. We were on a different mission and wanted to be free and unbridled in our Gospel presentation and lyric content. The mainstream wanted us to soften that message. I get that. I really do. It was like oil and water.

These dilemmas have faced people of faith since the very beginning. When should I be vocal with my beliefs to the watching world? When is it better to be quiet? These are questions all of us have to answer. Sometimes the answers vary depending on the circumstances. We face this dilemma at school, in the workplace, and in our everyday lives. I believe it was right for D&K, in that moment at Melodyland, with Capitol Records present, to be outwardly vocal about our faith even though it was career suicide for our mainstream aspirations. We knew who we were and why we were there. I get it and am comfortable with our choice. That is not always the case for everyone, though.

We Christians oftentimes feel we are obliged to speak our minds and offer a "biblical perspective" to every audience, at any time, regardless of the circumstances and the social ramifications. We also have a tendency to speak out, whether we have been asked to voice an opinion or not. This is not how Jesus often handled those opportunities. Although he never failed to tell the truth when he knew it was the right time, sometimes he held back.

I think about the time Jesus was asked if it was right to pay taxes to Caesar. There was a lot going on behind that question we might miss. Some of the religious people didn't believe it was appropriate for them to pay taxes because it involved using Roman coins with Caesar's head stamped on them, which they believed to be an idolatrous "graven image." Others wanted Jesus to oppose Rome as a dissident and even a revolutionary. The question was a trap. The chief priests were hoping to either catch Jesus preaching against Rome by saying not to pay taxes, or against the religious people by saying they should pay taxes.

Jesus asked to see the coin and then rhetorically asked whose picture was on it. The crowd answered that it was Caesar's picture.

Then Jesus threw them for a loop. "Render unto Caesar the things that are Caesar's and unto God the things that are God's."

His opponents immediately recognized the brilliance of his answer and shut up.

As I think about that story I find it fantastic that Jesus didn't take the opportunity to soapbox about all the bad things the Roman Empire was doing. He had the chance. They teed up the ball for him. Why didn't he take a swing? He could have talked about how Rome enslaved people. He could rebuke them for being entertained by gladiator contests where people were forced to fight to the death. He could have preached against the way they killed their infants to control unwanted pregnancy or how they worshipped pagan gods and had wild orgies. You name it. Jesus could have talked for three hours about the ills of Caesar and the Romans. He could have talked until the cows came home about those dirty Roman low-down heathen bastards. Or, he could have preached against the religious hypocrites who were trying to entrap him. But he didn't. He chose to hold back at that moment. There is much for us to learn from his wisdom.

There's an old proverb that says, "Preach the Gospel at all times. Use words if necessary." There is a time to preach verbally, and we should never be timid to do that. But we should live our lives in a way that points to God's grace whether we are opening our mouths or not. That's powerful stuff! It's not always so clear, is it?

THIRTY-THREE

SOLDIER OF FORTUNE

Petra was the biggest band in our genre during that time. They were great guys, and we had known them since the seventies. Dan Brock received a call from Paul Jackson, Petra's manager, asking us if we were interested in joining them for a fifty-city tour. Dan and I went to Nashville to meet with Paul and Petra's founder, Bob Hartman, to talk about it. We gathered at Bob's house in Franklin, along with our respective booking agents, and hashed the whole thing out. It was a happy coincidence that our *Streetlight* album fit the concept for their *Back to the Street Tour* so perfectly. As Petra was better known than we were, it was appropriate for us to play first. We were definitely not treated like a typical "opening band," though. They invited us to perform a fifty-minute set with full use of the sound and lighting rigs. We were treated extremely well by Petra and their staff. The tour was mostly booked into large arenas, which were much bigger than we were used to. Our recent tours were mostly in civic centers, colleges, and bigger churches.

The Petra/D&K tour attracted some large audiences and was arguably the biggest Christian rock tour ever staged at that point in time. We played for almost a solid hour every night and packed every possible musical moment into that set. Our last song was a seventeen-minute medley of some of our biggest songs back to back. Dana even included a couple bars of Jimi Hendrix's version of the "Star Spangled Banner." The crowd went wild and we received an encore every night.

Petra also put on one of their finest shows ever. They were consummate professionals. I watched them every night as both a fan and a student, determined to glean what I could from them.

As great as the Petra/D&K tour was, however, we were eager to get back to our own concerts. It was rock 'n' roll, for sure, but it was also missional. It was important to our core beliefs and calling for us to close each night with a word from Dana and to offer an invitation for the audience to respond and make a commitment to Christ. It's who we were, and it was the foundation of why we did what we did. We were sub-culture missionaries and were totally comfortable in our skin. That is what God created us to be. We overcame many obstacles along the way and learned a lot. But by 1986 we were really feeling effective. We were anxious to get back into our own element. When we saw people accepting Jesus, either for the first time or as a renewed commitment, and streaming toward the front of the stage each night, it really made all of the challenges and collisions worthwhile.

We continued to tour *Streetlight* throughout the spring and summer of 1987 to enthusiastic audiences. The music of that album really worked in a live setting—probably because so much of it was recorded live in the studio. It really connected us with our roots in every way.

With the release of *Streetlight*, we fulfilled our recording contract with The Benson Company/Power Discs. We were free agents again. This was an interesting time for Benson. They were acquired in 1980 by The Zondervan Corporation, which was a very large book and

Bible publisher that had owned a smaller music operation. Zondervan bought Benson and merged it with Paragon Records, which was owned by Bob MacKenzie and Wayne Ericson. It was Zondervan's way to become a market leader in music. Problem was, it was more difficult than they imagined to merge the book and music cultures of their businesses. In 1986 they were on their third president in just six short years. Bob MacKenzie was first, then Wayne Ericson. As we fulfilled our contractual obligations a guy named Bill Traylor was appointed to lead the company.

Traylor came from a Southern Gospel background, and we didn't know him at all. Zondervan severely restricted the company from spending money on marketing or promotion, and we weren't very happy about that. Sandi Patti and Carman, two of the other big artists on their roster, left the label and signed with a competitor. Suddenly DeGarmo and Key found ourselves as their best-selling artist, and we were out of contract.

This next phenomenon is nothing short of a miracle in the music business. Dan Brock, Dana, and I met to strategize about a new contract. Other labels were courting us and Benson wanted to re-sign us. We had options. We were determined to make the most of this rare opportunity.

Dan started off. "With the unsettled situation at Benson," he began, "the only way I could recommend you guys staying is, if they would grant you ownership of all of your songs and recordings, all the way back to day one. Them owning your catalog gives them an edge the competitors can't match."

"Do you think that is remotely possible?" I asked. "That never happens." I then added, "Dan, if you can pull that off we will give you a third of it all." Dana readily agreed.

Shortly after that meeting, Bill Traylor drove from Nashville to see us play in Birmingham, Alabama. It was the last night of the tour and after the concert was over, we were headed back home to Memphis, about a three-hour drive, give or take.

Bill said, "Hey, guys, I've got a custom van. How about I drive you back to Memphis instead of you riding the tour bus. It will give us a chance to talk." We agreed.

I sat up front, next to Bill at the wheel. Dan sat in the back seat, right behind us, with his head stuck right between Bill and me all the way to Memphis. Dana went to sleep in the back seat.

Bill let us know he understood the situation clearly. He was real nice about it. In fact, he said, "Look, I know Benson is going through really tough times. I wouldn't blame you guys a bit if you went somewhere else. So, I'm asking. What would it take for you to stay with us?"

I looked at him across the middle and past Dan and said, "Just give us back all of our albums and songs, and we will stay."

He was completely silent for a moment, and then whispered, "I understand."

So that's how it happened. Dan came up with a great idea and I happened to be able to deliver it at the perfect time. It worked.

Dan and our attorney, Richard Green, worked very diligently over the next several months to hammer out an agreement. Benson Records returned ownership of all of our past catalog of recordings, and the publishing rights to our songs to us. Future records would be owned by us on day one, but licensed to Benson for a time, along with the back catalog, exclusively for the United States. Richard Green came up with the idea to get ownership of the back catalog immediately, but license it to Benson for a period of years in the future to get Benson comfortable with the idea. Then for every new album we turned in, we got another album returned back to us. We retained all international rights from day one. It was a unique business arrangement. We were going to need to formulate a plan. We needed a company to house our intellectual properties, meaning our newly acquired master recordings and song copyrights. A new door was opening indeed.

THIRTY-FOUR

ROCK SOLID

When it came time to record again we wanted to continue with the more aggressive rock 'n' roll sound we returned to on *Street-light*. We also wanted to continue the "live in the studio" recording approach. We felt it gave us more of a distinctive "band" sound and it infused the music with an undeniable and palpable energy.

Dana wrote a little ditty with an old school rockabilly/blues riff called "Out of the Danger Zone." When we arranged and recorded it, however, it came out as a frenzied, totally out of control, rock explosion Dana basically screamed from beginning to end. I loved the edgy sound on his voice. It was a perfect way to open the record.

I wrote "Rock Solid," which became our biggest rock anthem over the years. I wrote the song as a duet so when we performed live, Dana and I had a chance to play off of each other vocally. It gave our concert another element of surprise. I hadn't sung a lead vocal on a D&K song since "Livin' On The Edge of Dyin'" on our second album, *Straight On*, in 1979. I think the notion of it actually unnerved Dana a little bit. He felt like his persona was rolled up as the lead singer of our band and didn't seem too keen to share the platform. I certainly was never pressing to be the prominent singer in our band, but I did want to sing lead when I thought it would contribute to our sound and performance. That desire ultimately led us to record solo albums a bit later as a creative release.

I also wrote "Brother Against Brother," which was aimed at infighting within the Church and against Christians attacking one another. I was pretty used to that kind of criticism due to our musical style. All of us early Christian rock bands faced it constantly. My gosh, I even remember our little girl, Shannon, coming home from the fourth grade one day with a church bulletin some kid gave her. It had a picture of me on the front. The picture was one used on a *CCM Magazine* cover. It featured me holding my key-tar up to my mouth while mock biting the keyboard with my eyes all wide, like some kind of maniac. It was a joke. The picture was widely circulated, so we were used to seeing it pop up here and there. The problem this time was the caption above my picture, which said, "The True Satan!"

Shannon asked me, "Daddy are you really the devil?" Then, she laughed and ran away, wanting me to chase her. She was joking around with me. Even in the fourth grade she knew I wasn't Satan. I hope so, anyway.

It seemed a lot of the problem fundamentalists had with us was we didn't conform to their accepted vision of what "Christian people" looked or sounded like. They almost never argued with our lyrics in the songs, or the things Dana said when he preached, or the other things we said from stage. It was never about the important stuff, just the surface stuff.

This next story shows just how shallow it can be. Christian music festivals flourished around the world starting in the seventies. Some were quite large, with crowds numbering over seventy thousand. Many were more in the twenty to thirty thousand range—which is still a lot of people. There were dozens of these events. Most were pretty "middle of the road" musically, focusing mostly on the artists heard on Christian radio. Some, like the Cornerstone Festival the Rez Band folks put on in Illinois, were more fringe oriented. We got invited to both types since we were a rock band and we had hits on the radio.

We were at the Fishnet Festival in Front Royal, Virginia, one of the more conservative events, when a young man took issue with me to my face. We had just returned from Australia, where I picked up a pair of black and white striped pirate pants and a long black coat that kinda looked like a cape. The clothes were outlandish, and I was proud of them. They have been immortalized in our *Rock Solid* video. If you would like to enjoy them for yourself you can find it on YouTube. I even had black buccaneer boots and a tie dyed shirt. You can thank me later. I thought it was cool.

That particular day, immediately following our concert, I was walking off the stage when a college-aged, clean-cut, handsome young man met me at the bottom of the stairs. I'm not sure how he got back there, because it was a secure area, but he was there all the same. He walked up to me, looked me straight in the eye, and very passionately asked, "Mr. DeGarmo, how does it feel to be conforming to the world?"

I stepped back a little and replied, "Just what do you mean?"

"Take a look at the way you are dressed," he said. "Your long hair; your weird clothes; that's what I mean. You are conforming to the world!"

"Will you take a little walk with me?" I asked. "I want to show you something."

I escorted him back up the stairs to take a peek at the crowd from the stage. All you could see was an ocean of people stretching a thousand feet in every direction. I looked at the young man and said,

"Take a look at all the people. Do more of them look like me, or do more of them look like you?"

He stammered a little. "Well, more of them look like me I guess."

"Ok then," I said, "According to your definition, you are the one conforming to the world."

He just stared off into space and slowly walked away.

It's easy for us to be critical of others who don't exactly look like us or agree with us on everything. We have a tendency to focus on the differences, rather than look for things we have in common.

We came to be known as "D&K" to our fans over the years. We decided to embrace that and name the album simply *D&K*. An artist designed a D&K logo that reminded us all of a Monopoly railroad logo. That logo became iconic to us for the rest of our career.

By far the very best thing that happened with the release of *D&K* was the "two for one" cassette giveaway. The concept was simple. If a person bought a cassette tape, they received a second tape of the entire album, contained in the same package, absolutely free. The additional copy was designed to be given away as an evangelistic gift to a non-Christian friend. It was a marvelous campaign. There were thousands and thousands of free cassettes given away by folks who bought the two for one package.

We received thousands of letters of testimonies from people coming to Christ as a result of that campaign. I still receive Facebook posts about the give-away program with that album and how much of an impact it had. I'm forever grateful to The Benson Company for helping us develop that effort, and to Dan Brock and our D&K publicist, Rob Michaels, for facilitating the program and seeing it to fruition. It took us all coming together to cover the costs involved. That effort was truly about building God's Kingdom.

One night in upstate New York, at the end of the D&K Tour, while we were leading the audience in "I Have Decided to Follow

Jesus," I noticed a lady come to the front of the stage with five children in tow. As was our practice, I led the folks who came forward
to a counseling room backstage where I prayed the Sinner's Prayer
with them as a group. I then gave them some words of encourage-
ment. Then counselors from the local area could speak one on one
with those who wanted or needed a more private conversation. We
used that format for years. At the end, we gave them each a copy of
the Gospel of John and encouraged them to see the importance of
finding a local church to attend.

At the very end of the counseling session that night a local fellow
came to me with the lady and the five children. She introduced herself
and each of her kids to me. All six of them made commitments to
follow Jesus that evening. That was the culmination of the D&K
period. That is what it was all about.

And with that, it was time to re-set once again. This time would
be different, though. Dana and I had been making records together,
pretty much every year, for over a decade. On one hand, a break
would be nice. On the other, musicians make music. I've never been
good at taking breaks. There was some trouble in the ranks, too. We
had some stuff to figure out.

THIRTY-FIVE

FEELS GOOD TO BE FORGIVEN

Once we got ownership of our masters and publishing back, we needed a company to manage them. Thus, in 1987, ForeFront Records was born. Ron Griffin, who worked with us as Benson's music publishing guy and then as our vocal producer, had both business and creative experience and was a good fit for our team. Dan and Ron were college buddies. Ron became a close and trusted friend to us as well. So close, in fact, Dan, Dana, and I decided to bring him in to run our newly created label. He paid his way, though.

We sold him a 25 percent interest in the DeGarmo and Key catalog in exchange for running the label on a modest salary until the debt was paid off. It was kind of a sweat equity deal. Ron worked hard and he was a great addition. Also, he could have been easily mistaken by his looks for Eric Clapton during *The Journeyman* years. In fact, he was! He was a good fit for us on several levels.

The initial business of ForeFront was to make international distribution deals for the DeGarmo and Key recordings. Through those efforts we were able to begin to fund the company. ForeFront signed a couple of other solo artists early in 1989. Ron produced and recorded their records, and we were proud of them. Unfortunately, neither project sold as well as we hoped.

The first ForeFront releases to sell well, ironically, turned out to be—at least in part—the result of some major tension building between Dana and me. The trouble began with me wanting to sing lead vocals a little more often on our albums. On the early albums I sang a couple of songs here and there, and I just wanted to do that again. Dana became really territorial and extremely weird about it when I brought it up. It seemed he felt I was moving in on his turf. I couldn't understand why he felt that way.

We were in bands together since we were kids, and I always sang lead a little. I already wrote a lot of the songs and managed much of our business. I couldn't imagine how my singing might intimidate him. I guess he just didn't like it. Dana was a better singer than me, but I think I can hold my own on a rock song or an impassioned vocal ballad.

I thought it would improve our live show to be able to play off each other more vocally. At the end of the day, though, Dana just didn't like the idea of it. In concert, I was always the wild and crazy one and Dana played the straight man. He didn't want to alter that mix.

Over the course of a few major fights, needless sleepless nights, and way too much drama, Dana, Dan, and I decided it was best if I recorded a solo album to keep the peace between us. In retrospect, I'm glad it worked out that way.

When I decided to record a solo album I wanted to do something really different from D&K. It was natural for me to reach back into the Memphis soul music that had formed me. I was excited to record a project that tipped my hat to those legendary performers from Stax Records and Hi Records. That music also suited my vocal style perfectly.

I asked Ron to produce the album. Ron is a great song man, and I needed some real objectivity in that department. Dana and I grew up as each other's professional critics, and I wasn't going to have his input this time around. Ron was the perfect choice. He didn't hold back either. I needed someone who cared enough to run me through the creative ringer.

I have to admit, when I started the *Feels Good* project I was pretty sensitive about my singing voice. Dana didn't help me conquer that one too much, either. I produced great singers for years, I knew what great vocals sounded like, and wasn't so sure I could pull it off for a full album. I didn't have enough of the confidence one needs to be a lead singer. Griffin said something to me one day in the studio I will take to my grave as a divine truth.

"Eddie," he said. "Do you know why Bob Dylan is such a great singer?"

I just looked at him and shook my head, "No."

"It is because he obviously doesn't give a f—-k what anyone thinks," he said. "If he cared what they thought he would probably never sing again."

I thought about that for a long while and came to the conclusion he was absolutely right. Half of the world thinks Bob Dylan sings well, while the other half wishes he wouldn't try anymore. It is so subjective, isn't it? It's a matter of taste really. I personally love Dylan's style and voice. He's great.

That was the exact thing I needed to hear.

Shortly before I recorded "Feels Good to Be Forgiven," my father died in an automobile accident. I was close to my dad and losing him impacted me in a big way. I wrote the song "Pickin' Up the Pieces" as part of my healing process. In fact, many of the lyrics on the *Feels Good* album were about folks who needed God's help to lift the burdens they were carrying around in this life. In retrospect, I think I wrote a lot of those songs to myself as I dealt with the loss of my father. I still miss him.

Doing my own album allowed me to release a lot of emotion. I was able to pour myself into the writing and recording of that album. Susan was so wonderfully supportive. I can remember playing her the initial tracks in the studio and us embracing each other and weeping. That was a special time in our marriage. I depended on her so much, and she was always there standing by my side, unwavering. It's always been hard for me to show my feelings and emotions. Susan has helped me learn how to connect with that inner side. I truly don't know what I would do without her.

My solo album was also a great way to support ForeFront. We released *Feels Good to Be Forgiven* in 1988. It sold pretty well for a "spin off" album. It was also nominated for a Grammy award, and I was nominated in the male vocalist of the year category for a Dove award. Some things are just too good to be true.

Dana went on to release his solo album a year later. It was called *The Journey* and it sold about the same, or maybe a trifle better, than mine. I think those efforts gave us the space we both desperately needed. We had been together since the first grade, my gosh! A little space was healthy.

As God usually does, he worked all those things for the good for both of us. The solo projects scratched a creative itch we had been feeling for a long while. They also helped our fledgling record label, and put us in the right frame of mind to record the next D&K album, which went on to become our biggest selling album ever.

THIRTY-SIX

THE PLEDGE

By the time we were ready to record *The Pledge* we had come through some real changes.

After playing with us for a decade, Greg Morrow left our band for a full-time gig as Amy Grant's drummer. I took it hard, but I understood his reasons. Dana took it really hard. Greg was the best drummer any band could ever hope for. On a musical level we knew it would be impossible to fill his shoes, but there was more to it than that. Greg had, more or less, grown up with us. It was like losing our little brother. That said, a gig with Amy was a step into a brighter future. I knew that to be true and was okay with his decision, but it hurt. It also meant we were suddenly in the market for a drummer.

I saw a local band called Junction play a few times around Memphis and was impressed. They had recently disbanded so I went on a search for their drummer. I found him through a friend named Jon Hornyak at Sounds Unreel Studio. His name was Chuck Reynolds, and he was good. Our timing was perfect. Chuck really desired a closer walk with God and was very interested in playing with us. We set up an audition, which he passed with flying colors, and we had our replacement for Greg Morrow.

We also decided Dana and I would back away from the production of the album for the first time. We entrusted those duties to Ron Griffin. He helped each of us with our solo records and worked with us on previous D&K projects so he knew what we were going for, what we were capable of, and how far he could push us. We liked his techniques and trusted his judgment. He knew how to deal with both of us pretty well.

We recorded the basic tracks for *The Pledge* at Ardent but did most of the overdubs at a couple of high-end studios in the Nashville area called The Castle and OmniSound Studios. Ron and his recording engineer, Billy Whittington, both lived in Nashville. It was easier for us to stop there before or after tour dates than for them to constantly keep coming out to Memphis, burning up I-40.

The recording process was different that time around. The full band was only together during the basic tracking process. I did all my keyboard overdubs without Dana being around and he sang his lead vocals and played guitar without me being present. It was the first time in years I didn't produce him, and he didn't produce me. As a result, the record came out sounding a little different.

I do believe *The Pledge* features some of the best songwriting of our career. Dana wrote "Boycott Hell," "Aliens and Strangers," "The Pledge," and "Who Will." I wrote, "I'm Accepted," "Hand in Hand," "Let's Get Upset," and "If God Is For Us." All those songs were received well by our fans and have stood the test of time.

"I'm Accepted" was a song that really surprised me. We received countless letters from people who were touched by that song and its message. I wrote it specifically for my daughters, who were in middle school at the time. I honestly didn't expect the song to speak to folks across all ages the way it did. Interestingly, before we recorded it we worked it up as a high energy, up-tempo rock song. The music just didn't fit the tenderness of the lyric, though, so we recorded it as a ballad, which is how I wrote it originally.

We were a bit surprised to receive some fairly harsh criticism for the song "Boycott Hell." We were used to controversy about being too loud or too rock 'n' roll, but this wasn't that at all. Some people criticized the song for having "Bumper Sticker Theology." I guess that has a kernel of truth in it. We always tried hard to come up with a title and a song that could end up being the theme to a "Summer Youth Camp" and plastered on t-shirts everywhere.

That was a badge of honor for us. It meant we were having a positive effect. The interesting point about that song is it was taken from a real live person and a true story. We had a friend who had the words "Boycott Hell—Accept Jesus" embroidered on the back of his jean jacket back during the Jesus Movement days. Two albums later I wrote a song called "God Good, Devil Bad," and received the same kind of criticism. It was also a true story about a real person I met who had "God Good" tattooed on one arm and "Devil Bad" tattooed on the other arm. You can't make this stuff up.

We knew *The Pledge* was special when we finished making it. We also knew the phrase "He Died For Me, I'll Live for Him" would have a tremendous impact on people. The song "The Pledge" was not really a commercial moment on the album, but its theme and message were right on target. It was who we were and it was the message we wanted to convey as a band.

For *The Pledge* tour we brought a Christian comedian named Steve Geyer and a brand new band to open for us. We had just signed the band to our new label, and they needed some experience on the road. They were called dcTalk. Ron Griffin often mentioned he had been listening to rap music, probably mostly RUN DMC back then.

He said he wanted to find a Christian rap act that could sing the choruses so youth groups could sing along. I have to give Ron the credit for having that vision. In dcTalk we found just that.

As an "added value" for the fans, I opened the second set with three songs from *Feels Good to Be Forgiven*. We added a saxophone/keyboard player for this spotlight and Michael Tait (from dcTalk) our guitarist Steve Taylor, and Dana lined up Temptations-style beside me to sing back-up vocals. Roscoe Meek, our monitor engineer, stood in to play guitar. It was a smoking band, for sure, and was fun music to perform. The crowd seemed to dig it, and it definitely brought a different flavor to the night.

We toured *The Pledge* for eighteen months solid. The album did incredibly well, both as the best-selling project of our career, and as some of the most effective ministry we ever saw. Between the solo projects, Dana wrote a book called *Don't Stop the Music*, we were endorsed by the NIV Student Bible, and ForeFront continued to grow. Things were really coming together.

THIRTY-SEVEN

LET'S GET UPSET

The way we ended up working with dcTalk was pretty interesting. Everyone knew Ron Griffin was looking for a commercially accessible rap group. One day a fellow named Jeoffrey Benward, who was one of the early ForeFront artists, gave Ron a demo tape a student gave him after one of his concerts at Liberty University. I'm not sure Jeffrey even listened to it, actually.

Ron was so excited about what he heard he rushed over to Dan Brock's house to play it for him. He was so excited, in fact, he couldn't even wait for Dan to finish getting ready. He played it for him while he was still in the shower. Dan called me and said they were so excited for us to hear it they were on their way to our show in Kentucky that night. It couldn't wait.

That night, in the back lounge of our tour bus, Ron played the demo tape of dcTalk and the One Way Crew. We then voted on whether to sign them or not. Dana wasn't a fan of rap music. He thought it might be a passing fad. In the end, though, he decided to go along with us. Ron, Dan, and I were all very excited!

We later found out the group had been pitched all over town and was passed on by every other record company. The same thing happened to me with D&K back in the day, so I was unfazed by that run-around. Through the years, I've been asked over and over again how a new, fledgling record company like ForeFront was possibly able to sign a band like dcTalk. My answer is always the same.

"Because no one else would."

In the early days of ForeFront Records our jobs were all pretty simple and straightforward. Ron, the only actual employee, ran the company and produced most of the albums. Dan helped Ron when needed, but most of his time was spent on DeGarmo and Key business. Those were the peak years of our career and it took all hands on deck to manage our affairs. D&K's job was to use our platform to help develop the bands and introduce them to the public. Dana and I thought it best not to share that we were co-owners in the label publicly. I actually didn't share that secret until five years later. After all, we were successful artists, and didn't want to confuse the audience or the industry by being seen as record company owners.

When we took dcTalk out on our eighteen-month tour for *The Pledge*, they were completely unknown. We were at the top of our game, and labels would gladly pay us to take their bands out as support acts on the tour. To justify taking dcTalk out as our opening act we offered them jobs as members of the crew. Toby "TobyMac" McKeehan sold our merchandise. Michael Tait set up our drums and backline amps. Kevin "K-Max" Smith was my keyboard tech. It might sound degrading, but it was a way for them to get a platform they otherwise would not have had.

In retrospect, hiring them as roadies was a bad idea in at least one way; they were not good roadies. In fact, they were terrible. We can all laugh about that now. Off-stage they were just about useless. When they performed, though, they were excellent—right on target. That made the whole thing worthwhile.

In 1990 I talked Tim Landis and Harry Thomas, the promoters of Creation Festival, into letting dcTalk take fifteen minutes of our headline slot at the festival. They were not booked to appear, so we gave them part of our time. Creation was the mother of all Christian music festivals, drawing between seventy and eighty thousand attendees to rural Pennsylvania each summer. Tim didn't want to do it at first. He said the fans came to see D&K. I assured him neither he, nor the fans, would be disappointed by dcTalk. They weren't.

I pulled the same maneuver at several other festivals that summer. Chuck Tilly, the organizer of Atlantafest, still tells that story. The rest is history. Before long the fans at our concerts wanted to see dcTalk as much as they wanted to see us—if they were pre-teens, maybe more. Clearly dcTalk was on fire.

As ForeFront began to heat up we signed more artists, including Audio Adrenaline, Geoff Moore, and The Distance. The label took more and more of our time and attention. Dan Brock spent more time helping Ron Griffin, too. The business was exploding and we were loving life. It may have been too much of a good thing, though. We ended up hitting a real tough patch we didn't see coming. Soon there would be plenty of pain to mix with the joy.

In 1990 D&K went out on a roughly twenty-date West Coast tour. One company was promoting all the shows. As the tour started, however, it became apparent the promoter had not done his job well. Business details were a mess, lots of tasks were being left undone, and the crowds were much smaller than we expected. Some shows drew a hundred people or less. No one knew we were even coming to town. Something was definitely wrong. We had never experienced this before in concert after concert. We were at the top of our game during this nightmare.

On that tour we were paid a straight percentage of the gate most of the time. We were comfortable with that arrangement because of our past success. Plus, we knew the promoter well and expected him to do a good job. Because the guaranteed fees were either low, or non-existent, we were losing thousands of dollars every night. We had around sixteen people on the tour in custom buses and were using a semi-truck for all of the equipment. It was very expensive.

Dana and I were extremely concerned—in fact, Dana was livid. He was thoroughly convinced Dan Brock was just too busy with the business of ForeFront to watch out for us anymore. It seemed apparent to him that Dan was not managing us properly and staying on top of our business. Although I have come to believe that Dan's role was a part of the issue, it wasn't the whole picture. There was something more complex going on. Our concert promoter was not doing his job at all, and we didn't know about it until it was way too late to fix anything. That's the plain and simple truth of what happened.

Our team was always proactive in staying in the loop of our concert activity and addressing issues long before we arrived in town if possible. These ill-fated concerts totally blindsided us.

After that tour, a deep fracture began to form between Dana and Dan. Looking back, I think it began long before that tour, though. It may have been Dana perceived Dan as siding with me over him in "The Vocal Wars" and surrounding drama that started us down the solo album path. Dan and I often seemed to see things from a similar perspective. At times that may have left Dana as the odd man out. I'm not sure, but I knew by that point it was getting serious. So serious, in fact, Dana decided he wanted to sell his ForeFront stock and was lobbying me to oust Dan as our manager. I couldn't believe what was happening. It was tragic. I felt stuck in the middle. This was no-win for me.

Dana and I met with Ron, Dan, and Richard Green, our attorney. Dana told us all he had made the decision to sell his stock in our record company. We had to come up with a way to do a valuation of what the stock was worth and Richard suggested a couple of ways forward.

In the meantime, Dana pressured me to end our management relationship with Brock and Associates. In fact, he told me he was seeking legal counsel about whether Dan mishandled our career so badly it might be considered legally negligent. I didn't believe that for a second, and did not want to go down that road at all.

Dan Brock was a loyal soldier for D&K and I felt it was wrong to tarnish his image after so many years of strong support. D&K was the center of my career at that point, so I did what I felt was the only thing possible. I called Dan and emotionally explained to him we were seeking to end our management relationship, and I had come to the conclusion it was only right for me also to sell my stock in ForeFront to create some distance between us. That was very difficult for me, as Dan and I were close friends. I'm convinced that telephone call began the process of eroding the trust we always held between us. I had multiple contractual recording and tour commitments with Dana I couldn't forgo for years to come, though. I was stuck!

When we received an independent valuation on ForeFront it turned out, even though we were only two years old, that our company was worth much more than any of us expected. Dan and Ron called me to explain they didn't believe they could raise enough money to buy both of us out. We would have to choose which one of us was going to sell.

A few evenings later Susan and I were at the D&K office in Germantown, packing up merchandise fans ordered through our newsletters. Dana dropped by right as it was getting dark outside. Susan brought up the ForeFront stock issue and what Dan and Ron told us.

"Dana, either you or Eddie can sell," she said frankly. "Which one will it be?"

Everyone who knows Susan knows how direct she can be. She just lays it all out there. I love that about her. It can get tense sometimes, but you always know where you stand. Sometimes I wonder how she would negotiate with the Russians.

The air was so thick in the room you could cut it with a knife. I asked Dana to join me outside for a few minutes. I told him I was leaving the choice completely up to him. If he wanted to stay, I'd sell my stock. If he wanted to sell his, I'd keep mine. It was totally his choice.

Dana looked me right in the eye and immediately said, "I prefer to sell mine."

So, that's what happened. Dana sold his stock in ForeFront Records in 1990, and D&K quietly severed management with Brock and Associates. I called Dan and explained I saw no other way forward and I promised to make the best of the situation. Dan extended a peace offering that helped us greatly. He felt awful about the massive tour losses we suffered. So, he decided to waive a commission payment due to be paid to him on a large royalty payment from The Benson Company. The royalties were several hundred thousand dollars, and every cent of it was used to help D&K pay off our massive tour debts. I've always appreciated that gesture. I tried my best to reconcile the relational breach he suffered in the loss of D&K, but I could tell it hurt him deeply. We just had to make the best of it.

THIRTY-EIGHT

AGAINST THE NIGHT

After a mostly strong 1990, the best way I can describe 1991, and the recording of D&K's twelfth album *Go to the Top*, is it was like a giraffe on roller skates—awkward and clumsy. We ended our long time management relationship with Brock and Associates, Dana was out of the ForeFront ownership group, and ForeFront was moving its distribution from The Benson Company, which was to be the home of D&K's future albums, to Star Song Distribution, a leading competitor. Everything was unsettled, and I was knee-deep in the drama, every day stuck right in middle of the crossfire.

Dana and I decided to invite Ron Griffin to produce *Go to the Top*. He did a fine job on *The Pledge* and was a good mediator of our creative dynamic. But things were awkward for us on a lot of fronts when we came together to record. The air was heavy when we were together. The album has some good moments, such as "I Believe," "Against the Night," "Family Reunion," and "Ultimate Ruler," but overall *Go to the Top* is my least favorite D&K album. The music stills feels unsettled to me. It sounds like it is lacking the passion and emotional electricity of our earlier work, or of our later albums *Heat It Up* and *To Extremes*, for that matter.

When D&K left Brock and Associates it fell on Dana and me to manage the large enterprise around the world. To tackle this properly we opened and staffed a Memphis office managed by Scott Winchell. We also had a Nashville operation with our production staff and equipment. The Nashville operation was first managed by Stan Letarte and later by Doug Jones. We had a better handle on managing the production office than the business office at first. The business office in Memphis managed all our interaction with the record companies and booking agents, along with publicists, interviews, travel arrangements, banking, royalties, and everything else that went on in the large business of DeGarmo and Key.

Not to disparage Dana in any way, but most people who knew and loved him would readily tell you business was not his first priority or gift. He had ample gifts in ministry, preaching, and teaching to make up for any business shortfall. The downside of this for me was most of the responsibility for the business of the band fell directly on my shoulders, and I was rusty to say the least. Dan Brock and his staff handled all of those matters for years while I was being an artist. Suddenly I needed to fill both roles. Dana did too. It was an immense amount of work for both of us.

It didn't help that the beginning of the *Go to the Top* tour was in Australia. From there we headed to Europe, which takes even more coordination. Chuck Reynolds, our drummer for *The Pledge* tour, had left the band. His replacement was an eighteen-year-old drummer from Memphis named Kevin Rodell. Kevin was an excellent drummer who played in the style of Greg Morrow and was a great fit for our band. He was perfect. I could close my eyes and almost hear Greg playing behind us and holding us together. Thank you, Kevin.

The *Go to the Top* tour continued with a long string of North American dates. We were able to bring ForeFront acts Audio Adrenaline and the rappers ETW as our openers on various legs of the tour. It only seemed right to help those artists reach an audience. Of course it benefited me as a ForeFront owner to get their names out there, but musically, the ForeFront artists were a good fit for D&K anyway. They were all misfits like us to a degree.

The first time Audio Adrenaline came on the road to open for us I hitched a ride with them to the auditorium from the motel. I remember being able to see the road passing by us through holes in the floorboards of their old rusted out van. It reminded me of D&K's Happy Truck days. Fortunately, they grew past that early stage of their career much faster than we did.

We filmed a long form video of several songs from *Go to the Top* when we returned from Australia. Stephen Yake directed the video and Ken Pennell, then the head of A&R at The Benson Company, assembled it. Ken worked with us from the late eighties as our creative sounding board with the record company. He was a great asset to us with his strong musical credibility, and we valued his input. I have always appreciated his contributions to D&K. The video turned out remarkably well. In some ways it feels better than the album to me. There are some hilarious Memphis locals who make cameo appearances in the video as well as excellent scenes from our homeland.

Filming that video was the first time I recall meeting Ken's teenage son, Marcelo Pennell. He was helping as a sound engineer for the video crew. Little did I know, as I witnessed that long-haired, goateed (longer than any I had seen before) kid wearing hi-top combat boots and short pants in the Memphis summer heat, that I was looking at my future son-in-law. He was just the right kind of "freaky looking" to fit in with the DeGarmo family. But that would be years later. He was still in high school.

THIRTY-NINE

IF GOD IS FOR US

Over the next year and a half, it became apparent I needed to move my family to Nashville so I could help out more with ForeFront. The label was exploding and growing by leaps and bounds. We released the dcTalk *Nu Thang* album and it was selling like hotcakes. We also saw early success with the first Audio Adrenaline album, and Ron produced a hit album called *A Friend Like You* for Geoff Moore and The Distance. Things were working at ForeFront. But things had become very tense between Ron Griffin and Dan Brock for some reason. I don't think I will ever totally understand what happened there. I worked at trying to get them together, but it just didn't seem to go anywhere. I couldn't get to the bottom of it. Neither seemed to care to work it out. It was sad. Ron and Dan were close friends since their college days. Something got personal and it was poisoning their relationship. Eventually Ron decided he wanted to sell his ForeFront stock and get out. It was very weird and uncomfortable for all three of us, but we set it up. It was then I allowed something to happen that came to visit me in waves of difficulty for years to come. Looking back, though, I still feel like I made the right decision.

At a breakfast restaurant off I-40, close to the Natchez Trace Parkway, between Nashville and Memphis, Dan Brock and I met to decide the best way to buy Ron's stock and move the company forward. We had a normal buy/sell provision in the company bylaws that gave the remaining stockholders the right to buy sellers' shares equally. I could sense through the conversation, though, Dan was still reeling from D&K terminating the management relationship with him.

I knew it was of paramount importance that he now pour himself into ForeFront. The company was doing well, but needed a steady hand. He never leveled with me about what went down between him and Ron, or perhaps between their wives Charlotte and Darlene, but it seemed like it was personal as well as business.

As we talked, I made a decision in my heart to allow Dan to buy a few more shares of Ron's stock than I would. That would give him majority control of ForeFront. I had D&K *and* ForeFront. He only had ForeFront and a soon to be expired contract to manage dcTalk. He needed to be affirmed and I knew this was the right thing for me to do. I also knew Dan was the right man for the job to run ForeFront.

He was always a great businessman and marketer. We needed him to be that for our company. Also, I felt it was important as an olive branch between us. I was going to move my family to Nashville and I wanted Dan and I to trust each other completely. We were only talking twenty-five out of five hundred total shares. In fact, I asked Dan to write down on a napkin a promise that he agreed to sell me ten of those twenty-five shares back when I decided it was right. That only gave him a five share majority. There was an appropriate time, many years later, when I gave that napkin back to Dan. He had forgotten about it. He was honorable and sold me the ten shares as he promised at breakfast.

On June 2, 1992, Susan and I moved to Nashville with our girls. Our oldest had just graduated high school and our youngest was entering tenth grade. The timing was the best it could be. It was still a hard move for us. We loved our home, our friends, church, and community in Memphis. Plus, D&K was a big deal in Memphis. In Nashville we were one in a million. I was still pursuing D&K diligently then, even though I knew inside I needed to prepare myself for the future. Those striped pants couldn't take me where I had to go.

When we first got to town, we rented a townhouse for a year to get our bearings. It was convenient for me as it was just around the corner from ForeFront. When I left to play concerts with the band, the tour bus could pick me up in the ForeFront parking lot. If for some reason we had to go south, the bus picked me up first and then went to Memphis. If we had to go north the bus drove to Memphis first.

ForeFront grew rapidly. After *The Pledge* tour, the label released my second solo album, *Phase II*, to strong reviews from critics and fans alike. One of the highlights on that record was my re-make of Bill Gaither's "Something About That Name." Russ Taff and Mark Farner (formerly of Grand Funk Railroad) performed as a vocal trio with me. Larry Howard, one of the greatest and most underappreciated blues guitarists in the South, played the solo on the track. The video featured a cameo appearance by Bill Gaither himself. Deaton and Flannigan were back as producers and their video definitely goes down as one of my proudest moments as a solo artist. Appearing alongside Russ Taff, Mark Farner, Larry Howard, and Bill Gaither was like playing with the Yankees.

FORTY

HEAT IT UP

B y the time we went into the studio to record *Heat It Up* things had settled down between Dana and me, between Dan and Darlene Brock and D&K, and between The Benson Company and ForeFront Records. I survived an amazing amount of crossfire, and it felt good to be done with conflict for a while. When I look back it really was a terrible season. No wonder I'm crazy. The good news is by 1993 we'd all made peace.

We asked Greg Morrow if he would be willing to record again with us for *Heat It Up*. It was hard to beat the team of Greg Morrow and Tommy Cathey. They were the backbone of our sound. John Hampton came back on board to co-produce with us. I was able to produce Dana's vocals again, and to capture his guitars. Dana produced my vocals and keyboards. We were definitely back in the zone.

We had a complete blast recording *Heat It Up*. Dana wrote the title track, as well as "Selective Amnesia," "Never Look Back," and "Divine Embrace." I wrote "God Good, Devil Bad," "It's My

Business," "Dare to Be Different" and "Talk to Me." The album came out really strong and we were very pleased with it. I see it as a close musical cousin to our *D&K* album.

As a release party, we decided to rent a music club in Nashville during Gospel Music Week to showcase the album. It felt like old times. We were able to get the Nashville Fire Department to send out a hook and ladder truck and a regular fire truck to park on the street with their red lights spinning outside of the club. Get it? "Heat It Up" and fire trucks? It was a lot of fun, and was exciting to feel fully back on our game.

We played to a packed house that night. It was an awesome way to launch the album.

The *Heat It Up* Tour included Geoff Moore and The Distance and a new artist named Karthi. Geoff and Karthi recorded for Fore-Front Records, so it made a lot of sense for me to work it out for them to tour with us. Geoff had been a friend of ours for years, trailing back to the Petra/D&K tour as Geoff opened a few of those shows. The *Heat It Up* Tour lasted about five months and went all across the U.S. and Canada.

The tour drew huge crowds in some cities, but struggled in others. That was typical of any tour, but this one was more jagged in that respect. Later I concluded we just didn't have a large enough organization to manage all the elements of a tour of that magnitude without a larger and more experienced office staff. From a business perspective we simply bit off a little more than we could chew.

From a ministry point of view, however, the tour was nothing short of fantastic. We saw thousands of decisions for Christ and countless lives impacted. The *Heat It Up* album sold well. We experienced a bit of a lull in sales with *Go to the Top*, which was a first for us and we didn't enjoy it. The marketing line for *Heat It Up* was "The Boys Are Back," and it proved true. Our momentum was back on track.

To capitalize on that momentum Dan Brock and I decided it was time to release a D&K "Greatest Hits" album on ForeFront. We had never released a compilation of our most popular songs and felt like the new wave of excitement made the timing good. We wanted to include a couple of new songs as well. I wrote a rock number called "Color Me Gone" and Dana wrote a power ballad called "I'll Come Out Fighting for You." We recorded those songs with Greg Morrow and Tommy Cathey at Greg's studio in Memphis, Crosstown Recorders.

ForeFront sent Dana and me on a twenty-one-city "promotional tour" visiting radio and retail. As a result, *Destined To Win: The Classic Rock Collection* sold well.

MTV's *Unplugged* series captured our attention. Essentially that was the way DeGarmo and Key performed in the very beginning, even before we released our first album. We were comfortable performing in the stripped-down, acoustic format. As a result, we launched the D&K Acoustic Café Tour in the spring of 1994.

We hired Susan and Sharon Anderson, her partner in DNA Designs, to create a special stage set for the tour. They fabricated this really cool café set with exaggerated features, kind of like what you would see in a Bugs Bunny cartoon back in the day. We loved it and so did the audience.

A brand new band called Big Tent Revival opened for us. It was their maiden tour. I negotiated a deal for ForeFront to market and distribute Ardent's releases. Big Tent Revival was their first release and a perfect fit for our "Acoustic Café" vibe. We hit about twenty-five cities and the tour was successful and very well received. It was the first of many Christian "unplugged" tours throughout the nineties.

I had recently purchased a southwestern style jacket and leather cowboy hat in Santa Fe, New Mexico. When we shot the photos for that tour I wore my new get-up. As I look back I think it was a bit of a mid-life crisis look for me. I finally cut my long hair (thank God) and I was looking for something new. Susan says I have had many a mid-life crisis since then. I was thirty-six then in 1981. I still had plenty of time to freak out.

We contractually owed one more album to Benson. For the next two years, I toured Thursday through Sunday with the band and worked at ForeFront Monday through Wednesday. I started that practice a year before we moved to Nashville. It was beginning to get the best of my family and me. Susan and the girls were in a new town and hardly knew anyone. It seemed I was always gone, and something needed to change.

It was always hard on our family to be separated that much, but now things were becoming frayed around the edges. Because Susan found her faith at our band practice all those years ago, she understood what I was about more than anyone. Still, being apart so much was very difficult on all of us. I can remember when the kids were little, sometimes they would hold on to my pants leg while I was getting on the tour bus to leave. It was heart-breaking and a big sacrifice for all of us. Thankfully, our family remained strong. I really give Susan much credit for that as she was the one holding down the fort.

I encourage anyone embarking on a career that keeps your family apart so much to consider it very carefully. If you are married, both sides have to be totally committed to what is going on. There is no room for division. It's not for everyone.

As we started to record *To Extremes* the folks at Benson began to talk about signing us to a new extended record contract. I put them off and stalled, but it kept coming back up. I already knew in my heart I was planning to hang up my D&K spurs and retire before we began recording *To Extremes*. We invited our original team of Greg Morrow and Tommy Cathey, and co-producer John Hampton, to join the project and lend their talents to the album. I wanted it to be just right.

I am proud of *To Extremes*. It displayed a heavier sound for us, which was a pretty honest reflection of the raw rock sound taking over mainstream radio in the nineties. Dana learned how to tune his guitar down to "drop D," which gave the whole thing a lower, crunchier tone. The album cover was controversial again. Susan and Sharon mocked up a joke cover featuring a black and white picture of our family dog, Wooly Bully. They also presented several other design options. To our surprise and amazement, the marketing team at Benson loved the "Wooly Bully" cover art. So, we went with it. It was "extreme" for sure.

TobyMac told me soon after, "Eddie, I knew you were going to pack it in when you put your dog on the cover." Maybe he saw something I didn't. I don't know.

I never wanted to be the old boxer trying to regain the title past his prime. I always wanted to hang my gloves up while things were good. A local Memphis music icon and friend of mine, Don Nix, once said to me, "Eddie, I awoke one day to find myself in the twilight of a mediocre career." That was a funny one-liner, but I never felt that way at any level. My time with D&K was fantastic. I was blessed. How many people get to say that?

Right after we turned in *To Extremes*, I went to Dana and had a tough conversation with him. I shared with him I felt it was time for me to pack it in and leave our dream band. I felt it was unfair for me to continue to allow Benson to throw big numbers at us to re-sign, knowing in my heart it was time for me to go. I also felt it was unfair for me to let Dana make plans that involved me when I was unsure I wanted to commit to them.

Not re-signing meant turning down hundreds of thousands of dollars. It was also difficult for me knowing how many lives were going to be impacted by my decision not to go forward. But I always wanted to walk away while things were really good. Things were still pretty strong for D&K in the marketplace, and I wanted to leave while it was still that way. "Always keep 'em asking for more," they say. That's the show biz motto and rule number one.

So, Dana and I shook hands, gave each other a hug, and I turned and walked away from what had been a fantastic career.

Now, I couldn't just walk away immediately. We had tour commitments on the books for about eighteen months into the future. We also had a slew of assets we needed to dispose of. We had a tour bus, a semi-tractor trailer, a huge sound and lighting system, a *literal ton* of merchandise, and warehouse space we leased to house it all. It fell to me to sell it all. It took me almost all of those eighteen months to move everything, but thank God, I was able to do it. My last sale was to rock icon Leon Russell. He bought all my keyboards, except my Hammond B3. I'll never sell that. In fact, maybe I'll get buried in it. It's big enough, but that's probably too weird, people would talk. I ended up donating my B3 to Trevecca University's music department where college students can put it to good use. That's way better.

We never toured the music of *To Extremes* formally. Probably just as well. Dana would have had a hard time keeping his guitar in tune. We had a few memorable concerts during the summer of 1994, but only a few.

The last DeGarmo and Key concert was at Kingdombound Music Festival in upstate New York that summer. It was an awesome experience playing to such a huge and wonderful crowd. It was bittersweet, but much more sweet than bitter. We had a great run.

Over our career, DeGarmo and Key received seven Grammy nominations and I received two others as a solo artist. We never actually won one, although some of my fondest memories are of taking our daughters, Breckon and Shannon, to the Grammy awards when we were nominated. I took each girl separately when she reached middle school age. We watched the show, rubbed shoulders with the stars, and danced the night away. That was the best! Also, DeGarmo and Key received around thirty-five Dove Award nominations. We never won one of those either. The GMA did later induct us into the Gospel Music Hall of Fame, though.

That encapsulates my transition from artist to record business executive. It certainly wasn't easy, and it involved some of the hardest decisions I have ever faced in my life. For me to leave my band was the most difficult choice I have ever made. I was just thirty-seven years old when I felt it was necessary for me to walk away from the dream God gave me so many years before. I dreamed of being in a band from the time I was a little boy. Dana and I had been friends since the first grade, and I was walking away. Dan Brock and I had been closest friends for over ten years, and I had to break our management relationship. That was tough stuff.

All of my experience learning the ropes back in the early days—learning how to survive as an artist on the road, learning how to write great songs, learning how to produce records, how to manage Ardent, and then all of the experience managing D&K—even all the stuff I didn't really even want to do—proved to be a training ground for what was to come next. I still had much to learn, but I had a solid foundation on which to build this next chapter of my life. All the painful on-the-job schoolin' wasn't for naught.

FORTY-ONE

IT'S MY BUSINESS

As so often was the case in my life, during the last several years with the band I was bi-vocational to the max. It seems to be the way it has always worked out for me. I burned the midnight oil managing all critical business for D&K and being out on the road most weekends, while also working with A&R and some marketing for ForeFront.

An important principle that worked for me over my entire career is when I began a new business I didn't have to be totally dependent on it for income during its fledgling years. I was okay doing whatever I could to make ends meet while the business got on its feet. The only way that worked was because I surrounded myself with gifted people. That's not always the easiest way to go, though. You have to be willing to give high quality workers their own space and some amount of self-management. They are leaders. You won't always get your way. I know I didn't.

Once the D&K chapter was completely closed, however, I was able to devote my full time and attention to the label. It was certainly no walk in the park. ForeFront was down to two partners: Dan Brock and me. The record company was exploding. We had just released dcTalk's *Free at Last*, Audio Adrenaline's *Don't Censor Me*, and Geoff Moore and The Distance's *Evolution*. All three were big hits and the workload was crazy.

I discovered when we first moved to Nashville the label's relationship with dcTalk was becoming strained. This was mainly driven by two factors. The first had to do with their new management. Dan and Darlene Brock managed the group for the first two years of their career. Then Toby (who was in the group) decided to set up a new management company called True Artists Management with two outside partners. His partners, Laurie Anderson and Dan Pitts, previously worked for Dan Brock and his wife Darlene at Brock and Associates and they also worked closely with D&K for many years.

Laurie was our booking agent at Brock in the eighties, and Dan grew up seeing D&K in concert from the time he was fourteen years old. He probably came to see us twenty-five or thirty times over the years, and we made a close bond as friends. He also promoted D&K concerts at Gordon College a few times while he was a student there. Dana and I introduced Dan Pitts to Dan Brock back in the day. So, when Toby left Brock and Associates to set his company up with people who worked so closely with us, it was only natural for that relationship to become a bit awkward. I think Dan and Darlene felt it more than I did.

The other dynamic factor in the increasing strain between dcTalk and ForeFront was, simply, their success. I've found that any time an artist experiences the kind of meteoric rise they were experiencing, everyone in town comes out of the woodwork, whispering. They whisper in the artist's ear he is being taken advantage of. They suggest the artist's career would be going much better if he or she were on their team. They plant seeds of discontent and confusion that can grow into major weeds. The result is a lot of paranoia. I think both camps were a little paranoid—dcTalk and us.

I did my best to create some basic trust between ForeFront and dcTalk. It was difficult at first. Prior to engaging full time, I didn't realize how charged the relationship had become. One night, while they were working on a record, I called the recording studio to speak with Toby. Their engineer answered the phone and refused to pass my call along because no one wanted to speak with me, including him. The engineer then hung up on me. I got in my car, drove to the studio, stopped the session, and fired the engineer on the spot—right in front of everybody. I informed them that as long as the label was paying for the recording session they didn't have the right to hang up on me.

I spent the next several hours allowing each of them to vent his feelings right at me. I did a lot of listening that night. By the time it was over, we at least got the train back on the tracks and moving forward. I even re-hired the engineer.

Funny thing, he and I have become good friends over the years. In retrospect, I'm not sure how smart it was to take control that way and stop the session. It seems kind of domineering, as I look at it now. But it was the catalyst to bring all the emotions out and to get us all talking.

Over time the relationship between ForeFront and our best-selling artist, dcTalk, got much better. Their album *Free at Last* was a smash success. It held the number one slot on the Christian album charts for more than a year.

Audio Adrenaline was in the middle of recording their album *Don't Censor Me* with producer Steve Griffith. I went to the studio one day and heard this quirky little song called "Big House." I immediately thought it was a smash hit and took a copy back to the office to play for Dan. He thought it was a smash too, so we began to crank up the marketing machine around the song. The problem was the band had mixed emotions about even cutting the song at all.

When we suggested they call the album *Big House*, Mark Stuart, the lead vocalist, said, "You know, I'm thinking about dropping that song. It doesn't really fit where we are going as a group. It's a little cheesy and too comedic."

After I picked Dan up off the floor, we made a compromise. "Don't drop the song," we insisted. "We'll call the album something different, but don't drop that song."

As wild as that may sound, considering how massive that song became for Audio Adrenaline, the story is all too common. When an artist works to craft his work into something commercial it can feel strange to actually pull it off. D&K experienced the same thing with our song "Destined To Win." Dan Brock and I wanted to name the album after that song and Dana wanted to drop it. Our compromise led to the album being called *Commander Sozo and the Charge of the Light Brigade*, for crying out loud.

That's what happens, though. Sometimes the product the masses want to invest in is not the same art the artist wants to convey. That's art meeting commerce. At that point you either learn how to compromise with integrity, or you land too far on one side or the other. The clever artist learns how to navigate those waters while remaining true to himself and crafting a product people want to spend their hard-earned money on.

Rebecca Smallbone was fourteen years old the first time we met. Her father, David Smallbone, was a well-known concert promoter in Australia. Although D&K never worked with him there, we had definitely heard of him. He fell on hard times, so he decided to move his wife and five children across the Pacific Ocean to Nashville.

The first time I saw David in Nashville was when he showed up at my front door asking about his boys possibly mowing our yard.

His wife Helen and daughter Rebecca were cleaning houses and thought we might hire them as well. That was how our paths crossed at first. The whole family was doing whatever odd jobs it took to get by. David earned a lot of respect from me and from others during that period. I knew all about being down and out, flat broke, and respected anyone who was willing to work hard to make ends meet.

A few months later David asked me if I would be interested in coming to hear Rebecca sing at church. I didn't even know she was a singer. I was looking for a female artist who was interested in singing to her young peers. At that point most of the popular female artists in Christian music were in their thirties and beyond. There didn't seem to be anyone singing directly to a teenage audience, which is the market ForeFront was most focused on.

Rebecca Smallbone, it turned out, could definitely sing. She also had a strong sense of her own creative and ministerial identity. She was talented, had something to say, and possessed poise well beyond her years. She was ready to sing for her peers. We decided she needed a more common stage name for performing. Her grandfather's name is James so it was natural for her to take that name. We put a "St." in front of it because it sounded statelier. Needless to say, it suited her well. Rebecca St. James was fifteen years old when we recorded her first ForeFront album.

We found the Smallbone family very refreshing to be around. David and Helen really worked hard to raise their kids in a wholesome way by limiting "worldly influence." As a result, Rebecca was a truly innocent young lady. For example, when we decided to record a Christmas album, Rebecca and her producer, Tedd T, decided to re-make a version of The Beatles' "Happy Christmas." It was a big hit in Australia and she liked the song and wanted to put her personal spin on it.

Rebecca was a very focused and spiritual young woman. Every session she was part of began with a group prayer between her, the musicians, and her producer. I still remember being in the control room of Tedd's studio when the prayer began. The custom was we held hands in a circle, then Rebecca would open the prayer, and during the prayer different people would add to her prayer as it went around the room. The lights were dim and the studio vibe was thick with lava lamps, beads hanging from the doorways, and nomadic looking musicians standing around the room holding hands.

Rebecca immediately began to pray intently: "Lord, we are going to record 'Happy Christmas' today. So, I lift up John Lennon to you that you would save his soul and bring him to you. He's been running from you for so long."

I opened my eyes to see everyone else except Rebecca had their eyes open as well, looking around the room. I looked over at Tedd and his eyes cut left and then right. Then he looked at me like he needed direction and support.

After a period of awkward silence, Tedd T spoke up and grunted, "Hmmm, ahhhhh." Then he said, "Uh, Rebecca, you know we all love John Lennon, but he's been dead for over ten years now."

Rebecca looked stunned and just said, "Really? That's sad." She didn't know. Sheltered she certainly was. She did okay, though. Interestingly, later her brothers spent years experimenting with different musical styles and identities before landing on their sound. They are now called For King and Country and are bringing the Smallbone legacy to a whole new generation.

FORTY-TWO

DARE TO BE DIFFERENT

Way back in the summer of 1974, our "Christian Band" played a series of Saturday night concerts in the parking lot of our church in East Memphis. We set up on a flatbed semi-truck trailer and rocked. It was a busy street corner so there were a lot of people stopping to listen or walking by. It was also across the street from a major shopping area, so that helped.

We played a song or two and then different folks would get up and share their stories or some thought from the Bible. Usually the youth pastor of our church gave a closing sermon and offered folks a chance to receive Christ as their savior. It was kind of like a rock 'n' roll tent revival, but without a tent. The summer nights in Memphis are warm and the humidity is thick enough to cut with a knife. Sweat poured off the band and everyone else in the audience. It was marvelous.

At one of those revivals a thirteen or fourteen-year-old young man walked forward and dedicated his life to Jesus. His name was Pat Scholes. Twenty years later he was in charge of Ardent Christian

Music in Memphis. Pat went to work at Ardent as an intern in the late seventies while D&K were recording at the studio. Over the years he had a tremendous Christian influence on the founder, John Fry, as well as our frequent co-producer John Hampton.

When Ardent decided to become active in producing Christian music, Pat came and met with me at ForeFront to see if we could help them. They formed a record business with several partners, including Dana Key. He was back in the record business after selling his stock in ForeFront.

Their first artist was a fellow named Steve Wiggins. Steve recorded an album for Sparrow Records, working with my good friend Peter York. The album didn't meet expectations in the marketplace so Sparrow decided not to make album number two.

Pat said they wanted to re-introduce Steve under the band name "Big Tent Revival." Spence Smith, Steve's drummer and longtime friend, was also to be a big part of the band. Pat then played one of the group's new songs. It was called "Two Sets of Jones'." I was smitten.

Over the course of the next few weeks I hammered out what is commonly known as an "imprint deal" between Ardent and Fore-Front. It would be Ardent's responsibility to sign artists and make the records. It would be ForeFront's responsibility to market, sell, and distribute those records. It was a great way to expand ForeFront's product line, have great artists and records to sell, and work with friends at the same time. A few years later they signed a Memphis rock band that definitely shook things up in both the Christian market and the mainstream.

Back before we made the move to Nashville, I occasionally sang and played piano at our home church, Germantown Baptist, on the rare Sundays when I was in town. One Sunday, after singing one of those "special music" songs at church, an elderly gentleman lumbered up slowly and asked me a question.

"Eddie," he began, "I have a favor to ask of you. My daughter recently lost a long battle with cancer. She was married with children. Her fourteen-year-old son, my grandson, is having an especially difficult time dealing with his grief. He is a big fan of your music and is into playing music himself. Would you happen to have time to visit with him? His name is John."

"I would be more than happy to see him," I replied. We exchanged phone numbers.

About a week later, I suited up with my jeans and my black leather motorcycle jacket and took my Harley to visit John. It sounded like he was into rock 'n' roll, so I figured I would show up in rock 'n' roll style. I pulled into his driveway, got off my bike, strutted to the front door, and rang the bell. A few moments later, a young man answered. I introduced myself and told him I was there to see John.

"I'm John," he said abruptly, "but before you come in, I have one question for you." He looked me straight in the eye and said, "Why didn't God heal my mother? Can you tell me that?"

I was taken aback, as those were the first words out of his mouth. But very quickly I felt the Lord give me words of my own. "Who told you God didn't heal your mom?" I asked. "She got healed. That's for sure. You're just not able to see it yet."

To this very day, I'm convinced God gave me that message to deliver to John Cooper.

Over the next few years, I saw John's band play a few times and became friends with him. When I moved to Nashville, however, I lost touch with him. One day, several years later, I received a call from my old friend Rick Miller. Rick was D&K's first booking agent and was always an avid supporter of us. I knew that he'd returned to college, got his ministry degree, and was pastor of a growing church in Memphis. He told me there was a band in his church he felt had potential. He asked if he could send me some of their music to consider for ForeFront. He then said they had a bit of a peculiar name. They called themselves "Skillet."

The music blew me away. It was a very unique and crazy blend of hard rock, blues, jazz, and classical, mixed together with singing and a whole lot of screaming. I loved it. I immediately called Rick to tell him so. He said, "Hey, do you remember a kid from your old stomping ground in Germantown named John Cooper?"

"Sure."

"He's the kid singing and playing bass. Skillet is his band."

We had just signed two rock bands, Bleach and Grammatrain, to ForeFront. It was 1995 and the modern rock and grunge scenes were exploding. Dan and I met and listened to Skillet and felt we might be able to serve them better by introducing them to the Ardent folks. The band was from Memphis and needed some time to record and properly develop, and we thought Ardent could be a good home for them. If Ardent signed them, we would still be fully engaged by promoting, marketing, selling, and distributing their records.

I called Dana, who was the head of A&R for Ardent, and told him the Skillet story. I overnighted the music to him, but didn't hear back from him for a few days. I finally called him and asked if he received the tape.

"Yes," he said, "But I'm not sure what we can do with this. I don't know how much I like it, actually. I don't think it has a good chance of selling."

Ardent was having good success with Big Tent Revival and was in dialogue to sign another roots and folksy band called Smalltown Poets at the time.

"You around tomorrow?" I asked. "'Cause I'm driving down to see you and John Hampton."

So, I went to Memphis the next day and pleaded my case for Dana and John to sign Skillet. I reminded them the band was from Memphis, so there would be no travel involved. The music was definitely edgy, experimental, and different from their other artists. But I had a gut feeling the talent, drive, and passion were there with this band. I thought it would work in the marketplace. Dana and John came around. So did Skillet.

I've been asked countless times about what I look for in a new artist or songwriter. Who gets signed? How come some get the opportunity and others don't? To answer, I usually approach the question from a fairly pragmatic perspective. It can be a difficult question to answer, because so much of it comes down to intangibles, but I have developed a guiding theory, with a corresponding set of principles, based on my experience.

For one thing, I always looked for character before talent. I really wanted to know the character of the artists, and the qualities and values they possessed, before I would sign them. Qualities like work ethic, integrity, honestly, regard for people, and trust, were absolutely essential to me. I've found that in this life character will carry you much further down the road of success than talent alone ever could. Mind you, talent is very important as well, but if you can find a talented person with character, the sky is the limit. Then you've got something special.

When it comes to evaluating talent, I actually developed a type of graph on which I broke it down into three main categories. I have to tip my hat to Dana for helping me craft this theory. We ruminated over this issue, consuming massive quantities of Doritos and coffee for hours on end on our tour bus in the late eighties and early nineties. This is what we came up with.

There are three main types of talent in musical artists. The first is songwriting ability. The second is virtuosity, or how well you play an instrument or sing. The third is charisma. In the mainstream they call it "sex appeal."

If an artist has an overwhelming amount of talent in any one of those three areas, it can carry a career.

For example, Bob Dylan could be an example of that in the songwriting category. He has so much talent writing songs, it doesn't matter how well he sings them or the amount of charisma he displays. It doesn't mean he doesn't move the needle in the other two categories, because he clearly does. It's just he has an overwhelming amount of talent as a songwriter. Other examples of that kind of talent could be artists like Aimee Mann and Willie Nelson.

Celine Dion is a good example of an artist in the virtuosity category. She sings so well no one pays much attention to whether she writes songs, or even if she's particularly charismatic. That doesn't mean she can't write or doesn't have charisma, but when she hits those big high notes in full voice, nobody cares much about anything else. Artists like Phil Keaggy, Al Green, Kelly Clarkson, Bela Fleck, Josh Grobin, Yo Yo Ma, and others are more highly regarded for their virtuosity than the other categories.

One could argue Elvis is the ultimate example of an artist who was dominant in the charisma, or sex appeal, category. I can think of no more charismatic artist than him. He sang fine, but was certainly not a virtuoso. He wasn't much of a songwriter. But the power of his performance, or even a still picture of him, was undeniable. There was so much electricity in the air when he was around, and he was so doggone handsome when he came on the scene it didn't matter what else he did. A modern equivalent might be someone like Taylor Swift, Justin Bieber, or Adam Levine of Maroon 5.

Sometimes artists may excel in more than one category, which certainly gives them a better chance at success. Bruce Springsteen is a great writer, and his charisma is off the scale, but no one would put him in the Hall of Fame for his singing ability alone. Adele would fill these two categories fully today. She a great singer, and her charisma and charm are as endearing as it gets.

Occasionally an artist comes along who excels in all three categories. He or she has a ton of charisma and is a great writer and performer. The Beatles come to mind. Sting, Michael Jackson, Prince,
or Beyoncé are other great examples. These artists are extremely rare.

In Christian music I believe dcTalk fit that bill. They were a triple
threat, for sure. We've seen those gifts with others as well. These days
it might be Lauren Daigle or Chris Tomlin.

When I was considering whether or not to work with a new artist at ForeFront, I thought through those important elements after he
or she left my office. It was important to understand where this
person's strengths were, and which type of talent would be the mag-
net to attract an audience.

In our world it was also critical every artist had something to say.
Christian music is a lyric-based genre. You can have the charisma,
the virtuosity, and the songwriting skills, but if you're not passionate
about delivering a message, this isn't the scene for you.

There are a few other factors that have little to do with talent,
but are incredibly important. The first is what I call the "maniac factor." I have never signed an artist or songwriter who in some corner
of his or her career or psyche wasn't some kind of maniac.

It's the someone who would call me at midnight wondering why
the Walmart in Tuscaloosa didn't have his CD in stock, or why Spo-
tify wasn't featuring her on the genre page. They would leave no stone
unturned. Sometimes the maniac was the artist or songwriter. Sometimes it was a manager. Sometimes it was a spouse. But, there was
always a maniac hiding under a rock somewhere. It might seem
weird, but I found it to be critical to the success equation. I needed
the maniac's help. Without that passion—or even obsession—it probably wouldn't happen for them. They had to want it more than anyone else, including me.

The second non-talent-based factor is uniqueness. Does the artist
stand out in the sea of faces? We can argue whether or not Johnny

Cash is a great technical singer, but none of us wonder whether it's him we are hearing when his music comes on. He is undeniably unique in his sound. That is a very important factor as well. In the end, talent is subjective. We all have different tastes, and we all like different music. Uniqueness is more objective. We all recognize something different. Of course, it has to be pleasing to enough people for it to work. I'm not talking about just being bizarre.

The cancer of any art form is indifference. You need people to either love you or hate you. But they *have* to care. They have to *notice*.

At the end of the day, however, it usually comes down to a great song. A great song can do more for an artist, songwriter, record company, agent, manager, or promotion guru than all other factors combined. It's the rue in the gumbo, the sugar in the cake batter, the sauce for the barbeque, the wine with a meal, the yeast in the bread, or the cocoa in the chocolate. Without a great song, little else matters.

There you have it. Those are my secrets of signing great artists and songwriters. I've been blessed and honored to work alongside some of the great talents of our time. These guidelines of mine are certainly not foolproof, it is just the way I approached it all.

In early 1995 the universe of Christian music tilted a bit. Jars of Clay released their first single, a hooky alternative pop song called "Flood." It was a smash hit on multiple mainstream radio formats and on Christian radio. The positive influence it had on the marketplace was significant. It also made a major impact within the Christian artist community. Suddenly most youth-oriented Christian artists really wanted to reach the mainstream "MTV crowd." That included just about the entire ForeFront roster.

Our label was always focused on that age group and when "Flood" rose to the top of the charts our artists wanted to achieve the same kind of "crossover" success as Jars of Clay. The problem was we didn't have an in-house mainstream radio promotion team at

ForeFront. We were totally tooled to reach Christian radio, Christian media, and Christian retail. We had to hire independent promoters if we wanted to reach the mainstream radio audience. That proved to be a challenge for us as a label, especially with a few of our major artists.

Earlier in 1995 I introduced Audio Adrenaline to John Hampton at Ardent. In addition to the work he did with D&K, John achieved a lot of mainstream success with artists such as Gin Blossoms, Jimmy Vaughn, and Robert Cray, among others. He and Audio Adrenaline hit it off. They went into the studio and recorded *Bloom*, which I still think is one of their best albums.

Later that year ForeFront released dcTalk's *Jesus Freak*. That album is still a milestone for the entire genre of Christian music. I remember the first meeting Dan Brock, Greg Ham (our head of sales), and I had with Toby about the project. He told us he and Mark Heimmerman wrote a song called "Jesus Freak." The band tested it in a few concerts overseas and received an incredible response from audiences. Its heavier, grunge rock sound was definitely a musical shift for the group.

Lyrically, it was an interesting twist for me personally. "Jesus Freak" was a derogatory term people like us were called back in the Jesus Movement of the seventies. It was never used positively, but was kind of like a religious version of a racial slur. If you were a "Jesus Freak" it meant you were out of your mind—some sort of religious fanatic. As I think about it, it was probably spot on, even though it was meant to be condescending.

I was very excited Toby wrote a song that reclaimed the word and used it as a badge of honor. It was subversive in the best possible way. I'm still proud to have been a part of that song's history, both as a co-owner of the label that released it and as one of the people who unleashed dcTalk upon the world.

In 1996 "Jesus Freak" was the first rock song to win Song of the Year at the Dove Awards. It was one of the greatest moments Dan Brock and I shared together. *Jesus Freak* was the final album in dcTalk's contract with ForeFront. As grand as its success was, however, I knew it would be next to impossible to re-sign the group to a new contract. Like I said, the Christian music universe had indeed tilted, the mainstream was coming into play, and it was going to challenge everything.

FORTY-THREE

STRESSED

In 1995 ForeFront Records was hotter than Louisiana Hot Sauce in a pot of Cajun gumbo. We had a roster of fifteen artists of our own, plus eight others through Ardent Christian Music. Our lineup was one of the strongest in the industry. We were the proud home of dcTalk, Audio Adrenaline, Rebecca St. James, Geoff Moore and the Distance, ETW, Code of Ethics, Bleach, Grammatrain, Eli, Seven Day Jesus, Michael Anderson, The Normals, Larry Howard, Considering Lily, and the D&K catalog. Our Ardent family brought us Big Tent Revival, Smalltown Poets, Skillet, Satellite Soul, Clear, Todd Agnew, Brother's Keeper, and Dana Key's solo work.

Other companies started knocking on our door back in 1994. Mergers and acquisitions were happening everywhere in the music business. One of the first to come calling was Wes Farrell and his Music Entertainment Group, the company that owned Benson. Although we both liked Wes quite a bit, and enjoyed our D&K related business with him, it didn't feel quite right. Zomba, the mainstream label behind Backstreet Boys, N Sync, and Britney Spears, made some overtures to see if we were interested in selling to them. Again, it didn't feel right, but it did get Dan Brock and me talking about the idea. We didn't start ForeFront with a plan to build and sell it, but a number of things changed along the way and I was getting more and more interested in the idea. Brock was not.

Despite all of our success, 1995 and 1996 proved to be very difficult years for us. At that point ForeFront was the largest independent Christian record company in the world. It was starting to feel, however, that we needed to be more than that. Many of our artists were eager to at least have the potential to cross over into the mainstream music world and were pressuring us to make those opportunities happen.

Most of our competitors had been purchased by mainstream companies and thus were able to suggest to artists they might have a better shot at reaching the rest of the world if they left us. EMI Music purchased Sparrow and Star Song Music. Zomba purchased Brentwood, Reunion, and Essential Records. Word was in and out of mainstream ownership throughout the 1980s and was at the time owned by Gaylord Entertainment, with mainstream distribution services through A&M and Epic Records. When it came to mainstream access, for whatever that might prove to be worth, ForeFront was at a distinct competitive disadvantage.

Although it wasn't necessarily true artists would have increased access to mainstream radio and marketing promotions just because their label happened to be owned by a secular company, that didn't keep various people from making that claim.

As an artist I could completely understand the desire to reach the whole world. The mainstream can be enticing and alluring. It's a bigger market with more recognition and the possibility of greater financial gain. I knew that firsthand. It's why I signed a record deal as a kid in high school. Plus, I knew what it was like to have mainstream elements reject the music I was doing simply because of its spiritual content.

Then there were all of the various times D&K brushed up against the mainstream. There was Mercury's interest in our second LP *Straight On* back in 1979. There was Bill Ham's interest in the *Mission of Mercy* record. There was Capitol Records and the "Every Moment" disconnect. I knew all about the temptation of the mainstream, and I honestly wanted our artists to have every opportunity available to them. But I also knew the odds were long. Again, as much as an artist wants to reach that world, often that world doesn't want him or her back.

There were also personal problems brewing at ForeFront. Dan Brock and I were always great business partners. We achieved a lot together. Our friendship, though, had taken a beating. I believe D&K severing management ties with him years earlier was the beginning of a major blow to our relationship. Also, my decision to shut down D&K probably left me a little emotionally fragile at the same time. That was my lifetime dream that was now gone. It's hard to write about this, but the tension between us and between our wives was definitely contributing to my interest in selling.

Darlene Brock always worked alongside Dan at his business. She was personally involved in everything. Throughout the D&K years, especially before we moved to Nashville, Susan and Darlene were best of friends. When we made the move, however, I could see stress fractures showing in their friendship. Darlene became the manager for Geoff Moore and The Distance, and at the same time she worked for ForeFront, but Susan didn't. That was the case for years and always completely okay. Over time, though, it began to take on its own weird tone.

For one thing, Darlene was increasingly uncomfortable with Susan coming around the office. I'm not sure how or why that started,

but it became apparent she just didn't want her there. Maybe Susan
was fraternizing with our employees too much for Darlene. Susan still
has friends to this day from elementary school and high school.
People like her and like to talk to her. Maybe Darlene was just overly
territorial and didn't like Susan on her turf. I don't know, but it was
very unsettling for Susan to sense Darlene's feelings.

Then there was another very specific event that became the proverbial last straw on the camel's back. ForeFront needed to hire an art
director, and I wanted Susan to get the job. That was her area of
expertise, and she held a degree in graphic design. She did numerous
album covers and various art and marketing projects for many different artists. Dan wouldn't go for it. That bothered me. Dan had
majority control of the company though, and he could make that call.

I allowed that to happen when I let him buy a few more shares of
stock from Ron Griffin. Dan making those kinds of calls on his own
was a new reality for me. I wasn't used to it. Then I made an awful
mistake. I told Darlene that if they in fact made the decision not to
offer the job to Susan, she needed to pay Susan a visit, face to face,
and explain why.

It did not go well. Darlene went to our home to explain her rea-
soning to Susan. It turned out, though, Susan never wanted the job
in the first place, and told her so. She said the atmosphere around the
Brocks felt oppressive to her. I understand why she would feel that
way. Needless to say, their meeting ended in flames. In fact, I can't
imagine a worse ending without someone going to jail. It was just
awful.

At that moment I knew the relationship between the Brocks and
DeGarmos had been blown to smithereens. Susan was hurt. Not by
Darlene's lack of offering her the job, but by losing a friend. I was hurt
too. Susan was my girl, and I intended to stand with her. How could
it be any different? Something had to give. To this day I still can't

understand what really happened. I don't know if I'll ever understand how things like that can go so bad. As I mentioned, it's uncomfortable to even write about. I think it's important, though, so I'm doing my best.

Thus there were both personal and business reasons for me to want to consider selling the label and parting ways with my long-time friend and associate. Dan and I had several long conversations about it, but we didn't agree on much. It's hard enough to consider letting go of a business you spent so many years building even without a decaying friendship complicating things. I'm sure it was hard on him too. It's not like he was made of stone.

We placed a provision in our company bylaws called a "put/call." It meant one stockholder could buy another one out based on a particular maneuver. The potential buyer would "put" a price to the other partner. The other partner had ten days to either sell his shares to you at that price, or to turn it back on you and buy you out at the same price. That mechanism keeps the price honest and helps to avoid uncomfortable situations between partners.

It was an aggressive move to undertake for sure. I did my due diligence and came up with a strategy, a fair price, and investors to back me. I was going to buy Dan out. It was kind of like being in a gunfight at the OK Corral. He would have the opportunity to match my price and buy me out, but only had ten days to make a decision. I had to get the details just right. I was about to pull the trigger.

My office at ForeFront was right next to Dan and Darlene's offices. We shared one executive assistant. I came to work one morning and went upstairs to my office, put my briefcase down, and turned back to the door to see Darlene standing there. "Excuse me, Eddie," she said, "but I found this binder downstairs on our conference room table and thought you would want me to bring it to you immediately."

She handed me the binder, and I was floored. It contained my personal copy of the ForeFront corporate bylaws, with my hand-written notes related to the buyout all over it, as well as all of the legal correspondence and accountant information related to my plan for the put/call. Wow! It was a shocking development, to put it lightly.

I always kept that binder in the credenza in my office. Somehow it ended up on our company's conference room table completely out in the open! My mind was racing. I would never have left it out like that. Impossible. Did someone come into my office, go through my stuff, find the binder, and leave it out in the open with all of my strategy on its pages for everyone to see? I'll never know for sure who did that. I guess I was naïve to leave it in my credenza unlocked, but I never would have expected that. Over the years I've had several suspicions of what happened, but no answers. Who knows, maybe it was an angel.

Later that afternoon Dan and I were alone in his office going over various albums, marketing, and general label stuff in our weekly meeting. When we were all but through, Dan lowered his head a bit, looked up at me, and said, "You know I've been doing a lot of thinking. I've come to agree the timing may be right for us to sell our business and become part of a larger entity. Things have changed in the Christian music business."

I nodded in agreement. That's exactly what I had been saying for some time.

Dan went on. "Eddie, I believe it is best if we both stay with this together and ride the horse to the barn. We are great as a team."

I looked back to Dan and said, "If you are making me a firm commitment to sell ForeFront and move our business to a different level by becoming part of something bigger, I'm with you. I agree with you. It is better if we ride the horse to the barn."

Dan and I never spoke of my corporate bylaws being left out in the open. It really didn't matter at that point. We were in agreement so there was no need to force his hand. Later that year he even supported the hiring of my eighteen-year-old daughter, Shannon, in the A&R department. Dan and I were well into our forties and desperately needed someone young and native to the culture to be our eyes and ears. Shannon was the perfect fit to help us stay current.

That's the down and dirty story of how I came to sell ForeFront Records.

In the spring of 1996 we entered discussions with EMI Music to purchase ForeFront. Bill Hearn, the CEO of EMI Christian Music Group, was leading the charge for EMI. Richard Green, who represented D&K for years and also handled our business affairs for ForeFront, had recently been named general counsel for EMI Christian Music Group. He also worked to facilitate the sale of Sparrow and Star Song to EMI. They were building something special there we felt good about. With the foundation of Sparrow and Star Song, EMI and Bill Hearn seemed very committed to building the Christian genre. ForeFront was a perfect way to fill out the roster for the newly formed company.

The deal closed in June of 1996. It was a great day. We felt the move positioned our artists in ways we couldn't as an indie. We were hopeful for our future. It also alleviated a lot of stress between Dan and me.

As Bob Dylan had sung so many years earlier, "The times, they are a changing."

FORTY-FOUR

COMPETITION

When Dan and I sold the company to EMI we had to commit to stay and run it for a few years. That only seemed natural to us, and we didn't want to abandon our artists anyway. Dan was our president but focused mostly on sales and marketing as well as managing the company in general. I was our executive vice president and focused on signing artists and songwriters and managing all content creation, including music, art design, videos, and anything else of that nature. I always thought of myself primarily as a songwriter, then as an artist and producer, so that role was a natural fit for my skill set. I was also always the guy on the road figuring out how to sell another t-shirt, so I guess I was more instinctively interested in sales and marketing than I thought.

One thing I didn't anticipate about selling ForeFront to EMI was the amount of criticism we would receive from some of our peers. Many thought we "sold out to the man." Some rebuked us for becoming "worldly" through our new association with the mainstream. Some cried we "made a deal with the devil," while others interpreted Paul's command not to be "conformed to the world" in Romans 12:2 as somehow related to Christian businesses. When the Bible was written there was no such thing as a Christian record company or book publisher, so I'm fairly sure that is not what Paul was talking about.

I was used to criticism and had become quite adept at accepting rebuke. But this wasn't anti-rock stuff, or a bunch of out-of-bounds TV preachers; these were my friends. It reminded me of the "New Satan" church bulletin Shannon was given all those years earlier. I guess when you try to do new things there will always be people calling you the devil.

I spent over twenty years working for Christian music companies owned by large mainstream global conglomerates. I've been asked many times by friends, family, and church leaders if I was ever asked to compromise our content or beliefs for the sake of business. Generally speaking, the answer is no.

There was one time, though. And it was a doozy.

In 1996, shortly after we sold ForeFront to EMI, I got a surprise visit from the head of EMI North America. His name was Charles Koppelman, and there was something he needed to speak with me about. He called just a few minutes before coming by, and I had no idea what was up. It felt like a surprise visit from my high school principal. When he showed up in his chauffeur-driven car, I was even more intimidated.

EMI had just signed Prince, who at that point was going by the name "unpronounceable symbol" for a combination of creative, political, and marketing reasons. I always wondered what his mother called him then. They'd released his new album, *Emancipation*. When Mr. Koppelman arrived my assistant brought him straight up to my office. After a few brief moments of introduction, he got right to the point of his visit.

"Did you know we just signed Prince and released his new record?" he asked. "Have you heard it?"

"Not yet," I said honestly, "but I plan to. I've long been a fan of his earlier work, like 'Little Red Corvette' and 'When Doves Cry' and other stuff from back when he had a name you could spell and not just a symbol."

Mr. Koppelman continued, "This album has a Gospel song on it, and we need some help promoting it. Would you be open to marketing it through your Christian radio channels?"

That was certainly not what I was expecting. I needed to handle this carefully and respectfully. I thought about what he asked me for a moment and then spoke up. "Mr. Koppelman," I began, "when we promote an artist and their music to the Christian networks, churches, and media, it carries a lot of responsibility for us. Not only do we promote their music, we promote a lifestyle and a belief system. Our church, radio, and media partners take this as seriously as we do. They trust us. Since Prince doesn't reflect a Christian walk or faith in his lifestyle, and hasn't professed even to being a Christian that I know of, if we were to use our name and relationships to promote him to the Christian market I think it could really damage our credibility to our partners and to the customers and fans of the artists we represent.

"I don't want to be judgmental," I continued. "That's not my point. I don't personally know Prince. But I see the lifestyle he promotes, and it does not seem compatible with our mission and who we are as a company. That being said, Mr. Koppelman, you are my boss, and I respect that. If you insist that we do it, we will. But I want you to know it will seriously wound our company."

He looked at me mildly. "I had no idea," he admitted. "I never thought of it that way. We would never do anything to hurt your credibility and what you represent. We don't want that either. Forget I ever asked."

Then he got up and left.

That is the only time I have ever been asked to do something that pushed the limits of who I am as a Christian. And once this powerful representative of the mainstream music world understood the ramifications of what he was asking, he immediately rescinded his request. These guys are smart.

One of the true highlights of my ForeFront years was working alongside and learning from our attorney, Richard Green. He was the one who really taught me the business side of music. Richard was a music business veteran. He represented D&K from the early eighties and was ForeFront's legal counsel for many years. He took me under his wing and acted as my mentor. He also became one of my closest friends. Guys like that are priceless in this life. Richard became the head of business affairs for EMI Christian Music Group and was instrumental in helping Bill Hearn at EMI convince Dan and me to become part of the group.

Watching EMI Christian Music Group come into being was truly impressive. At the time, EMI was one of the "Big Five" music companies in the world. For a company like that to take such a serious interest in Christian music was an interesting development for someone like me. I vividly remember all those times the mainstream companies expressed some interest in D&K until they found out what we were all about. With EMI it was now different.

Bill Hearn had a passionate vision to expand the Christian music genre. He worked alongside his father Billy Ray Hearn when EMI first purchased Billy Ray's Sparrow Records. After Billy Ray retired, Bill took over the helm as CEO, and he successfully led the company after EMI acquired Star Song Records and Distribution. Star Song was the home of several very successful artists of that day, including Twila Paris, Petra, David Meece, Newsboys, and many others. Star Song was also ForeFront's distributor. Once they were added to the group it made perfect sense to round out the lineup by purchasing ForeFront.

Bill is the consummate record man and one of the very best I've ever come across. He lives it, breathes it, and eats it for breakfast, lunch, and dinner. The three years Dan and I spent running ForeFront under EMI and Bill Hearn were productive years. We were able to partner with Virgin Records, also an EMI company, to re-sign dcTalk to a new record contract. Virgin began by taking "Between You and Me" from the *Jesus Freak* album to mainstream radio. We achieved some good success there.

Audio Adrenaline released their answer to "Jesus Freak" in a song called "Some Kind of Zombie." Rebecca St. James released "Pray." We also had a big hit with "What Would Jesus Do" by Big Tent Revival and the accompanying album collection of the same name. We even enclosed a "WWJD" bracelet in the clear spine of the CD jewel box. That was Greg Ham's idea. He was our VP of sales and did a good job tapping into an important cultural trend of the day.

Greg was our longest running ForeFront employee. In fact, when he first started with us in the late eighties his job was to pack and mail order D&K merchandise to fans. He was a college student at the time and absorbed every part of the record business like a sponge. Out of our thirty-five or so employees, he was focused on sales growth and was fantastic at his job.

ForeFront was firing on all eight cylinders and it showed. Our artists were commanding radio and sales charts and dominated their fields in the various awards shows. Our artists garnered four out of the five Grammy nominations in their category in 1999. We were flourishing.

As the end dates of our employment contracts approached, Dan and I talked about whether we wanted to continue with ForeFront or move on. Dan came to the conclusion he really wanted to move on. The corporate world of the record business was something he didn't feel compelled to continue with. I get that. I really do. It's a much different experience than owning your own business and operating it independently.

In some ways, being in a big company can provide better access and resources to help your artists. In other ways, though, it can be frustrating. Layers of corporate bureaucracy can make it hard to make quick strategic decisions and performance is constantly scrutinized through "metrics" of every kind known to man. That didn't appeal to Dan at all. He was not a committee man. I wasn't either, but my job seemed more fun in a lot of ways. I got to make records and videos. He got to make budgets and sales projections.

I told Dan I decided to stay with the company after our employment contracts expired. EMI already made it clear they wanted us to stay. I felt called to make music that impacted people's lives. That was my gift, and I felt I served best by staying with ForeFront. He didn't really debate my decision. He simply said, "I always thought we would leave together. We started it together, and I always figured we would ride off in the sunset together." I'll never forget him saying that.

When we told Bill Hearn Dan was going to leave but I was going to stay, I felt compelled to explain my desire to be given Dan's role of president. Looking back, I see that as presumptuous on my part. More than a little bit of my ego was involved. I never even considered there would be a different way to move forward if Dan left. I assumed it meant I would be promoted. When I told Bill I wanted that role his response left me speechless.

"I'll have to think about it," he said.

It turned out Bill was considering Greg Ham, our VP of sales, as Dan's replacement as president. I knew it wouldn't work for me to stay if that was indeed Bill's choice. Greg Ham is a good man, and the contest wasn't about that, I just knew in my heart I couldn't stay on if Greg made the cut. It wouldn't be fair to him, or to me for that matter. I also felt I would do a better job. Who knows if that is true or not, but just ask any United States presidential nominee if he or she will make a better president than a rival. Of course the answer would be yes, regardless. Over the next few weeks, I made my case to Bill to be made president and I'm sure Greg made his as well.

Bill chose Greg. When he told me, he asked me to stay in my current role and even offered me a ridiculous raise to stay. "You know you won't really work for Greg," he said. "You founded the company. You will be by his side." But I knew it wouldn't work. I resigned immediately.

I was confused and upset. How could I, the founder and creative leader of this enormously successful business, be passed over like that? It hurt me deeply and I don't think I'll ever fully understand it. I'm fairly sure the Brocks never really supported my decision to stay and run the company. I'll never really know. Dan's words haunted me: "I always figured we would ride off into the sunset together."

As painful as that whole experience was, I now see it as one of the most wonderful turn of events in my life. It really seems to me that God, in his infinite wisdom, knew had I settled into that role I never would have created Meaux Music or *!Hero the Rock Opera*. The next chapter, it turned out, was critical in my development. It would prepare me to build and run the largest Christian music publishing company in the world. God was absolutely in control, even though it hurt.

FORTY-FIVE

ULTIMATE RULER

Just a few weeks after resigning from ForeFront I got a call from Bill Hearn asking to see me. Neither of us mentioned ForeFront when we met. Bill opened the conversation by asking me if I would be willing to help him with two things. He went on to say CBS Television, in conjunction with the Vatican, was producing a three-night mini-series titled *Jesus* to air on TV on Easter of 2000. It would be released as a motion picture in theaters internationally, but in North America it would be a major television mini-series event.

He went on to say Capitol Records and Sparrow Records obtained the soundtrack rights as well as the "Inspired By" rights. His hope was to create an album with well-known mainstream artists alongside top Christian music artists. He invited me to serve as the album's executive producer along with himself, Evan Lamberg from EMI Music Publishing, and Mike Curb from Curb Records.

I knew Evan through the years as one of the top creative guys in music publishing in the world. Of course I knew Mike Curb from my days with Pat Boone and Lamb and Lion Records a lifetime ago. Bill went on to explain I would be the hands and feet of the project because he, Evan, and Mike had a lot of plates spinning. I was intrigued and excited to create something special with these guys. Little did I know where it would lead me and what it would teach me along the way.

This was an unprecedented opportunity to work at the highest levels of mainstream media to impact culture. I was very excited and honored to be involved.

CBS Television committed to an enormous budget for the production. It would be released globally, simultaneously. The project was also being produced in conjunction with the Vatican's apology for 2,000 years of anti-Semitism. The Church was finally admitting that the Gentiles were just as responsible for the crucifixion of Jesus as the Jews were. That was a really big deal to a lot of people. It was the first time the Church formally admitted to having the blood of Christ on its hands. Throughout history the Jews were castigated and persecuted for having caused the death of Jesus. They were chased all over the world as a result.

My first task was to fly to New York to attend a meeting set up by the show's producers and CBS television executives. The purpose of the meeting was for them to present the magnitude of the project and to introduce those of us who didn't know everyone involved. The meeting was held in the boardroom at EMI Music Publishing, the largest music publisher in the world, at their mid-town Manhattan offices.

Evan Lamberg met me at the door, as gracious as ever. Evan served as EMI's VP of Creative, East Coast. We met a few times through the years and worked together from time to time looking for just the right song for one of my ForeFront artists to record. Years later, Evan and I crossed paths again. He became my boss as president of Universal Music Publishing, North America when EMI recorded music was purchased by Universal Music Group. He helped Bill Hearn (my other boss at Capitol) and me create Capitol CMG Publishing, which is the largest publisher of Christian music in the world.

When I entered the boardroom I didn't know anyone else present. There were movie producers, CBS executives, film and DVD distributors, the director, and many others involved in the project at various high levels. One of the show's producers, Russell Kagan, stood at the head of the massive table. As everyone took their seats or lined up around the walls of the overcrowded room, Russ addressed us all.

He introduced himself and said, "I am so honored and appreciative that each of you are here today. I realize all of you are experts in your fields, and this is possibly your first exposure to this project. Before I say another word, I want to make a commitment to you; it is our utmost goal to make the best f—-king Jesus movie ever!" He struck his chest with his right hand as a dramatic pledge. He didn't have a single thought about the language he used to describe a film about Jesus. He was just proud.

Now this is different, this Southern Baptist-raised boy thought to himself.

That's the mainstream world. They can't know what they don't know. We Christians often expect them to think, act, and *be* like us. We judge them when they aren't. I agree there are limits to socially acceptable behavior in society, especially with underage people. But too often we circle the wagons against secular folks for just being secular.

We church folks are often guilty of not showing simple kindness and love toward the non-Christian world. That doesn't mean we have to accept public lewdness, unjust practices, or indecent behaviors. It does mean, however, there is no excuse for us not to be kind and respectful as we recognize human dignity in folks with different views than ours.

Russ Kagan, Saul Melnick, Evan Lamberg, and many of the other folks involved in *Jesus: The Miniseries* became good friends of mine through the project. The mini-series turned out to be a hit worldwide. The record delivered a number one hit with "I Need You" by LeAnn Rimes. The album contained outstanding performances by 98 Degrees, Lonestar, Sarah Brightman, Edwin McCain, Hootie and the Blowfish, dcTalk, Steven Curtis Chapman, Yolanda Adams, and many others. I was very proud to have been involved with it.

To impact culture, we have to be willing to be a part of culture.

The second thing Bill Hearn asked me that day concerned a very young artist named Stacie Orrico I signed a few months before I left ForeFront. He asked if I would be willing to stay on with Stacie as a sort of advisor and mentor.

Stacie was just twelve years old when I signed her. She was also one of the most gifted singers I have ever come across. She was very young, though, and would really benefit from the kind of guidance I could offer. Bill and Greg Ham felt it was a good idea. I felt a certain responsibility, being the one who signed her. I was also a big fan of her family. I readily agreed.

When I met with Stacie, she told me her musical influences were R&B pop singers in the vein of Brandi, Monica, and TLC. Those were the popular artists of that genre in the late nineties, and Stacie was a big fan of their vocal style. She was a little white kid who sang like a black R&B singer. I was familiar with that phenomenon growing up in Memphis. That's pretty much how they described Elvis.

As soon as I started looking for songwriters and producers to work with her, I realized how few contemporary R&B producers there were in Christian music stylistically in sync with what was going on in the mainstream pop/R&B genre of that time. I worked with Tedd "T" Tjornhom, with Rebecca St. James, Code of Ethics, and ETW. Tedd had some mainstream R&B history when he worked with Dez Dickerson and Prince in Minneapolis. He produced several other hip-hop records as well. I tapped him to work with Stacie, and they came up with some good stuff.

I also came across an African American producer, Michael Anthony "Mookie" Taylor. He was immersed in R&B music and got right to work making sure her sound was legit.

I also wanted to make sure Stacie properly approached the Christian music market. I brought in Mark Heimmerman as a third producer. He experienced great success with dcTalk and had a solid feel for pop music.

It worked like a charm. Stacie hit it off with all three producers. Each one brought a bit of a different flavor to the mix, and it all blended extremely well together.

We weren't into the project very long when both Tedd and Mookie separately asked me if I could help them with their music publishing. They had been writing songs with Stacie and neither one had a publisher. They needed some guidance about how to properly get their songs set up and published. Tedd also asked me if I would consider managing his producing career.

Shortly after that I founded Meaux Music Publishing. The word "Meaux" has some meaning. It's not the sound a kitty cat makes, even though I've heard it pronounced like that from time to time. It is based on the original French spelling of DeGarmo, or "deGarmeaux" as it was known back in the old country. In fact Pierre deGarmeaux landed in Albany, New York, in the 1600s. However, coming from Memphis, I also really like the true pronunciation of Meaux as "Moe," as in "Mo music," "Mo money," "Mo betta," "Mo barbeque," etc. You get the idea. It fit my personality. It was also easy to clear the trademark.

My first signings to Meaux Music were Tedd Tjornhom and Michael Anthony Taylor. That raised a few eyebrows at EMI and in the music community because both of these guys were known commodities in the industry. I went on to sign Pete Stewart of Grammatrain and Marc Byrd, who was in a rock band called Common Children. Both of those guys were go-to producers and writers. Pete was working with TobyMac and Michael Tait on their individual solo projects.

Marc Byrd wrote several very well-known songs, including co-writing "God of Wonders," which was recorded by Third Day and went on to become one of the most sung worship songs in the world. I first heard about him through Brad Ford, who was a founding member of the band Bleach on ForeFront, and who toured with Marc's band Common Children.

We signed several more songwriters at Meaux, including Robert Marvin, Anthony Phelon, Christy Byrd, Nathan Lee, Paul Meany of Mutemath, Shannon DeGarmo, and others. Meaux was definitely growing by leaps and bounds. We were placing songs on a lot of albums and our writers composed their share of hits. All that took place in the first two years of the business. We had some serious meaux-mentum!

FORTY-SIX

BLESSED MESSIAH / !HERO

There was definitely something special about the music and art of the 1960s. There was a creative energy passing through the atmosphere. It's probably hard for younger people to appreciate, but the explosion of culture that happened when I was a teenager and continued into the seventies was about much more than just music.

I loved and studied all of it. The British Invasion brought us The Beatles, The Rolling Stones, The Who, Cream, Led Zeppelin, and so many more. American artists responded with grit, grease, and guitars of their own. Hendrix, Joplin, Buffalo Springfield, The Grateful Dead, Creedence Clearwater Revival, and all the rest were the soundtrack of my coming-of-age.

It seemed every few weeks some radical new sound or sight came down the pike. All rules were off. The young had the culture's reins firmly in hand, and we were determined to change things. That was my culture. That was my generation.

Those of us who found our faith during those years were deter-mined to apply the creative energy of the day into our own spiritual pursuits. It wasn't some kind of calculation back then. It was more like instinct.

I grew up playing in rock bands, so that's what I continued to do as a Christian. It made perfect sense to me. But one thing I always wanted to do, and never had the chance, was to write, produce, and stage a full-blown rock opera. Shows like *Tommy, Hair, Godspell,* and *Jesus Christ Superstar* really blew my mind. Heck, I asked Susan to marry me after we saw that last one.

Rock operas, in many ways, were the ultimate expression of our cultural revolution. The heartwarming musicals like *Oklahoma* and *The Sound of Music* gave way to socio-political dramas. They took rock 'n' roll to Broadway and the West End in London.

Besides sounding and looking cool, those productions were per-fect for diving deeper into the social message and ideas lurking within the music. They reflected, and helped to shape, the values and ideas of the counter-culture. I dreamed of creating an updated, modern, culturally relevant, rock 'n' roll reimagining of the Jesus story. I wanted it to be something that would reach unbelievers and encourage believers. I wanted to include a wide range of musical styles right in step with the youth of the day.

I started really thinking about writing an urban rock/hip-hop opera about Jesus while I was still on the road with D&K. Life was a bit too busy at that point to really do anything about it, though. Then the ForeFront years filled most of my time with label work. During that time, the idea came back alive. I was driven to see it come to reality.

The concept was simple. What if, instead of being born 2000 years ago, God decided his Son should come to earth today? I placed the story on the gritty streets of New York City, today's cultural epicenter. I couldn't fathom a modern musical on the streets of New York without incorporating hip-hop music, so I did.

Jesus would be surrounded by street gangs. The disciples were a gang. The religious authorities were a gang. The Romans were the cops and government figures. My hope was the contemporary setting would allow the audience to relate their own experiences to the story of Jesus.

I was going to need help, and lots of it. I took the idea to my dear friend Bob Farrell. Bob had experience writing major long-form thematic works, including *Le Voyage*, *Emmanuel*, and *Savior*. I knew nothing about theatrical music, but I could see the play with my mind's eye. I knew how I wanted the music to sound. I shared my concept with Bob and invited him to co-write it with me. He immediately said yes.

Writing always came easily for Bob and me. We were a good team. This project definitely put us to the test, though. We started by writing the title track, "Hero," while on vacation with our wives in 1994. We wrote it on a beach in St. Thomas. That was the easy one. No suffering there. The rest of the musical, however, gave new meaning to the word "grueling."

!Hero was my version of "the agony and ecstasy." It took over five years to write. Staying true to the boundaries and dynamics of the Gospel story was our top priority, but we definitely needed to take some creative and dramatic license with how we told it.

Translating the social, religious, and cultural tension that made first century Israel such an explosive powder keg into a modern, urban setting was a major creative challenge. Sadly, it doesn't seem the world has become any saner in the last 2,000 years. It's not that far-fetched. The world is still a nasty place. I was determined to capture the proper amount of intensity through the songs, the sets, and the brief spoken parts—not a simple task.

I had never written a play before. I had a lot of learning to do. My lack of experience was both an advantage and a challenge at the same time. We weren't held to preconceived ideas of what plays or musicals should be. We were limited only by our imaginations. I also had no idea how challenging that kind of writing was.

As if writing and producing a large-scale musical wasn't enough, I also wanted a book version of *!Hero*. I reached out to Stephen Lawhead, who was well established as a best-selling author by that point. It had been nearly twenty years since he was D&K's manager, but we never lost touch with each other.

I sent him the demos for the songs just to see if he thought there was a book in it. He suggested we try to create a graphic novel of the story. I had never heard of a graphic novel; Stephen explained it was like a sophisticated comic book. His son Ross was an illustrator and they agreed to develop a graphic novel for *!Hero* Once it was completed they began to work on a three-part novelization of the whole thing, too. Although those novels were never completed back when *!Hero* was touring, I'm happy they will soon be released. Good things come to those who wait, I guess.

The music on *!Hero* was ambitious, to put it lightly. The soundtrack included thirty-two songs performed by Michael Tait, Rebecca St. James, Mark Stuart, T-Bone, and several other artists. Pete Stewart agreed to produce the album. It took him a full year to record it.

Along with the record, there was a stage play to produce, and the whole thing needed to be able to tour. It took a staff of thirty-seven people to make it all work. It was certainly the most massive live production I ever undertook. Once things were up and running with Meaux Music, that was exactly what I did.

Our little company was operating at full capacity to say the least. We had only been in business for two and a half years at that point.

!Hero was a much more expansive, and expensive, undertaking than I expected. The final product, however, was turning into something really special. It was a massive amount of work, but worth it all.

And then, just as *!Hero* was nearing completion, my life and career took another unexpected turn.

One day Bill Hearn and Richard Green asked me to join them for a lunch meeting. I didn't know what the meeting would be about, but I knew they must have something in mind. We went to a small, quiet, boutique restaurant where we could talk.

Richard began by giving me props for Meaux Music and what we were able to build in such a short time. There were nine specific songwriters we successfully signed despite direct competition from EMI Christian Music Group. We went head to head with the biggest publisher in Christian music and were nine for nine. Among other things, that definitely got their attention.

Bill asked if I would consider becoming the president of EMI CMG Publishing.

Wow. I told Bill I was honored to be asked, but wasn't sure it was the right time. "I'm having a good time building Meaux Music," I said, "and it's too early for me to sell it."

Then Bill really caught me off guard. "I agree," he said. "You can run them both at the same time if you want. I think there are some things we can do to reduce any potential conflicts. If we can agree on those things, I see no issue with you running both companies."

That was a surprising offer for sure. I thanked them both and asked for some time to ponder. They graciously agreed we would circle back around in a few weeks.

I went home and discussed the idea with Susan. On a professional level it seemed like a great opportunity to be back with what I considered the premier company in Christian music. On a personal level it made some sense as well.

Much to my financial chagrin, I rode the tech bubble of the late nineties all the way to the heavenly heights of the market. When the bubble burst in 2001, however, I rode it all the way back down to the pit of investment hell. In retrospect, I have to give Susan credit for seeing the meltdown coming. I must also take the fault for being stubborn and blind to the truth. I sure wish I listened to her at the time. We were stung, but still completely okay. It was a good lesson for me to learn. Susan has always said, "Eddie, you are great at making money. Unfortunately, you are also one of the greatest at losing it."

Buy high and sell low. That's my motto!

Together we decided the opportunity to run EMI CMG Publishing was too good to pass up, especially given the fact I could continue on with my endeavors at Meaux Music.

I went to dinner with Bill Hearn and accepted the offer. We talked a lot that night about different facets of the music business and how it was changing. He told me about some exciting momentum they were experiencing around newer styles of modern worship music. One UK band in particular, called Delirious, was really moving the needle, not just at radio or in terms of sales, but by putting out songs people wanted to sing at church.

That's a big part of the music publishing business, and it was becoming increasingly important. Modern worship music was still relatively young then. Bill also told me EMI CMG was in dialogue to acquire half of a British catalog of worship songs called Thank You Music. They saw promise with the fledgling genre in general, and this group of songs in particular.

Modern worship was different in that the songs were the big stars, rather than the artists. It was also all about church, not crossing over into the mainstream. In many ways this new movement reminded me of the early days of Jesus Music, since long gone. There were even massive festivals where tens of thousands of young people gathered to sing songs about Jesus. It was definitely an exciting new development.

I explained to Bill I didn't know much about modern worship or the music publishing aspect that supported it. I said Meaux published a few songs like "God Of Wonders" and "Show Me Your Glory," which were showing promise and growth in the Church and that was about the depth of my knowledge.

"You'll pick it up quick and do just fine," he said.

Famous last words.

FORTY-SEVEN

REBEL FOR GOD

I n a span of just a couple years I transitioned from co-owning and forging the largest independent Christian music label in the world to being an unemployed entrepreneur once more. Then, after building Meaux Music, I became a playwright and stage producer. Then, just like that, I was presiding over the music publishing resources of the largest company in Christian music. It was a time of rapid change, fast learning, thrilling success, and tragic heartache. It seems that's the way life rolls for me.

I began my new position at EMI CMG Publishing on April 1, 2002, precisely three years to the day after leaving ForeFront. It was an exciting time for sure, but much was required of me. I was by no means any kind of expert in the business world of music publishing and had no experience managing a publishing entity the size that EMI CMG operated, so I had plenty to learn. I was a good song man, though. I was good with songwriters and artists, but had only dived as deep into the business of music publishing as my independent roots would allow. I had a lot to learn about my new world. Fortunately, I had a great team to work with there.

The first major deal I had a role in was EMI CMG's acquisition of Thank You Music. I got to be part of the closing team on that very big transaction. John Paculabo, also known as John Pac, was the managing director of a British label and publisher called Kingsway Music. They were the company that owned the Thank You Music catalog. I met John years before with Bob MacKenzie of The Benson Company. Bob and John shared orchestras and studios in London from time to time, when they were both making records. It was a good way to control costs.

The negotiations to purchase half of Thank You Music started well before I joined the team, but it was my job to integrate the businesses and to make sure the songwriters were served well by our Nashville-based family. Thank You Music would be owned and operated as a joint venture between Kingsway Music and EMI Christian Music Group. Kingsway would continue to manage the business in the UK and Europe, and EMI CMG would manage it in the rest of the world.

Shortly after my first day, I flew to the UK with Bill Hearn and Peter York to meet the staff and songwriters of Thank You Music. I'll never forget that day. I met with Matt Redman, Tim Hughes, Stuart Townend, Keith and Kristyn Getty, and Paul Oakley, just to name a few of the very talented Thank You Music writers.

It was an interesting experience for me as most of the artists I was around and worked with up to that point came from more of a rock 'n' roll, hip-hop, or pop-based perspective within the Christian and mainstream music genres. It felt like the DNA of the worship artists and writers was a bit different. A lot of these guys and gals were bi-vocational, much like I was for the first four years of D&K. In their cases, though, most of them led worship music on a church staff and then wrote songs on the side. That gave them an interesting point of view about mixing business with the Church. I learned a lot about that issue in the years following.

John Pac taught me a lot about the world of worship music and the business that happens around it. He had a wealth of knowledge, loads of experience, and a passionate vision for the future. He was also a great teacher. Worship and business can certainly be a peculiar dynamic. We are peculiar people.

EMI CMG also operated a joint venture with sixstepsrecords, including sixsteps publishing, a brand new company grown from the ministry of college evangelist Louis Giglio, his wife Shelly, and the songs of his worship leaders, including Chris Tomlin, David Crowder, and Charlie Hall. Most people would know this group as the team behind Passion Music and the Passion Worship Events.

At that point, worship music was not played on Christian radio very often, so we needed a different way to promote the songs to the church. EMI CMG started a song promotion program called *Worship Together* a couple of years before my arrival. The goal of *Worship Together* was to introduce new modern worship songs to worship leaders around the world. That was also right around the time websites really became a popular tool for marketing. When I joined the company, the WorshipTogether.com site had some 80,000 members of worship leaders. I was blown away by that number back then. When I retired, thirteen years later, we had grown that program to reach over 750,000 members worldwide, and incredibly we published seventeen of the top twenty worship songs in the world. I'm still in awe we were able to build the membership of WorshipTogether.com that dramatically. It became a very powerful voice to get the songs recognized.

A pastor once shared with me, "Eddie, of all the things you have been able to accomplish, your publishing of worship songs may be your most significant contribution to the Church. For the first time in history, Christians worldwide are able to know of and sing the same songs in worship to God. You have been a big part of helping that happen." I never thought about it in that way before. I'm honored to be part of building that kind of unity in the Church. That's important stuff.

I recall a meeting I had with Chris Tomlin. He came to my office one day pretty down in the dumps. He sat on my sofa and looked up and said, "Eddie, why won't Christian radio play my songs? I just don't understand."

Fortunately, I had quite a bit of experience with that question.

"Chris," I said, "You know, I've seen this before. Radio wouldn't play D&K when we started either. It was too new and too different for them. They wouldn't play dcTalk because it was labeled as hip-hop in the beginning. Just give them time. They will come around. You'll see."

Well, the rest is history. They saw the light. Worship songs now make up a massive chunk of Christian radio stations' playlists, and Chris Tomlin is one of the best-known artists and songwriters in the market.

Modern worship music is a worldwide movement within the Christian Church that has affected the industry and the public in profound ways. There is much to be celebrated, of course. This music has helped millions of people sing to God in a way that is authentic to their culture. There are also some areas of concern. The industry of worship has taken that age-old quandary of ministry and commerce to new extremes. I've lived in that conundrum for several decades, but it's even hit a new level for me. Nobody ever thought of the term "Worship Celebrities" before, either.

FORTY-EIGHT

OUT OF THE DANGER ZONE

A few months after I started my new job at EMI CMG Publishing I invited Bill Hearn over to our home to listen to the finished recording of *!Hero*. I was in the process of funding and producing the project independently and was nearing a release date. Pete Stewart put the final touches on the recording, and I was very proud of it. It took almost two hours for us to listen to the whole thing. When it was over, Bill said, "I think you may have something special here. Let's discuss how we can help you release it."

We ultimately negotiated a distribution agreement for *!Hero: The Rock Opera* between Meaux Records and EMI CMG distribution. Meaux Records was a new company I started to operate alongside of Meaux Music.

I'm forever grateful to the artists who sang the roles on the recording. Michael Tait was our Hero, Mark Stuart, from Audio Adrenaline, was Petrov, and Rebecca St. James sang the part of Maggie. The album also contained performances by the rapper T-Bone, Matt Hammitt from Sanctus Real, John Cooper from

Skillet, Michael Quinlin, Nirva from TobyMac's band, Nathan Lee, Bob Farrell, and Paul Wright.

It was a gargantuan task to release *!Hero* and bring it to market. I began by hiring several expert consultants to help with the sales and marketing, web presence, social media, publicity, tour marketing, and art direction. It also became a major family project. I hired my oldest daughter, Breckon, to be the project manager. Her job was to coordinate all the different pieces. She had been a school teacher for several years, but was taking a break to raise her two children while finishing her master's degree. Breckon was always highly organized and efficient. I knew she would be great in that role, and she was.

Apart from the product release, there was a tour to put together, and there was a separate staff for the tour. Bob Farrell rehearsed the five-piece band and worked with me to put the show together. Teresa Davis rehearsed the six dancers and worked with the choreographer, Todd Hannebrink. Ian Cattle was the tour production manager. Eric Welch produced the video backgrounds and screens.

Eric later directed and filmed the *!Hero* live DVD. My son-in-law, Marcelo Pennell, who is married to Breckon, was charged with oversight of all audio mixing and sound design prep in advance of touring. Marcelo is a very talented recording and mixing engineer. We had massive amounts of video and audio to sync up, sound effects to be edited and so forth. He nailed it all.

Of course my dear wife was the costume designer. As I have mentioned, Susan is excellent with all things artistic. She taught graphic design at a college level for twenty-two years. She can also sew anything, design anything, make anything, paint anything, and do anything. Oh, and she can cook. *I taught her everything she knows.*

Okay, she hasn't read this, and will probably smack me big time when she does. But seriously, without the support of Susan none of this would have happened. We funded the project together and she was an enormous help in getting it staged. The point here is *!Hero* was a family affair. All hands were on deck—and then some.

I was managing all of those moving parts and a new full-time job. I took that on while serving as president of EMI CMG Publishing. I was also running Meaux Music with its staff and roster of writers. It was a lot. I'm not complaining about it, even though it took me sixteen hours a day—on a short day—to manage it all.

It was obvious something needed to change in the long term for me to survive, thrive, and do the tasks before me well. I was doing too much. I have learned a very important key to success is focus, and whatever you do, you must be able to do it well. That is much more important than doing many things at once. Quality always eclipses volume, especially if you can't handle the volume. That is when you are most at risk to let everyone around you down—most likely yourself.

In December of 2004 I sold another company to EMI when they purchased Meaux Music and integrated all our writers into their publishing family. Meaux had grown tremendously in just over four and a half years, but Susan and I were ready to move on. I was getting a bit weary from running two separate companies. It made sense for several reasons. Besides, I was able to continue working with the Meaux writers and producers through my role as president of EMI Christian Music Publishing. It was a win for everyone.

My time at EMI Christian Music Group was fruitful and fulfilling. We were positioned well in multiple genres of music, including modern worship, rock, pop, and were even making good strides in mainstream country and pop. We grew the business well beyond EMI's in-house record labels over the years. We became song publishers for writers outside those borders, including Casting Crowns, Third Day, Matt Maher, Mutemath, Kirk Franklin, Fred Hammond, Leeland, Ben Glover, and many, many others.

The modern worship genre was exploding all over the world, and our songwriters were leading the charge. Unbelievable songs were coming from Chris Tomlin, Matt Redman, David Crowder, Brenton Brown, Tim Hughes, Martin Smith, Stuart Townend, and Keith Getty, to name just a few.

Our contemporary Christian writers were topping the charts as well, with hits by TobyMac, Switchfoot, Steven Curtis Chapman, Rebecca St. James, Stacie Orrico, Newsboys, Ben Glover, and Audio Adrenaline.

We were number one in the industry and the largest Christian music publisher to ever have existed in the world. Where do you go from there?

FORTY-NINE

SOLDIERS OF THE CROSS

My dad was a pretty good harmonica player. He could hold his own on a guitar, too. At the mature age of just twelve he ran away from home to hop trains around the country during the Great Depression. He learned how to blow harp from the hobos sitting around their campfires. His love of music never faded. Music was always around our home when I was growing up.

Dad was also an electronics and gadget geek. We always had the latest in stereo equipment and recording devices. We owned one of the first cassette tape recorders on the market. It was made by R.C.A. and the dog-gone cassette tape was about the size of an iPad.

True to his musical roots, Dad was a big fan of Southern Gospel quartet music. Memphis happened to be the home of the annual Quartet Convention. Every year dozens of quartets and thousands of fans gathered at Ellis Auditorium down by the river. They held "All-Night Singins" during which one group would come on stage right behind another group until the break of dawn. My dad loved those "Singins." He dragged me along with him, staying up into the wee hours of the morning to hear the tenors holding out high notes while everyone else held on to something else.

That was my first introduction to Christian music on a professional level. Beyond that, my knowledge of Christian music was limited to singing hymns at church. The guys in those Southern Gospel groups were always dressed to the nines, with matching suits and matching colored shoes. Heck, sometimes even their hair color matched. The ladies were dressed impeccably well, in the fanciest dresses money could buy. Their hair was often piled so high on top of their heads I imagine the Bride of Frankenstein would have been envious. I took it all in. I really admired the showmanship, even though it could be a little over the top by any standard. But boy oh boy, could those folks *sing*!

They also travelled in style. They had the best, flashiest, tour buses, and they displayed them for all to see outside the arena like a glamorous diesel chorus line stretching all the way around the building. You could tell they were awfully proud of them. I was amazed by how shiny everything was—even the people.

In 1972, when I found the faith and became a Christian, we were at the tail end of the hippie era. The world was in the last gasps of the counter-culture revolution and many of us young people, whether Christian or not, liked to think we were anti-materialistic. We were anti-shiny.

During our humble beginnings as a Jesus rock band, Dana and I talked about how we were going to be different. We rejected the stuff we saw being consumed and popularized by the world. We pledged to say "no" to both the trappings of secular rock glamour and what we perceived to be the materialistic trappings of the Southern Gospel world. We were going to do things God's way. No glitzy showmanship for us. No sirree!

A few years later, after we experienced some success, I remember looking at myself in a mirror before we stepped on stage one night. I was dressed in a shiny suit. When we left town that night, we rolled away riding in a shiny tour bus. Hmm…

Then the inspirational artists of the early 1980s came around. They said, "We are not going to be like the Jesus rock bands. We are going to sing songs that can be sung in church on Sunday morning. We are going to do things God's way."

A couple of years later along came success. One day they too looked down and saw they were all wearing shiny suits and traveling in shiny buses.

Then along came the grunge movement of the early nineties. The Christian artists of the day proclaimed, "We are not going to keep God's music closed up inside the church. We are going to do things God's way and carry the music to the masses via MTV and mainstream radio."

Success snuck in. Even the alternative rock groups and grunge groups saw they were wearing their "flannel version" of shiny suits, and they too traveled in shiny tour buses.

Then the modern worship movement was born. Those guys loudly shouted, "We are going to recapture God's music and bring it back inside the church and sing it directly to God. That is how it is supposed to be. We are going to do things God's way, not like the artists who want to be in the mainstream."

Now, many of the worship artists wear shiny suits from Urban Outfitters and travel on shiny tour buses.

I can hear you saying, "Come on now, Eddie. You're becoming cynical in your old age."

I assure you, that is not the case. My point is just this: shiny suits and shiny tour buses are just what happens any time success creeps into most anything in life, whether it is the Church, our work, or ministry. It's as simple as human nature. Success isn't a bad thing as long as it is viewed properly and the proper expectations and values are assigned to it.

However, true success is not about money, fame, or even the number of baptisms you perform. Success is about following God's will, no matter what it may be or where it may take you. I've known people who would be considered very successful in the world's eyes, but are some of the unhappiest folks I've ever met. And it happens in all walks of life, not just music. Businessmen and preachers face the exact same challenge. One could run a Fortune 500 company or be a pastor at a mega-church with a popular worship and arts ministry, but still be a failure in life. Success is not about the numbers, ultimately. It's about obedience. Sure, sometimes obedience leads to abundance. When it does, thank God for it and keep your head on straight. Sometimes, if a person isn't ready for it, that kind of success can be the worst thing that ever happens to him or her.

Success, as described in the Bible, is pretty straightforward. It is only comprised of two primary points:

Point #1: Love God with all of your heart, soul, and mind.

Point #2: Love your neighbor as yourself.

Both are easier said than done. Volumes have been written on each point. It's good to ponder what it means to love God with everything you have, and what it means to love your neighbor completely. But that really is the simple truth. That is what success is.

Part of our problem is when the Church acts like a business it risks taking on the values and priorities of a business. We start judging our success as Christians, or as ministers, by metrics used to judge success in a corporation. I think in the end it is better when church is more like church, and business is more like business. When we mix the two it can get messy. I'm not saying it's always wrong. I'm not saying that at all. I'm just saying that things can get messy with a capital M.

Sometimes things can get weird fast. Is that what church should really be about?

FIFTY

DIVINE EMBRACE

ASCAP, which stands for the American Society of Composers Authors and Publishers, is a performing rights organization that licenses radio and television stations, public venues, websites, and others to use copyrighted music. Dana and I were both affiliated with ASCAP throughout our songwriting career. In 2007 ASCAP asked if they could honor DeGarmo and Key at their annual Christian Music Awards dinner for our lifetime contribution to music. They also asked if we would be willing to perform a few songs at the program. It was an enormous honor.

But thirteen years had passed since we performed together. I was excited, but also more than a little nervous. I called Dana and relayed the opportunity to him. After laying out the details and asking for his opinion, he simply said, "What do you think?"

I told Dana I would be game if Tommy Cathey and Greg Morrow happened to be available to join us. If we were going to do it, I wanted our performance to represent the full force and fury of what we once were. Dana thought that was a great idea. Amazingly,

both Tommy and Greg, who were two of the most sought-after musicians in the entire country, happened to be available for that date.
That seemed like some kind of miracle right there. They thrived in
their post-D&K careers. Truthfully, they were always better musicians
than Dana and I. We could just write songs.

We played four songs that night to a house packed full of friends,
co-workers, and members of the industry. ASCAP presented us with
their prestigious "Horizon Award." I have to say; I think we tore it
up. Dan and Darlene Brock came. Bill Hearn and my whole crew from
EMI CMG Publishing were there in the audience. Several of our top
songwriters were there too. Susan, our girls, their husbands, and our
grandkids were even there. Yikes! They had never seen Grandpa "Mo
Mo" rock like that before. All in all, it was a wonderful evening. Dana
and I had a ball.

After the news of that short set got out, we received several invitations from around the country to perform. Neither Dana nor I
intended to resurrect the band, but it was a lot of fun to get together
once a year or so and play for folks. We played a special reunion show
for Dana's church later that year and then again at the Cornerstone
Festival in 2008 alongside our old friends in Rez Band.

In May 2010 we played our final show at a biker's rally sponsored
by Lifeway Christian Stores. That was an interesting dynamic for
sure. The show was at a retreat center in North Carolina. About a
thousand bikers gave us a rousing welcome. It was great! Oliver North
was the featured speaker that night, too. Had you told me back in the
eighties someday we'd be playing for a thousand bikers at an event
sponsored by a Christian bookstore chain and Oliver North would
be the speaker, I'd have told you that you'd lost your mind. Life can
still surprise me sometimes.

I needed to drive back to Nashville after the concert to catch an
early morning flight. My son-in-law, Michael Carpino, who is married

to my youngest daughter Shannon, was due for our annual fly-fishing trip to upstate New York. Michael's from that part of the world and can translate for me when the folks up there can't understand my southern drawl. My phone rang at about one in the morning as I was driving. It was Dana.

"Man it was great seeing you," he said, "and it was great getting to play together again. I sure would like to do it more. Would you be open to that?"

I told him I was.

He went on, "Wouldn't it be great if D&K made it into the Gospel Music Hall of Fame this year? Johnny Cash is on the ballot too, and I think it would be cool since we're both from Memphis."

D&K was nominated several times previously, but had yet to get voted in. I'm told sometimes it takes a few nominations to make it.

"Yes," I said, "It would be amazing to get inducted alongside Johnny Cash. That would be the coolest, actually."

We dreamed about it for a few minutes on the phone and then hung up.

That was the last conversation I ever had with Dana Key. He passed away a week later from a pulmonary embolism. Life is fleeting, isn't it? My friend is gone.

Dana's family asked me if I would provide a eulogy for his service. Of course I would. He and I were best of friends from the first grade. We were really more like brothers than friends. The family informed me the plan was to have a private graveside service for their immediate family, and then to have a celebration of his life at the church Dana pastored a couple of hours later. That is where I would deliver his eulogy. His sister invited Susan and me to the private family service, since they considered us part of the Key family.

The family service was scheduled to begin at 10:00 a.m. Mind you, this was June in Memphis, Tennessee. I'm pretty sure summer humidity was invented in Memphis. As we gathered around the gravesite that morning we were already dripping with sweat. Suddenly, Dana's brother-in-law, Wright, nervously rushed up to me and asked if he could speak to me alone.

He took me to the side and said, "Eddie, I just got a call from the preacher and we royally screwed up. He thought the service was for 11:00 a.m., and he is still forty-five minutes away. What are we going to do?"

From the looks of the folks standing around in the heat and humidity, especially the elderly folks, I knew we couldn't wait on the preacher. They would have wilted. I looked back at Wright and whispered, "You open with a prayer and I'll close. No problem."

So, I ended up preaching Dana's funeral. I was honored to do so. But that was the first and will be the last funeral I preside over. It makes sense. It really does. I'm sure Dana is still laughing about it. Now that I think about it, I'm pretty sure that's the only time he ever stayed still and quiet while I was talking to him the whole time we knew each other! That's pretty funny. I sure do still miss him terribly.

That afternoon we celebrated Dana's life at his church. It was packed to capacity. I was honored to speak of what Dana Key meant to so many around the world. We shared some kind of fantastic adventure together where our dreams as kids actually came true. God took control at the absolute perfect time in our lives and set us on a different path. His path. I'm still amazed at the work he allowed us to do and the lives he allowed us to touch in building his kingdom. What a journey it was! I am forever grateful to have worked alongside, been friends with, and to have known Dana Key. I loved him like a brother. We were blood.

Later that same year DeGarmo and Key were inducted into the Gospel Music Hall of Fame right alongside our hero, Johnny Cash.

It was just as we'd dreamed. Dana would have been awfully proud.
I know I was.

FIFTY-ONE

I USE THE "J" WORD — TO EXTREMES

From 2002 to 2010, EMI CMG Publishing almost tripled in size. From 2010 through 2014, we almost tripled again. We represented over 300 songwriters worldwide. To say we had a good run is a gross understatement. We were blessed to represent the best in virtually every Christian music style and genre, from the "scream-o" bands with Tooth and Nail Records, to hip-hop with Gotee Records, to rock with ForeFront Records, pop with Sparrow Records, Modern Worship with sixstepsrecords, Thank You Music, Hillsong and Integrity Music, to foot stomping Gospel music with Kirk Franklin, Smokey Norful, Vashawn Mitchell, Andrae Crouch, Motown Gospel, and a host of others. It was a stunning lineup and I was proud to have served them all.

In September 2012, EMI Music, our parent company, was split up and sold to the highest bidders. Half of the business went to Sony Music and the other half, which included the Christian Music Group, went to Universal Music Group. Universal already owned another Christian music publishing business called Brentwood-Benson Music

Publishing. Brentwood-Benson was run by a good friend of mine by the name of Dale Matthews. Our new parent company, Universal Music Publishing, was also run by another very good friend of mine named Evan Lamberg. He and I worked on the *Jesus* movie and mini-series together, among other things.

EMI Christian Music had only been a part of Universal for a few weeks when Bill Hearn and I heard from Evan. He asked us to have a meeting with him and his boss, Zach Horowitz, around the notion of combining the forces of EMI Christian Music Publishing and Brentwood-Benson Music Publishing. It didn't make sense for Universal to keep the two businesses both within the same system but separate.

Christian music is a niche in the global music market and it was inefficient to operate the two entities separately. Combining them would be a complicated process and would create a behemoth Christian music publishing had not seen before.

Because of EMI CMG's strength in our market and maybe due in part to mine and Bill's long-term relationship with Evan, I was asked to combine and lead the businesses under the direction of Bill and Evan. It was an extreme honor for me.

I spent the final two years of my career combining EMI Christian Music Publishing and Brentwood-Benson Music Publishing into a massive new company named Capitol Christian Music Publishing. I was blessed to represent most of the top songwriters of Christian music all around the world. It was an honor and quite a responsibility—especially for a kid from Memphis who grew up playing in rock 'n' roll bands. Who would have thought it? Not me!

From the time I was a little boy, I always wanted to be able to retire when I turned sixty years old. I'm not sure why. It was just a goal of mine. When I turned sixty I made the decision and walked away from Capitol Christian Music Publishing. I was sitting on top of the world in my career and expertise, so more than a few friends asked me why I would do such a thing. Universal and Capitol asked me the same question—more than once. I just knew it was right in my heart.

Susan also knew it was right. It was a very similar feeling to when I walked away from DeGarmo and Key, only more so this time around. I felt strongly I was allowed to plant the flag on top of the mountain and now it was time to find another mountain—maybe.

One of the last executive management meetings I attended was the Universal Music Publishing Group's global conference in Santa Monica, California. I was joining leaders from all over the world who ran the Universal Music Publishing Businesses in their respective countries. There were leaders there from Europe, South and North America, Mexico, the Middle East, the Far East, Australia, and several other countries and territories. One of the features of the meeting was each representative was given a twenty-minute time slot to give a brief presentation and overview of his or her local business. The point was for the business units to discover new ways to synergize and work together on licensing and marketing each other's songs and music.

The individual presentations were fantastic. Each representative showed a "sizzle reel" video of his or her local writers and artists and then presented an overview of each business. This was followed by a time of questions and answers from the other attendees. There were around one hundred of the top music publishing executives in the world there. I saw and heard everything imaginable, from Korean hyper-pop music to Egyptian rap music (which sounded like a cousin to American hip-hop, but was rapped in Egyptian). I heard Chinese rock music and Middle Eastern symphonic music. It was an incredible assortment for every taste and palate, and it was a great way to learn about the publishing business around the world.

When my time came, my team produced a stunning "sizzle reel" of songwriters and artists from the wide and diverse world of Christian music. The reel included video clips from TobyMac, Chris Tomlin, David Crowder, Kirk Franklin, Hillsong United, Switchfoot, Underoath, Britt Nichole, Michael W. Smith, and others. I was very proud of how our music stacked up competitively with the music I heard from around the world.

After the video I gave a brief overview about how our music differed from mainstream music in terms of marketing and the various revenue streams. I spoke of the magnitude of Christian radio, the unique importance of CCLI (the organization that surveys the songs sung in churches), and the massive amount of print music that our industry produces for church use. I also spoke about the large amount of Christian music being licensed for use in popular mainstream motion pictures and television programs. That fact is usually very eye-opening for people who don't realize Christian music has the reach and relevance it does.

After I concluded my presentation and even before I asked for questions, a well-known music attorney stood up and said, "Eddie, you have to help me. I know you, and I know you are involved in Christian music. But before you played your video reel I was completely prepared to hate it. I just knew I would hate it because it was 'Christian' music. I have to tell you, though, the opposite happened. I really liked what I heard and saw. Now, I'm completely confused. What makes this stuff 'Christian' music? It sounds as great—and the videos look as good—as anything I heard or saw today from around the globe. I don't understand why it has to be Christian."

Standing in front of that audience, with music industry leaders from around the globe staring at me, I offered a silent prayer that God would give me exactly the right words in the moment.

"David," I said, "When you are an artist and songwriter, you write about things important to you and your life. As a writer you present your values to the listener, either subtly or directly. You write about the feelings you have about love lost and won. You write about things you observe in everyday life, whether beautiful or ugly. Hip-hop writers might write about the street. Pop artists write and sing about young love and relationships. Country writers talk about rural America and pickup trucks. Christians write about their faith and values. That is what is most important to them."

Then I looked at the audience and said, "Those of you who have read the Bible know it includes every subject under the sun in its pages. Therefore, Christian songwriters have a wide and very deep well of material from which to draw. They can write about love lost, love found, pain, murder, adultery, hope, despair, good and bad, despicable characters, and kings or queens. It's all in there. Christian songwriters want to present their values and their observations to the audience just the same way any artist does. Therefore, we can have Christian songs that contain subjects and stories from many perspectives."

I could still see some furrowed brows and could sense a little confusion from those in the audience. "Perhaps the best way to explain it," I said, "is to tell you about my life. I started playing in bands as a youngster growing up in Memphis, Tennessee. By the time I was sixteen, music was a serious part of my life. My band signed with a major label, and we were popular around town. I thought it was a big deal. I was 'on my way.' Then, when I was seventeen, an incredible thing happened. I had a lightning bolt experience with God and I gave my life to Jesus. It was a radical thing.

"Everything changed. Everything. I began to write songs about my faith and about what happened in my life because that stuff was important to me. I wanted to share my experience, my feelings, and my observations with others through my music because that's what artists do. I actually didn't realize I was writing 'Christian music' until others pointed that out to me. I was simply writing about what mattered most to me. That's what all these artists are doing. I hope that explains what Christian music is about."

Whew! That was heavy. I'd worked for mainstream entertainment companies for twenty years and never had an opportunity to share my story and my faith *personally* like that before—especially to music business leaders from all over the world. I was long known as "the guy who made Christian music," but this was personal. It was different and very powerful. I'm honored God had it happen that way. I didn't plan it and couldn't have.

After I stopped speaking, Evan Lamberg came up and gave me a bear hug in front of the whole group. Then he said, "I've known Eddie DeGarmo for twenty-five years and there is no finer guy, and no better Christian music publisher than him. I am proud to have him on our team."

I was blushing.

I often wonder if anything I said that day changed anyone's mind about what Christianity is all about.

TO EXTREMES

One of the last concerts DeGarmo and Key performed was in 1994 at the Mall in Washington, DC. We performed on a stage atop the steps overlooking the Reflecting Pool, facing the Washington Monument. You know the spot in the movie when the eponymous Forrest Gump takes off to hug Jenny as she wades through the Reflecting Pool towards him? That's where we were.

The event was sponsored by "True Love Waits," a sexual purity program introduced by the Southern Baptists. They organized the large Washington, DC, rally as a way to promote sexual abstinence before marriage. They created a stunning visual by planting over 200,000 one-foot tall crosses across the Mall as a memorial and tribute to the unborn children lost to abortion due to unplanned pregnancies. "True Love Waits" was a powerful program teaching sexual abstinence as a viable alternative to birth control.

D&K was invited to perform at the rally for over 25,000 youth who traveled to DC from all over the country. I recall it was a beautiful but very hot July day in our nation's capital. We arrived the night before, and we went out to the concert site early to catch a glimpse of the myriad of crosses being placed carefully on the grassy Mall. It looked like an endless military cemetery with crosses as far as I could see. It was quite powerful.

As I stood on the platform looking across the Mall I couldn't help but notice a man dressed in a robe and sandals, doing his best to look like Jesus. He was carrying a full-sized cross just like Jesus carried over his shoulder, and was slowly dragging it through the massive crowd of teenagers in front of the stage. I knew I had to go speak with this guy. This was something I had to know more about.

Frankly, he was quite a sight. I made my way down from the stage through the throng of onlookers gaping at the man who looked way too much like Jesus. He made it through the crowd and was standing at the edge of the huge memorial to the unborn. The bizarre contrast of this normal-sized man, with his full-sized cross, against the sea of small crosses was a vivid and powerful image. I walked up to him. His head was bowed and he was looking directly at the ground, seemingly bent over from the weight of the massive timber resting on his shoulder.

"Why do you carry this cross around?" I inquired as gently and respectfully as I could. "Jesus did that for you so you don't have to. Do you realize that?"

He lifted his head and looked straight into my eyes and said, "I believe we are to be partakers in the sufferings of Christ, brother. That is why I must carry this cross around on my back!"

I looked down, to the spot where his cross met the ground.

"Then why do you have that little rubber wheel mounted to the bottom of your cross? So it will roll easier?"

He looked at me, and a smile appeared across his lips. "Everyone has their limits, brother. Everyone has their limits." He then turned and slowly walked away.

I guess that is right. *Everyone* has his limits.

Over the years, I've often thought about that strange encounter and always come home to the same simple truth.

Isn't it amazing and awesome God's love has no limits?! That's the deal.

ACKNOWLEDGMENTS

A big thanks to John J. Thompson. I've written plenty of songs and even a musical with a stage play, but never a book before. When I completed the first draft of the manuscript, I wanted an experienced writer with another set of eyes to help me make it better. I asked John J. Thompson to take that job. He acted as my editor, sounding board, and clean up man. We worked together for several months re-arranging, editing, re-writing, and sanding on the manuscript endlessly. I thank John profoundly for his contributions. The book is much improved due to his selfless work.

Also, a big thanks to Gary Terashita. After I completed my work with John, Regnery/Salem Publishing came on board. I thank Gary at Regnery/Salem for his final editing work. He took the tome I gave him and worked with me to polish it to the finished book it is now.

Thank you to Marji Ross at Regnery for her belief in me and wanting to carry this book to the world.

A major thank you to Louie Giglio and TobyMac for contributing the forewords to *Rebel for God*. Your words are so gracious and humbling to me. I am forever grateful that we are friends.

Thank you to Chip McGregor and McGregor Literary for representing me and my work. You are the best.

Thank you to my lifelong friend Dana Key and our D&K band members over the years:

Greg Morrow and Tommy Cathey are known as the definitive DeGarmo and Key band. You guys are awesome.

There were many others who played with us over the years including: David Spain, Mel Senter, Max Richardson, Kenny Porter, Terry Moxley, Tony Pilcher, Marty Perry, Rusty McFarland, Steve Taylor, Chuck Reynolds, Kevin Rodell, Mark Pogue, Jimmy Marks, Brent Milligan, Paul Lameroux, and Marty Paoletta.

Thank you to all of our D&K crew and support staff with our touring; especially to Chris Taylor, Madison Sherman, Charles Gilliland, Gary Westman, Stan Letarte, Doug Jones, Mark Rogers, Bill McGoldrick, Rich Furchen, Mark Davidson, Mark Horne, Bill Rinks, Roscoe Meek, Ray Gaston, and Mike Christian.

Thank you to our drivers:

Gary W. Jines, Jim Deswarte, and Carl Jones for keeping us between the lines.

Thank you to our record producers:

Ron Capone, Joe Hardy, John Hampton, and Ron W. Griffin.

Thank you to D&K's personal manager, Dan Brock. You were a huge part of our mission and making D&K thrive.

Thanks to Stephen Lawhead, who was our manager during the beginning years and believed in us first.

Thank you to the management team at Brock and Associates for your belief in our ministry and keeping the D&K machine finely tuned including: Darlene Brock, Laurie Anderson, Pamela Muse, and Teresa Christian.

Thanks to Dan Pitts for coming out and supporting all of those D&K concerts back in the day. It meant a lot to me.

Thanks to Stephen Matthews and his dad for driving (and flying) all those times to see D&K play. Your enthusiasm was awesome.

Thanks to Richard Green for your wonderful friendship. We are buds!

Thanks to my friends at CCLI: Howard Rachinski, Malcolm Hawker, and Gary Christianson.

Thanks to Pat Boone and Doug Corbin at Lamb and Lion Records for taking a chance on a rock band.

Thanks to Mike Curb, who partnered with Pat Boone to sign us.

Thank you to Mary Lynn Robbins for her A&R guidance at The Benson Company. She helped us with some pivotal albums.

Thank you to Ken Pennell for his A&R contributions at The Benson Company. He came on with us beginning at Streetlight working alongside of us through our last album.

Thank you to Rick Miller, our first booking agent. You were a brave man to take that job.

Thanks to Scott Winchell for running our D&K operations in Memphis.

Thank you to Rob Michaels for his incredible support and ideas with our mission and publicity.

Thank you to my business partners in ForeFront Records: Dan Brock and Ron W. Griffin.

Thanks to Greg Ham and our entire ForeFront staff back in the day. Incredible things happened through your dedication and hard work.

Thanks to all of the many ForeFront artists that made it the exceptional label that it was.

You guys impacted a lot of lives.

Thank you to all of the artists, cast, and crew of *!Hero: The Rock Opera*. You guys gave your heart to it. Thanks to Bob Farrell for writing it with me and helping to bring it to life on stage.

Thank you to the executive team at Capitol Christian Music Group who I worked beside for so many years: Bill Hearn, Richard Green, Peter York, Rick Horne, Ken Pennell, Greg Bays, and Erin Carter.

Thanks to Evan Lamberg at Universal Music Publishing.

Thank you to my Capitol CMG Publishing crew for helping me build our music publishing into the magnificent business that it is today worldwide. You are the best.

Thank you to the many artists, songwriters, and producers that I was honored to work with over the years. You inspire me.

Finally, thank you to all of the fans of my music. You are the greatest. Also, thanks to the countless people that have been impacted through the work of the artists and songwriters that I was privileged to walk alongside. May God bless you all.

For information about author speaking engagements, please contact Info@AmbassadorSpeakers.com.